NOT THAT I'M BITTER

To Hannah

NOT THAT I'M BITTER

HELEN LEDERER

MIRROR BOOKS

MIRROR BOOKS

Copyright © Helen Lederer 2024.

The right of Helen Lederer to be identified as the owner of this work has been asserted in accordance with the Copyright, Designs and Patents Act, 1988. All Rights Reserved. No part of this publication may be reproduced, stored in a retrieval system, or transmitted in any form, or by any means, electronic, mechanical, photocopying, recording or otherwise without the prior permission in writing of the copyright holders, nor be otherwise circulated in any form of binding or cover other than in which it is published and without a similar condition being imposed on the subsequent publisher..

1

First published in hardback in Great Britain and Ireland
in 2024 by Mirror Books, a Reach PLC business.

www.mirrorbooks.co.uk
@TheMirrorBooks

ISBN: 9781917439060
Hardback ISBN: 9781915306654
eBook ISBN: 9781915306661

Photographic acknowledgements:
Helen Lederer personal collection, Alamy, Reach Plc,
BBC Archives, Shutterstock, Getty Images

Every effort has been made to trace copyright,
Any oversights will be rectified in future editions.

Editor: Christine Costello

Printed and bound in Great Britain by Clays Ltd, Elcogra S.p.A.

MIX
Paper | Supporting
responsible forestry
FSC® C018072

Contents

Muff Dive	9
Family	18
The Big Wheeze	26
My Teenage Diaries	31
Hand Relief	37
Heartbreak	45
Therapies	53
Drama School	60
Stand-up Comedy	70
Thrush in Edinburgh	85
Fat	94
Doing '80s Comedy	102
From Stand-up to TV	109
Naked Video	113
Two Timing	120
It was All Going so Well...	127
and then I Met a Man	134
West End	140
Stand-up & Single Parenting	146
Divorce on Stage	153
Comedy Crasher	159
Absolutely Fabulous	164
June Whitfield	172
New Agent	176
Husband... the Sequel	184
XL Extreme Diet	194

My Play	202
Reality TV	210
The Jewish Question	221
Celebrity Big Brother	230
Agents and Me	246
Deathwish	253
Gastric Band	259
'Let Go' from Newsnight	269
Back to the Beginning	279
Showing Off	285
Acknowledgements	297

> 1. Muff Dive
> Swimming frock
> Camel toe
> FAT

I'm standing on a diving board with my arms in the air looking at a red light. A producer is lurking hundreds of feet below me looking worried.

She calls up, 'You're not showing enough.'

I hiss back, 'It's been agreed. No camel toe.'

But the producer wants more.

'Do not dive until the red light goes out,' she says, adding, 'And look scared, but in a funny sort of way.'

A few weeks before, I'd been shopping for Christmas gifts when my agent rang.

'I've been asked if you want to do a reality TV show...'

I put my bath bombs back on the counter. Someone wanted me for a job. This felt pleasant.

The agent was still speaking '... and they want you to dive.'

This, less so.

'Dive. Where?'

'Water.'

I had no idea if I could dive. I didn't even know if I could jump into a pool – I'd got into the habit of lowering myself in via the steps in the shallow end to protect my highlights.

'Why?'

'Because it's Splash! A new diving show. With Tom Daley. Everyone has to dive.'

'Can't I still be in it and not dive?'

'No, they've already got Jo Brand.'

'Why? What's she doing?'

'Judging.'

Of course she was. And it was with a dull sort of sadness that I knew I would now have to dive, in public, for money.

The red light goes out. I tip myself forward and make myself fall into nothingness…

* * *

I was ten years old when I first discovered not everyone finds the same things funny. My mother was looking grim. I'd just started on my evening Nesquik when I was summoned downstairs.

'I've just had Mrs Finch on the phone.'

'Oh, yes?'

'She noticed some ink on Sarah's knickers this evening. Do you know anything about that?'

'Ink?'

'Yes, apparently somebody had used a biro?'

'A biro?'

'Yes.'

'There were a pair of eyes on her…' my mother paused, 'bottom… which Mrs Finch says hadn't been there when she left this morning.'

I said nothing.

'Mrs Finch says she's rather concerned.'

Until Mrs Finch's concern, I was in a really good mood. We'd all had such a laugh, and now this…

'We were just doing a game where I was a surgeon,' I began, 'and I drew these eyes as part of the operation, and it was so funny and…'

'I'll have to tell her you were showing off,' sighed my mother, and went off to phone Mrs Finch to apologise.

'Showing off' were the words adults used to describe my need to be hysterical. This was meant as a criticism. Occasionally I got praised when a bit of levity was needed to sort an awkward moment the grown-ups had created for themselves, but mostly it was punitive. The problem was how to read the room. Would my behaviour be praised or punished? I spent most of my childhood making myself and other people laugh and then being told off for it.

When I led a highly successful stink bomb campaign as a 10 or 11-year-old in the upper third, our class got detention, which is where I thought we should leave it. But when someone I considered a close friend suggested I should own up, *as well*, I felt betrayed. Surely I'd just initiated one of the funniest comedy spectacles our class had ever seen? Why get into more trouble? My lack of morality went hand in hand with being funny, along with a sadness about having a fatter bottom than most of my peer group. Not all comedians have fatter than average bottoms, but most of us aren't normal. I'm not particularly proud of that. But I am funny. So, I guess that I knew from an early age that my ideal job would have to be in the field of public humiliation, writing, and performing – later known as Stand-Up Comedy.

So, how did I get from being what my mother called a 'show-off', to an '80s stand-up comedian, to appearing with other comedians on TV – usually in their shows, not mine – to standing on a diving board on prime-time telly, worrying about my camel toe?

It's not as hard as you might think…

NOT THAT I'M BITTER

I invite you to imagine a time when women didn't do comedy unless they were fat, an impressionist, or promoted by a man. Younger readers – be happy you weren't around in the '80s. But I was. I need to write this. I need to understand how a short, asthmatic show-off had to invent her own club because no-one else would have her in theirs.

When I did my first stand-up gig in 1981, I noticed an anomaly. There were hardly any lone women on the circuit in London. In fact, women on the comedy circuit at all appeared to be rare. Apart from two tall, strict female comedians who made points about the miners' strike in their set, it was mostly men. I didn't make any points. Political or otherwise. My main subject was me.

I didn't have anything else to go on. Apart from Millicent Martin who got to sing a satirical song at the end of each *Frost Report* and Joyce Grenfell who performed whimsy in an evening dress on the BBC – there were no female Les Dawsons or even Bernard Mannings as role models. Women tended not to initiate jokes, and anyway, we were still needed to be the butt of most of them.

It must be hard for today's female comedians to believe there was a time when it was unusual to be given a slot on the bill and if we were included, there could only be one woman at a time. Now, you can't move for women on panel games, or women who produce, direct and play themselves in a sitcom.

Womanly comedic warmth is everywhere – we name our children after each other's pets and appear in each other's podcasts or friendship travelogues on TV.

But in the '80s, BBC sitcoms reflected the opinions of the male commissioners. One famous head of 'light entertainment' was heard to say, 'Don't laugh, this is the wife,' as he arrived at an awards event. So, it was no surprise when Felicity Kendal won 'rear of the year' and got cast as the lead in a few comedies at the same time. There was an appetite for women to be both sexy and funny – as long as they didn't initiate the laughs. And since laughter depends on a moment of recognition, we weren't used to women driving the comedy in the '70s and for a TV audience to laugh, it was decided, they needed to be shown a world they knew. And so it was that June Whitfield was the feed for Terry, while Felicity fluffed her pet rabbit in *Solo* and waited for a man.

But, somehow, in the midst of this middle-class, humorous, softy sexualised, landscape, Victoria Wood got commissioned by Peter Eckersley to write and star in her own show *Wood and Walters*. Jon Plowman followed soon after, by championing *French and Saunders* while Humphrey Barclay championed Emma Thompson.

And me? I'd already missed the boat. In 1984, the championing slots afforded by these admirably enthusiastic, male commissioners were taken. Three women stars at a time was enough. Where would it end if you had four or even five female-led comedies covering comparable ground on TV at once? The funny male comics offered choice; women offered duplication.

I was either the wrong person at the wrong time or the right person at the wrong time or, more worryingly, at the right time but the wrong person. And asking for comedy work in the '80s by a woman was seen as ambitious and unsightly. There was little support. I was described as 'vulnerable' by another comedian, which was a surprise, especially as I had my own car.

Being blonde and a stand-up wasn't straightforward, men were prepared to be intrigued by my 'individual' personality up to a point, particularly if they planned to hit on me. The phrase my professor may have used when I played Rita in *Educating Rita* in 1989 sums this up: 'You either hate Rita or you fuck her.' The moment a female comedian walked on stage, the audience felt the right to assess their fuck-a-bility. When I was introduced by Ben Elton in *South of Watford* in 1984, the cut-away shot shows a man in the audience looking fascinated at my crutch area and trying to make sense of how one of these could have turned up on a stage.

The way to deal with this was loose trousers and therapy.

The second therapist decided I had what's known as 'above-average anxiety', as if I was supposed to be pleased. She told me, 'Helen, for someone who hates authority figures, failure and being humiliated in public, you've chosen the very career that will most likely offer all of these in one continual cycle of adrenal excitement.'

One time I turned up for a gig at The Comedy Store with my woollen singlet and the sensible, loose trousers. I'd not been on very long when I heard someone in the audience shout out, 'let's see your clit!' in a confident sort of way. I wasn't familiar with the word 'clit' at that time, even though by then, I'd lived in a squat and been down the Dordogne in a canoe.

I had to say, 'I'm so sorry you want to see my... what?'

In the end I just said I hadn't brought it with me that night and hoped I was off the hook. In those days, there was a strip club in the same building. And the clit-seeker may have taken the lift to the wrong floor.

The comedy circuit was the only place I wanted to be. And apart from the mix of fear, adrenaline and one clit inquiry, it also led to being in other people's shows.

'Don't crash my laughs,' warned Rik Mayall once – and I never did. I'd do the feed, wait and make sure I remained in character. I didn't want to be seen to be overdoing it. I was very earnest in the '80s. Like a comedy secretary.

Some of the famous people became my friends and some of them didn't. Some of them hated me. They still do. Some of them I slept with. It was expected in the '80s and '90s.

For someone who was told I was 'distinctive looking' and fully prepared to ride an exercise bike on stage at The King's Head in front of a largely hostile and occasionally curious audience, I was unusually passive and acquiescent when it came to sex. I'd do it because I wanted to. Or because I didn't.

This was pre #MeToo. And I was never good at saying no. It took longer. And it went against my upbringing and my need to please my father. Most of his family had perished. Surely I could summon up the good manners to agree to a bit of sex if someone had the temerity to ask…

Nowadays the canvas has changed, but in those days, recreation in the workplace was often sought through the genitals.

I was more concerned about my actual comedy material than the Casting Couch as a road to employment. How would it work? Were people issued contracts before or after the deed? Were people issued a contract before a blow job or just expected to wait and hope for a small part? It was all a bit vague… and since there were fewer conversations about being a victim in the '80s, people cracked on with or without the wandering hands.

Did my career turn out to be the one I envisaged? Reality TV hadn't been invented in 1980, so being cast to go down a river on a barge with someone like Angela Rippon or Michael Burke and be filmed pitching a tent, for no particular reason, wasn't taught at drama school. On the other hand, when the *Celebrity Big Brother* shrink asked me: 'Do you cry easily?' I replied, 'The higher the fee the more sincere my tears of gratitude.' Actually, I didn't say this. The brilliant Rab C Nesbitt writer Ian Pattison wrote it for me as a gag.

But having a familiar face means it's never a surprise when I'm stared at and never a surprise when I'm not. When I found myself being stopped by two policemen for driving in a bus lane, one of them thought I might be their dentist, so I had to list a few TV shows I'd been in to clear that up. And, on this occasion, avoid a fine.

But I'm grateful for the opportunities I had. I don't go around announcing, 'I was always the bridesmaid,' because that would be a weakness. No-one likes humble in showbiz. But for the past 30 years, people have asked me, 'Why aren't you on telly more?' particularly when I'm in a pub or a garage, so I've decided to blame myself. It's certainly a good place to start.

I was happy to be in *The Young Ones*, *Girls on Top*, *Bottom*, *Happy Families* and *Ab Fab*. Most actors from those shows are now legends. I had my chances. Did I waste them? Was it because of self-sabotage, inconsistency, fear, or timing? Or amphetamines?

In my TV comedy career, I didn't create these shows and therein lies my dilemma. Shouldn't I be grateful? Why do I judge myself for what I'm not, rather than what I am? Was my mother right? Or my therapist? Or all my therapists? Was doing stand-up part of a lifelong deathwish?

On the occasions when I succeed, I wish my father were still alive so that he could see me do something other people like. When I fail, it's immediately bleak. If I was watching myself on a bad night, I'd be appalled and have to hide.

More recently, producers have stopped asking why women aren't funny because they've been told not to now, and at least we've moved on since the days of the clit request… haven't we?

I'm going to try to make sense of how the comedy world evolved with me in it, and what it did to me and what I did to it. My storytelling may be seen by a younger generation as a bit irresponsible, especially with today's clarity about acceptable behaviour. In my day, the difference between 'kinky' and 'dodgy' was a bit blurred, which I'd like to think has paved the way for the conversations we are now able to have about consent. In those days, sharing a less than perfect night with someone was one thing, but finding out you had to spank them as well, when it wasn't even your idea?

Nowadays, thrill seeking, sex toys and boundary breaking are inevitable, whereas in the '80s, selling the *Socialist Worker* outside Kensington Tube station was seen as a daring and passionate belief system for some.

In those days, if we came across someone who seriously 'leched', the general idea was to maybe report them and then wait 20 years for something to be done about it.

Turning events into funny stories was how I got my laughs. And if you couldn't laugh... then you weren't a comedian, and I really wanted to be.

But, deep down, this book is to prove that I was there. It's going to be busy and a bit awkward. There may be parts that appear boastful, which is going to be tricky to resolve. But performing is meant to be seen by the public. So, if that's okay with you and if you're still here, let's begin...

> 2. Family
> Czech ✉
> Posh refugee
> Isle of Wight

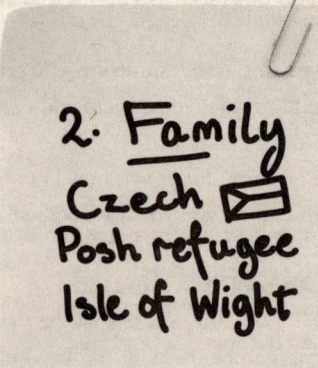

I was 13 when I learnt there was a name for people of mixed heritage.

'What's a half-caste?' I asked my friend Francis.

Stephanie and I were reading the problem page in Petticoat magazine. We'd become curious about a published letter from someone calling herself a 'half-caste'.

'We are,' said Francis.

It felt good to be told I was part of an official club without having to do anything to earn it. What were the chances? Francis' father was half-Nigerian Italian and her mother was Scottish gentry.

'Really?' asked Stephanie, sounding as pleased as me.

'Stephanie's half-Gibraltar and you're half-Czech. That's a half-caste,' explained Francis.

'And half Isle of Wight,' I added, for extra lineage.

This may explain why we all got on, apart from our shared interest in shoplifting in Lewisham.

* * *

Both my parents had slightly odd middle names. My father's was Klaus, which was embarrassing because of its association with Santa, and my mother was gifted the middle name of Effie. Not dissimilar from 'Effie off'. This may explain why my sister and I were given 'Patricia' and 'Margaret' by way of compensation.

Basically, half my family was foreign. Or that's how I explained my surname to people because the repetition of letters could be annoying. I'd have to say 'Yes, Lederer? That's E, R, twice. So sorry.'

If I brought friends home, they sometimes asked why my father talked funny. He had a clipped accent that wasn't quite English. However, my father wanted to be as English as possible and had particular ideas of what not to say and what not to do. I don't know where these behaviours came from, but they were nevertheless instilled from an early age. My sister and I were never allowed to say, 'pleased to meet you,' it had to be, 'how do you do?' If a boyfriend happened to offer up a casual, 'pleased to meet you,' when he met my parents, I knew I'd have to chuck him sooner or later.

My father was born in a rather smart spa town outside Prague. The Lederers appear to have led a happy existence with skiing holidays, picnics and maids. When he was seven, he smeared his lederhosen in butter to stop them looking new and got into big trouble, but this was not the reason he was sent away. It was because his father had the foresight to know they would not be safe if they remained in Czechoslovakia. If you were a Jew, a cultural Jew or even a tiny bit of a Jew, you would end up in a camp or shot, so arrangements were put in place for my father to get round that early on. An English teacher was paid to take my father and two other schoolboys on a train and then a boat to England. This may sound similar to Kindertransport, but it is more bespoke, since

Captain Morgan had already been their English teacher in Teplitz and there were only three of them escaping.

Somehow, they had been found places at Margate College for boys and a school uniform was cobbled together in some haste. None of the boys spoke much English, had seen the sea or knew anything about cricket, but they had got out in good time. A year later my grandfather arrived, followed a few months later by my grandmother and my aunt who managed to get on one of the last trains before all travel was forbidden. Both grandmothers were sent to the Theresienstadt ghetto, while friends and other family were all deported to Auschwitz.

My father told me he'd been lonely as a boy which made me feel awkward because I wanted to think of him as tough. Vulnerability in a parent was too heartbreaking to think about, so mostly I didn't.

But one day, during one of our rather filling suppers in Eltham, I decided to tell my father about a Norwegian girl who had joined my class. She couldn't speak English and no-one spoke to her at lunch. He became so adamant that I speak to her the next day that I wished I hadn't brought it up, but I knew I had to do it. Embarrassingly enough this obligatory act of kindness was observed by Miss Thomas who was on lunch duty and I was singled out in front of the whole class for being kind. I wasn't kind. I'd done it to please my father.

My mother Jeanne met my father at a club in London where many Czech and Polish students gathered after the war. Her background was very different from his. We never heard her sing, unlike my father who would break into song on long car journeys which felt very open and free compared with other adults who lived in Eltham at that time. But she was always happy to tell us she was from the wrong side of the Isle of Wight (and bought shop-made pastry to prove it. And once, in the '70s, she purchased a bri-nylon, loose cover for an armchair, which was either impressively modern or irredeemably lower middle class).

She left the island at 17 to go to university. Then she was recruited to Bletchley Park. She told us it was that or the Land Army and there'd be more sitting down as a decoder. She was decoding and keeping secrets at the same time my Czech grandfather was eavesdropping on captured German generals at Trent Park in North London as a 'secret listener' and reporting his findings to British Intelligence. They didn't know about each other. Too secret. Then she got a job in the Board of Trade, which was where women went if they wanted interesting jobs that men did at the same time. I'm not sure what exactly she did at the Board of Trade, but 'negotiating deals with other countries' and 'allocating resources to certain industries' are likely areas of activity.

Sadly, she didn't have very long to do it, because women in the '50s were expected to give up their careers once they got married.

My mother seemed relatively resigned to this. Except for when our two-toned maroon and grey Ford Anglia wouldn't start in the winter, and then she would say 'bugger' which sounded quite glamorous. My sister and I felt rather thrilled to glimpse this darker side. Or maybe her dependency on the Ford Anglia was more of an escape from being a housewife than we realised.

But usually, she seemed very self-contained, which came in handy when dealing with the Czech side of the family. Jeanne was outnumbered by the Lederer women and she knew it. My aunt Brigit's bond with my grandmother was intense. We called my grandmother 'Little Baba', which was embarrassing if you thought about it for too long. We called my grandfather 'Big Baba', because he was. Thankfully, we called my aunt by her real name.

My father was loved with a passion by both Little Baba and Brigit. They were a team, and my mother was a far too modest and sensible Isle-of-Wighty scholarship girl (even allowing for a potentially boastful Grade 8 piano accreditation) to compete. She would often cook up a nice ham with cloves on it and place it on the hot plate, otherwise known to be an electric plate warmer in the shape of a tray on legs, as her way of being agreeable to her foreign in-laws.

My father's sister's family never discussed being Jewish, escaping Hitler, or any aspect of that part of their lives that was distressing or sad making. I only discovered my cousin Netty hadn't been told about the Jewish relatives when I brought it up with her as a teenager. We'd been to see Glenda Jackson in *Sunday Bloody Sunday*, about a polyamorous relationship which needed a bit of unpacking in the '70s, but clearly not as much as the Jew thing. She had no idea. Her parents may not have been thrilled that I was the messenger because, until then, none of their neighbours knew either.

And I could see why our side of the Lederers could be seen as a bit lacking in values and liberal. We didn't live in a house with a drive, we didn't go to boarding school and even more controversial was the fact that I was allowed a leather jerkin at the age of nine. One of my first experiences of having my enthusiasm crushed was when I bounded into our sitting room to showcase my brand-new leather jerkin to our babysitter. There was a beat, before she collapsed in a heap of hysteria. My short, fat frame encased in adult leather with white stitching around the neck and hemline was too much for her. I rushed upstairs to sob in the box room. The babysitter followed me, somewhat chastened, and had to beg forgiveness for a long time before I felt able to come out from the suitcases. I have never worn leather in a jerkin since.

When we stayed with Brigit, the difference between the two sides of the family became quite marked. All the grandchildren were expected to say, 'Please may we get down from the table' after each meal. But then the two cousins would scamper off purposefully to brush their teeth. My sister and I would wait awkwardly for them to come back, wondering if we should have brought a toothbrush.

with us as well, and why hadn't our mother told us to pack one. We didn't do teeth cleaning after meals in Eltham.

But being more modern and liberal had its triumphs. My mother introduced both cousins to the miracle that is called strawberry Nesquik. If it wasn't for her, they would never have known that you could just add granules into a drink to make it pink and even add a straw for sheer excitement. As far as Brigit and Little Baba were concerned, milk had to be boiled in a milk pan and was never, ever pink.

The Lederer gatherings were very important. Apart from overeating, we'd sometimes have to go for a walk to get fresh air. Little Baba would take us up to Whitestone Pond and tell us things about the world which I wouldn't completely understand but went along with. She introduced me to the phrase 'on the contrary', which for many years, I thought meant 'on the country'. Whenever I heard the words, 'On the country, Helen…' I knew to brace myself for a debate.

Being disagreed with by Little Baba was considered a compliment and a way to expand my mind. I would make one statement, and then Little Baba would contradict me. I knew this was being done for my own good, which was just as well, since I always wanted to please her. Her somewhat masculine, authoritarian tone could be quite loud in shops, but we would hold hands, play rummy and once she tipped me off about a *Play for Today* with a young couple kissing that she thought I might like. I was shocked. I was 15.

Little Baba's diary was usually full. When they first arrived in Hampstead, many refugees would stay with them, and when Big Baba died, her diary was kept full with bridge parties, concerts, and in one case a trip to see *Emmanuel in Tokyo*, with her best friend Marianne Grunfeld. When I suggested there may have been some nudity she told me she just shut her eyes at the nude bits. She can't have seen much of the film.

And then Little Baba's children died. My aunt at 45 and my father at 51. She took herself away to grieve. And when she came back, there was less room for the rest of us. We sensed the pain and the sadness, but wanted to be approved of, so we didn't dwell. I was the youngest and least interesting. I was also the silliest, according to the non-blood uncle.

When I was in my twenties, my sister asked me to drive Little Baba to her house in Maidenhead for lunch. I had made this journey many times up the M4, but suddenly, with Little Baba in the front seat of my hastily-cleaned-up Hillman Imp, I panicked. Out of anxiety I told myself that today, the M4 would probably be the wrong road to take, so I veered off the road I knew and got quite lost. It didn't take long for Little Baba to remark that, in her experience, housing estates and factories were not usually to be found either side of the M4. We were late for lunch and Little Baba had not been fooled.

Whenever I'm with an elder or person of authority, I'm usually braced for some kind of criticism. By mistake, I behave badly, as if playing into what I see is their disapproval of me. This is all done in panic, but it's how I mess up auditions, forget my lines or say the wrong thing to an agent, exactly when it matters. Basically, quiet people and authority figures are my two worst types of people to be stuck with, especially on a Zoom.

My family's high standards and expectations shaped me. My mother wanted me to do what I was told, and my father wanted me to take risks. Both came from a place of love and worry. I wanted to please my father by being an adventurer, but I wanted to avoid getting things wrong to please my grandmother and my mother. People pleasing began early and covered most areas of my life except when I prayed. Then I was free to ask for things that only I wanted. I'd start with, 'Dear God, please let there be no burglars, murderers, kidnappers or ghosts in this house tonight or any other night', which covered all timing options, and then I'd end with, 'And please let Gordon call me this week and ask me to the Colfs Disco'.

Although we knew about my father's reason for coming to England, there was no suggestion that we were full-on Jewish. There was a brief phase when my sister and I went to Sunday school in a church in Eltham, but this was to meet boys. My father would even drive us there and say, 'If you decide to believe in God, I won't stand in your way.' I knew he didn't mean it which is why I decided to get into praying in a big way. It felt secret and thrilling and rebellious. But it was also good to have time in the car with him. In those days it seemed normal for a father to stay out of the house in the daytime and only come home in time for a huge, three-course supper.

My father died when I was 21, before he got to see me do stand-up. I couldn't have done it when he was alive because I couldn't risk disappointing him. I often feel that my ambition was realised by one tragic heart attack. I lost my father. I found a voice.

3. The Big Wheeze
Showing off
Hysteria
Stunted

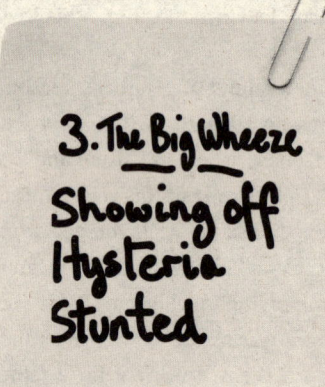

The year is 1960. I am five years old and for some reason I'm halfway up a mountain in Austria with German-speaking children who are all staring. I don't speak German. My father won't even buy a German car.

For some reason I've been left on my own by my parents to take part in a skiing lesson. The teacher screams at me that I must now ski over a precipice and into oblivion. The other children are waving their sticks at me. They are all cross as well. I do what I'm told and prepare to die. My ski falls off and I see it hurtling down the mountain. I lie in the snow, alone.

I'm the only pupil with one ski, a runny nose and I know that no-one kind will ever come and find me. Then I hear this strange noise. A tiny strain of high-pitched sawing. It's getting louder and louder. Is it someone yodelling? A goat herd?

Then I realise that the sound is coming from me... it is my first wheeze.

* * *

After the wheezing incident, I was taken to our family doctor in Eltham for some kind of explanation. The sawing noise was called asthma.

'Dr Ferguson says you mustn't laugh or get over excited,' said my mother on the way home in our Ford Anglia, adding rather sternly, 'or you might die'.

From that moment on, I made it my business to become hysterical whenever I could. This not only upset my parents but also made me happy. Particularly when friends came around. There was a power in laughing when I knew we weren't supposed to. And I got funnier with an audience. This was when I first realised, I liked to make people laugh.

'Stop showing off Helen,' was something I heard a lot. Even when I wasn't showing off, they were on the lookout in case I keeled over and died. Which in turn made me paranoid about being judged while I was having forbidden fun. My phobia about having anyone I know in an audience started this way.

On the positive side, the asthma explained how I became a fat, funny, attention-seeking adult with above-average anxiety about being laughed at and an issue with authority figures. As well as resentment and sadness about anyone who didn't think I was fun. At the beginning, when journalists had to ask, 'Were you always funny?' in an accusatory sort of way, the asthma explanation worked well.

For most of my childhood we lived in a 1930s detached house in Eltham, with a red door and a front and back garden. We had a parquet floor in the hall with wooden panels on the walls and basins in the bedroom that no-one used. Eltham had one Woolworths, one swimming pool, one library and, in the late '70s, the arrival of a Wimpy Bar almost put us on an equal footing with

Bromley. There was also a bespoke bra shop up a side road, a Tudor-style pub and a teacher training college where we got our babysitters from. When they arrived, they were told to watch me in case I had an asthma attack, which might have been too pressurising, so we got through a lot. Only the one who laughed at my leather jerkin seemed up for return visits.

While the downside to asthma was not being able to breathe, the upside was being off school and using the time to plan games. I was easily the most popular person for coming up with original things to do at break time. One game that stands out was called the Sanitary Towel Game. There wasn't too much to it. My friends and I would all assemble in the Fiction Library during lunch break and we'd all become sanitary towels. That was the game. I was always Doctor White because it was my idea, Mary James was Doctor Green and someone else was Doctor Red. The game would then proceed something like this:

'So, Doctor Green, what are you doing today?'

'Well, Doctor White, interesting you should ask. We are doing more sanitary towel work actually, in the sanitary towel factory.'

On one occasion, when we were being sanitary towels, we forgot to go back to the classroom after break, because we were laughing so much. Miss Thomas, my form teacher, opened the door. We froze. Everyone was told to go back to the classroom. Except me. She asked me to stay behind.

By now I was familiar with saying the wrong thing and braced myself. I didn't enjoy getting into trouble. It made me feel sick. Even now when I see a policeman on a motorbike, I worry how easily I could be in prison and always make sure I stop eating my apple if I'm driving, or any other action that may provoke attention.

But instead of telling me off, Miss Thomas asked me if there was something worrying me.

'Yes,' I said, blinking.

Miss Thomas looked pleased.

'My grandmother is dying?' I suggested.

'Really?' Miss Thomas looked suddenly kind.

In fact, Little Baba was in great health. She could be playing bridge this very minute, or seeing another *Emmanuelle* with Marianne Grunfeld, for all I knew. But it occurred to me, my home life would now be investigated.

'But no-one else knows about her dying. I mean, I know obviously...'

'How do you know?' Miss Thomas was being gentle, which was pressurising.

'Er... because I overheard them... talking.'

This was an early lesson. You can never tell one lie unless the lie is excellent. But on this occasion, I was allowed back into the classroom.

Miss Thomas was very, very kind to me after the Sanitary Towel Game episode. I knew I wasn't deserving of her kindness but at the back of my mind, somewhere, I knew she disapproved of my popularity. It wasn't normal.

In light of her new leniency, and with the fake dread of Little Baba dying at home, Miss Thomas decided to allow me to perform a talk show in front of the whole class. Since I was an avid fan of *That Was The Week That Was* and had already been doing David Frost-style interviews in break time, I leapt at the chance for a wider audience. My TV guests didn't get to say very much. But it worked. It caught the mood, the moment and everything else. At the end of the performance Miss Thomas looked at me for long enough to make it feel a bit odd. Then she announced, 'You will be famous one day.'

We should have left it there. Instead, Miss Thomas commissioned me to write and stage a play for Open Day. It was a disaster. I ditched everything I knew and loved (David Frost and messing about) and ended up copying Enid Blyton to make sure it was imitative and, as it turned out, entirely bad as well. The title was something like *Great Uncle Henry Comes to Stay* with very poor jokes and one-dimensional characters. I had peaked with my David Frost aged 10. I had to wait 45 years to get that feeling again, which turned out to be reading out loud from my novel and getting clapped with certain words. Budleigh Salterton Literary Festival was worth waiting for.

The rest of the time, rebelling didn't make me happy, but I still did it. Miss Abraham, the headmistress, never trusted me after she was told about me cheating in my French test. The fact that I had become a cheat was a surprise to both of us.

'I was just looking at the envelope with the French words on it, that happened to be on my lap at the same time as the test,' I explained with genuine concern in case she got the wrong end of the stick.

I was more of an accidental rebel than an intentional revolutionary, but the need to initiate fun was always there. Maybe it was being kept off school while I wheezed my way through six terms at Malory Towers, but being able to create hysteria for me and my peers was everything. And my skill at filling Lederer silences with a sense of fear my fillers might cause offence, rather than soothe, fitted well with the risk and allure of stand-up comedy.

My very first memory of hysteria was lying on the sofa, watching *Zoo Time* when someone said 'bum' on camera. At first, I was taken aback. Didn't they know that the word 'bum' was possibly the most funny and rude, banned word ever spoken? Bum meant... well, it meant a bottom. I was beside myself. I laughed until I cried. I couldn't stop. By now I had rolled off the sofa and was wheezing and gasping for breath. My sister wasn't laughing as much as me. Maybe more staring with concern. My mother had to hurry in and say, 'Look what you've done now, you've spilt your milk'. Which was true, I had. On the plus side I hadn't urinated. Or died.

4. My Teenage Diaries
Levis ☺ ☻ Boys

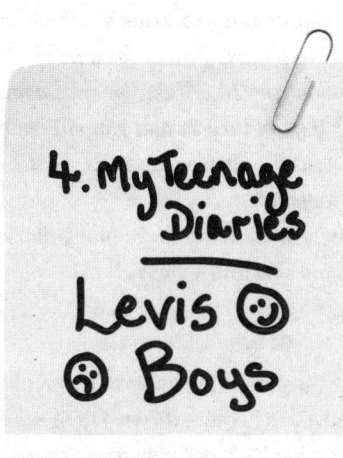

December 29th, 1969. I'm 15 years old and I'm in Eltham High Street looking for something to buy with a £1 Boots token. I cross the road to avoid Woolworths as this is where I nearly got caught shoplifting a 'Pan Am' mini-purse with Mary James. Woolworths is on the same side as Eltham Library where I stole the book about the Siamese twins, Chang and Eng, who fathered 21 children.

I can't find anything I like in Boots that works for me for a pound, so I start walking home. I don't steal anything. Just as I step onto a zebra crossing something miraculous happens. A Riley car draws up and Dave Wood winds down the window and calls me over. I know Dave Wood. He is the brother of Pauline Wood, who I know from Guides. Pauline smoked and was older, so I was never in her set. Dave is way older than me and one of the best-looking boys I've ever met.

'Get in,' he says.

In 1969, if a boy you know tells you to get into his car, you get in. Dave tells me he is on the way to Sidcup to buy some windscreen wipers.

Later we go back to his house and drink a coffee before he runs me home. Dave asks if he can take me out for a drink. My parents say yes, as long as I'm home by 10 o'clock. I'm cross about this, but we go, and I enjoy our time in the Fox and Hounds. Afterwards, Dave comes back for more coffee. Before he leaves, he asks me if he can take me out again sometime.

Later that evening, I write about Dave in my diary: 'He is rather nice. I'm in a muddle… Typical. V happy.'

* * *

When I hit puberty, my need for hysteria was replaced by a new interest: Boys. I know this because it's written in my *Melody Maker* diary. I have nine similar diaries. So, when I was contacted by the producer of *My Teenage Diary for* BBC Radio, to see if I'd written any diaries in my teens, I was ready for her. It was 2019, and since my daughter had already read most of them, they were easy to find on her bookshelf.

'It's odd that you seemed to know so many boys,' was all she would say after reading *Melody Maker 1969*. Adding, 'and were quite sad.'

I turned up at the BBC studio clutching at least seven, in case Rufus Hound or indeed the audience might wish to see my evidence. They didn't, but I put them on my lap for authenticity.

'I think I can see a theme building,' said Rufus, after I'd read out the first few entries.

Apart from one only slightly upset mention of the Biafran famine, along with a nod to the Moon landing in 1969, my diary was focused solely on two main interests: Boys and Levi's. In the front of *Melody Maker 1969*, I wrote:

Everyone is very excited about the Americans going to the Moon. Maybe I'm not as excited as I should be, but my parents most certainly are. I don't know what else to say, but I'm determined to keep writing this diary all year. Some more extracts…

SUNDAY JULY 20TH

One of the most boring uneventful depressing days of my life. Everyone madly excited about the Moon. Stay up ever so late watch it on TV. They land! Had to go to bed.

MONDAY JULY 21ST

USA doing v well on Moon thank goodness.

FRIDAY JULY 25TH

Feel a bit depressed. Go to Lewisham. Look everywhere for jeans.

SATURDAY AUGUST 2ND

Went to town. Didn't find Levi's.

FRIDAY AUGUST 8TH

Went to town in morning. Sweated. Got Levi's! And Jethro Tull LP.

SATURDAY SEPTEMBER 27TH

Danny party. Great. Get off with Nick Cove (again). He says he'll come round tomorrow. Nervous.

MONDAY SEPTEMBER 29TH

Nick doesn't write or ring. Bit hard at first. Keep thinking about him. He goes to Manchester University on Wednesday.

SATURDAY OCTOBER 11TH

Go to Lewisham. Buy more Levi's.

SATURDAY OCTOBER 18TH

Colfe's Dance. Dance with five different boys. Miss Nick terribly! Ian says he'll come round tomorrow, but I'm not sure if I like him. I feel lonely. Want Nick so much. I also have tummy ache.

MONDAY OCTOBER 20TH

I must make myself dislike Nick Cove otherwise I shall be so terribly hurt, more than I already am. It's so difficult as he is the most good-looking bloke I know.

WEDNESDAY NOVEMBER 5TH

Hear that Nick Cove told Jenny to stay available all weekend as he was back from university. Depressed and cry. Worst week.

FRIDAY NOVEMBER 14TH

Forget Nick Cove, forget him, forget him, forget Nick Cove, forget him, forget him.

SATURDAY NOVEMBER 29TH

I love Dave Wood.

TUESDAY DECEMBER 30TH

Go to Eltham and change tights and go to library. Then Dave came round at 1.30pm. I'm a bit embarrassed, but he's not of course. We go to Wimpy Bar for a Coke. Like him more and more.

MONDAY JANUARY 5TH, 1970

I didn't write today because I didn't come in from bloody Jenny

Craig's party until 1.30am. Before the party, Dave called round for me with some girls and one boy already in the car. At the party he completely disappeared and that was that. Well, not quite. I grabbed hold of Phil and said 'kiss me' so that Dave could see. Cried all day – MUST MUST get over him.

TUESDAY JANUARY 6TH

Felt awful when I woke up and cried immediately. A really terrible day. Sounds stupid but I keep picturing Dave snogging with this girl and my stomach turns. I feel pretty wretched. By 9.30pm, I decide to attack the process of getting over him by praying, praying for help. By 10.15pm I'm almost there.

(My prayers could get quite long, because I always had to include the 'please let there be no murderers, burglars, kidnappers or ghosts', incantation at the end, as my generic insurance policy against being robbed, or killed. This would be on top of any more immediate and urgent prayer I needed to get in about Dave. My actual sleep time had to keep getting put back to cover this).

SATURDAY JULY 25TH

How I dread going to France. Today I love Gordon. I don't want to go.

SUNDAY JULY 26TH

Miss Gordon. Cry in bed. I love him.

SATURDAY AUGUST 16TH

Last day. I love Marcel and I cried. So did he. We sat on the quay and we mouthed words of love. What am I to do now? What? Sick on boat. Nice to see family again – cry in bed. How I hope Marcel writes – how I hope it's true. What of Gordon? I don't know.

It didn't take too long to resume relations with Gordon (one day according to my *Melody Maker 1969*), and very possibly I may not have read Marcel's letters properly. Or even opened them.

I was preparing for my first Saturday job as a waitress at Chez Maurice in Eltham when there was a knock on the front door. I looked out of the window to see two boys with rucksacks on the pavement. I realised it was Marcel with a pal on the doorstep. I ran into the kitchen to hide.

'Shouldn't you be at Chez Maurice?' My mother wanted to know. She may have been making marmalade. Or crab apple jelly.

'There's someone to see you Helen,' my father joined us in the kitchen.

I ran out of the kitchen and into the hall. I immediately phoned Christine, my friend, at number 27. I managed a terrified whisper so as not to alarm my father but begged her to come round immediately. This was an international emergency. While I cowered in the hall, my father told me to go out and speak to Marcel. He had left the door ajar.

I didn't want to say anything to Marcel without Christine. My father insisted. So I opened the door properly and stood on the doorstep looking helpless. Marcel had to search my face for clues because I was silent. Also, I'd forgotten all my French. Christine finally arrived, having run all the way up the road. She quickly assessed the situation.

'Helen, elle travail,' said Christine, addressing her remark to Marcel and looking authoritative. This was helpful.

I looked hopefully at Marcel. 'Oui, I travail now.'

He looked stricken. 'Tu es change,' he said.

It had only been a few weeks. 'Oui, je change,' I said, sadly.

I went to Chez Maurice to start my waitressing job. I got sacked for lack of adding up skills and being slow.

> **5. Hand Relief**
>
> VIP Escorts
> Squat
> Laura Ashley

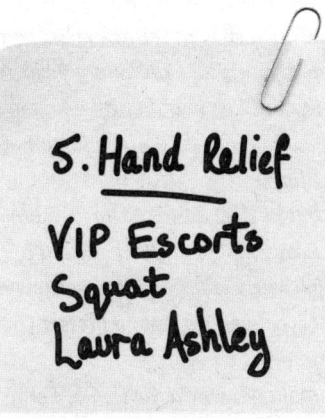

It's summer 1973, I'm in the back room of a massage parlour on Charing Cross Road. The words 'VIP Escorts' can be seen in neon lettering in the window. I think it was this that first attracted me. 'VIP?' I thought to myself, 'that's got to be good'.

I'm 19 years old and taking a year out after school. I don't call it a gap year because gap years haven't been invented yet. Instead, I call it my 'fucked up my grades year'.

The day before, I'd been job hunting around Leicester Square but hadn't had much success. It could have been my Laura Ashley skirt and desert boots – but of the two topless waitress establishments I tried, neither venue appeared ready to take a chance on me. So, when I saw the 'masseurs wanted' notice in the window on the way to the bus stop, I popped in to ask about vacancies. I was in luck. The boss told me to come back the next day to get trained. I was over the moon. I'd be trained as well as paid. Definitely something to make up for getting an E in A-level English.

I'm still wearing a short, light blue, woolly jumper to go with the Paisley Laura Ashley maxi skirt as this is my 'interview ready' look.

The boss arrives and points to a rail of navy blue tunics. Some of them are missing their buttons and they all look too small. I suggest it might be best if I carry on in the Paisley skirt and my woollen, if that's all right with him.

He doesn't object but he does decide to have a shower which seems an odd thing to do. I contemplate the bed in front of me while I wait. I assume the boss will talk me through the various moves when we start the training. Maybe there's a way to protect your back if you're bending for a long time.

He returns to the room wearing a towel. Oh, I'm to practise on the boss. Slightly weird now.

He gets up on the couch, lies face down, and suggests I start on his ankle. I pour some oil onto my hands. I start gingerly on his ankle. Then when I think I've done enough pressing down and around, I go up and then down his calf in what I hope to be a meaningful sort of way. I keep thinking how useful it will be when I'm trained. Another asset for adulthood, along with being able to drive and make a sponge from memory.

The boss says I'm doing great. I've got a good touch. I'm only on to my second proper boyfriend at this point and oiling ankles hasn't been a thing. I allow myself to feel encouraged.

Suddenly, from his lying down position, he says, 'You know, we don't ask our masseurs to have sex.'

I say, 'No, of course you don't – why would you? Goodness!'

Then he says: 'But we do ask them to offer relief massage.'

I have no idea what this means.

I say, 'Oh yes, right,' keeping my voice interested, while I pinch a knee cap.

The penny starts to drop when he turns over. He removes his towel and gestures for me to begin.

I look around the room. I don't know what I'm looking for. I can't leave. It will look unprofessional. Somewhere in my mind I'm thinking, 'Oh, this has gone to a new place now, but if I leave, it will look bad. I'll stick it out and hope for the best. Maybe I can pray if things don't improve'.

I have no idea what to do exactly for the relief section of the procedure, but 20 seconds later he has me up to speed on that one. Afterwards I make my move to the basin, to get at the soap.

Then I wait. I decide to pick up my shoulder bag and try to look satisfied that my job is now complete. As if I've successfully just handed him back his dry cleaning. Suddenly a woman in her twenties joins us. She's clearly been here before. It appears we are both to do the same kind of thing again, but as a team. I try to respond to her, as she eyeballs me across his privates. She's Australian and much more laid back than me, but nevertheless it's an odd way to get to know someone. I didn't feel it appropriate to begin with a polite, 'Did you train in Sydney?'

I seem to have forgotten my new skills, so I let the Australian lead. The boss makes some more high-pitched squeaking sounds. Then it seems we are all free to leave the building.

'He shouldn't have done that with you. I'm really cross,' says the Australian when we reach Piccadilly, as if we'd been on a visit to her naughty uncle and I was a frumpy friend up from Colchester.

Then I'm on the bus home in a slight daze, smelling of Cussons Imperial Leather and a wet towel.

* * *

Quick segue where I'd like to blame my old school:

It's different now, but in those days, Blackheath High School girls were expected to go to Oxford (there were often three of these in each class, often with fawn socks), become secretaries, or, if that didn't work out, get married. As a last resort they might consider teacher training college if they couldn't manage one of the other three. All of these behaviours would make it into the school magazine, under 'news'.

I was told to apply to a couple of teacher training colleges as it was clear I wasn't going to get married or be able to learn shorthand. I didn't get in. I put this down to our headmistress Miss Abraham's conscientious character reference where she may have been morally obliged to include the stink bomb initiative and cheating in the French test, and also because I didn't want to go to teacher training college. I might have said this at the interview or at least demonstrated some confusion as to why I might want to be a teacher.

I wanted to act, but the school's belief that a drama school was one step away from prostitution made me feel it wasn't worth mentioning to anyone. Or at least that's how it seemed. I don't remember any old girl, famous actress coming back on prize day to tell us to follow our dreams. The only famous alumni was Mary Quant, and she did tights.

Since my A-level grades weren't great, the only sensible thing to do was to tell everyone I was taking a year off and look at adverts for things to do that were scary and creative.

I found an adventure playleader course in Islington. The words 'play' and 'adventure' sounded like words a drama school would use. I immediately applied. I have no idea why I thought working with children was a good idea but put that to the back of my mind. I'd get two weeks of training and I'd learn how to play, which had to be better than staying in Eltham. And also, my parents were moving.

Once I'd completed the course, I was given the address of a playground and a place to live. Back then, 61 Hornsey Rise Gardens was a squat, although I didn't know it was a squat at the time because I had no idea people had to pay actual rent in those days. But it was a big house at the end of a cul de sac off Hornsey Road with lots of dustbins in front of it. I was shown around by Nicky who also ran the adventure playground and had the wildest hair out of all the squatters in the house. After a while he decided I was his girlfriend, so I went along with it. The other squatters were only slightly less hirsute, but had studied at LSE with Nicky, and were all older than me. Nicky was 27, I was 19.

Nick (not Nicky) was a 'voluntarily celibate', with an interest in making open-toed sandals out of old tyres. He had given a pair of these to Nicky. If they went out together at the same time, they looked like they were walking on the same bit of old car. The couple in the basement (the macrobiotics) made endless loaves of bread. The random French girl in the top room didn't stay for long. I interrupted her once when she was masturbating, and she left soon after. I did knock.

The most surprising thing about the job on the playground was not being asked to leave. But three of my least favourite moments have stayed with me.

One day a child called out to me: 'Miss, hey Miss!'

'Yes?' I said, smiling in an encouraging fashion. I may have been sitting on a roughly-honed swing at the time.

'Have you got any teeth, Miss?'

I had very small teeth then, which tended not to show unless I opened my mouth very wide, and that could have looked aggressive to young people.

Another incident was when a seven-year-old clung to me like a limpet and I cuddled him back, feeling strangely moved, only to find he'd nicked my purse.

The third memory is of sitting on top of the railway siding one afternoon, on my own, looking down at the wooden playground structure, with a severe pain in my side. I feared I might be having an early nervous breakdown. But it passed after an hour, so it must have been a muscle spasm.

After a few weeks of living at the squat, I'd moved into the attic room with Nicky who told me, among other things, that when the revolution came, he would be a true part of it. I didn't know where I would be when it came, but I knew I'd miss him terribly. I was also worried about the issue of violence which was kept vague.

When my playground job ended, Nicky continued to be a respected community leader and good with young people, while I needed to find some other work to pay my way in the communal kitty. I needed to be there in case he got off with someone else and anyway, riding on the back of Nicky's motorbike, going to films with subtitles, listening to Velvet Underground while puffing on a knob of hash, wouldn't be happening in Eltham. Or Chislehurst – where my parents were planning to move. I was at finishing school.

I was open to ideas for interesting jobs and Nicky decided his German friend Inge could advise me about hostess work in the West End. Inge explained that hostess work mostly involved meeting people and talking to them, which sounded doable. She did mention a topless option which came out of the blue, but I was committed. If Inge had managed hostess work so impressively, then so could I.

Nicky supported my job hunting. But when we got the bus together to Leicester Square to scout out some likely hostess-type places of employment, I began to have my doubts. Inge was a very different kind of person to me. According to her, being a strong woman meant being able to do what you liked with your body, but I was more interested in impressing Nicky and making some money, so he wouldn't chuck me.

We stopped at a restaurant that had pictures of girls in the window. I was wearing my usual outfit for interviews and asked to see the manager about vacancies. Nicky waited outside. The manager thought I was about to book a table. He actually said, 'What's a nice girl like you doing asking for a job here?'

On the way out, I was relieved he hadn't offered me a job, but that was only after I'd allowed myself a look at the other waitresses. I did not look the same.

'They're full,' I explained to Nicky, and we walked on towards the bus stop. This was when I saw the notice for vacancies for masseurs on Charing Cross Road.

After the training session, I reported for work the next Saturday to start my new job. I was shown into the back room where two other female masseurs were waiting for people to massage. They both stared at me. Maybe they hadn't seen a duffle coat before.

Eventually, the Greek masseur (lacy blouse in brown) reluctantly got up from her chair to show me a cubicle to rattle off a few instructions. She pointed at some oil and talcum powder. I knew she was going fast on purpose and didn't want to annoy her by asking questions such as 'which went on first?' Was it the oil, and then the powder, or the other way round? And how much of each? Too little and I'd be basting, too much and I'd be dealing with some kind of clay vase.

I heard the shop door open and peered out to see what a customer might look like in real life. A man was standing in the shadows, in front of the alcove of fake flowers. I could make out a mac.

It could be my turn next. I went over my training in my head. Oil, talc and possibly the add on. I'd have to ask the awkward question. I'd have to ask the unknown man in the mac if he wanted anything else. What if I knew him?

Suddenly I picked up my duffle coat and headed for the door. No one came after me.

This is a pattern in my life. Being an accidental rebel and now sex worker wasn't so different from stand-up comedy. The attraction to danger and fear is eventually what led me to perform. Most performers would agree it's best to stay on the stage once you've gone to the trouble of getting on one, but sometimes it's not.

NOT THAT I'M BITTER

Once, as Paul Merton may or may not be happy to remember, there was a regrettable occasion in Balham at the Banana Cabaret Club, when I knew it wasn't the right time to take to the stage. It was while I was being introduced that I came to this decision. Paul had to go on to be introduced as funny woman 'Helen Lederer'.

6. Heartbreak
First Love
Death
VD (I think)

My heart is broken. I know it is because I haven't eaten anything for two days, which is new.

I suddenly panic.

'Do you think it's dangerous?' I ask my friend Helena.

'What?'

'Not eating for two days.'

She takes one look at me.

'I think you'll be all right.'

The pain is terrible. Dave is the first person I have ever really fallen in love with. Properly loved, where I feel sick just looking at him. I bought him a battery for his car. It was an honour.

And now it's over. And it's all my fault.

So, this is how I learn that it takes four years to get over the end of a love affair.

* * *

NOT THAT I'M BITTER

It was coming up to September. My accidental gap year was coming to an end, and so was my fun. My one-off workshop in 'hand relief' would not be recognised as a qualification, so it was time to chase up the deferred place from Hatfield, to do something called 'social studies' promised the year before.

I was celebrating my 20th birthday in my parents' new home in Chislehurst when my father told me to look out of the window. I screamed and rushed out to touch my present. It was a car. A Hillman Imp, apparently.

I felt so lucky. And then I saw the duck. It was on the passenger door. The prospect of giving anyone any lifts in it became slightly less cool. But I was still very grateful. The best bit was being able to commute to a college that was relatively near the squat and keeping the boyfriend.

The first thing I noticed about college was the sheer volume of men in the corridors all walking fast. I'd never seen so many men at once, carrying folders.

Sanjeev Bhaskar was one of these, but I only found out he'd been there years later and we both had cubicles named after us. I felt obliged to turn up and cut the ribbon. It was the least I could do.

My scent at this time was called Chic by Yardley. A lot of people commented on my smell, but even allowing for this small success, I knew I wasn't going to fit in. Most of the women in my year didn't look old enough to have done anything that required initiative, apart from open their A-level results and get on the train from where they lived to Hertfordshire. There were two males and about 27 women including one mature student and two Christians, one of whom went under the name of Linda Fridge. I only mention this surname because it has stayed with me.

I sensed that, unlike me, many of them wouldn't have been afforded the opportunity to watch themselves having sex in front of a large wardrobe mirror, with their slightly older boyfriend. I decided this must be one of the main differences between those who'd had a gap year and those who hadn't, but I tried not to feel too superior. It was, however, rather lonely.

At the end of my first term, I met a short man with glasses called Tim. I felt a stirring. This meant I would have to tell Nicky. And I would also have to leave the squat. The biggest surprise was that Nicky seemed to mind. I had proved to both of us, I was capable of unkindness. And his mother would be sad. She liked me.

Even my parents had become quite fond of him. The first time Nicky had been invited for a Sunday lunch, my mother had been peering through our crochet-look net curtains from Heals, to know 'when to put the peas on'. Seeing Nicky walk up the path through the nets made me protective. I told my parents not to laugh at the dungarees as they were quite short, and they didn't.

But now I had another boyfriend. He lived in a house that was known as 'Beehive' since it was behind the Beehive pub. Tim was in the year above me, which gave him status even though he'd been allocated the smallest room. Until me, Tim hadn't had a proper girlfriend. Even so, I became jealous of a confident girl on the same landing once I found out she'd taken Tim's virginity. I toyed with fantasies about wanting her dead which was a very surprising reaction especially as she was always very pleasant to me. Her father was a don at Oxford and I couldn't help feeling she might be a slight disappointment to her parents. But then, we all were.

The Beehive people all called me Baby Doll. BD for short. This wasn't a compliment. I knew it had to do with me having a big head. And I was only included in the group as the girlfriend of Tim. A bit like living in the squat really.

After struggling with Tim's single bed as well as one of his housemates' interest in our toilet habits (a future psychotherapist), I was pleased to find a room of my own above a tropical fish shop called Marine Inn. The tanks vibrated beneath my mattress at night and a toasty smell of worms and rotting eggs followed me around upstairs, like a warm balm of fungal fish food and algae.

The landlord allowed me to hang a pair of Laura Ashley curtains, as long as I promised to keep his musty, unpleasant ones in a bag for someone else to enjoy when I moved out. I had a coffee table made out of an old drawer and my guitar was kept propped against the wall to offer a hint of musicality. It was perfect.

I lived there with Liz and Ronno who were on the same course as me, although neither had taken a year off or been given massage work experience. There was no sitting room and the shared kitchen was so small we had to hold our toast above our heads for space. This may also have been the reason our cycles became synchronised.

In 1975, just after my 21st birthday, my life changed completely.

The Christmas holidays had started and I was back at my parents' house. I had been out with my father in the day, buying presents. We had returned home in good humour, both of us enjoying our connection after a few months apart. For some reason I lay awake that night.

I heard my father go into the bathroom. Soon after this I heard groaning. I got out of bed and found the bathroom door open. He was lying on the floor. This didn't make any sense. Everything felt wrong. I'd never seen anyone die before. I called out for my mother. She came immediately and dropped to the floor to cradle my father's head, but I knew he was already in another state of being. The shock of this ending and the love of my parents' relationship were bound up on the bathroom floor. I had to be the adult. I called an ambulance.

Not long after we arrived at the hospital, a young doctor came to tell us quite briskly that my father had died. He was 52.

There was nothing else to do but drive back from the hospital in disbelief. Everything felt unreal except for the ache in my chest.

My father was the person I loved more than anyone else. Now it was my turn to cradle my mother. We didn't know what to do. She had collapsed on the floor, so we both just sat together on the hall carpet.

'It's not fair,' she said. I'd never seen my mother cry before. People like my mother didn't cry. She'd always been organised and self-sufficient. I spent the next few years trying to banish this memory because I didn't know what to do with it. I'd stand in the shower and feel the grief. A new relationship had begun. I would now have to look after my mother, but without her knowing.

My father was a magnet. Even my school friends looked up to him. I was still trying to think of ways to impress him after I'd left home, which is still within the normal range of having a cool parent.

In the 1960s he took a year out from his normal job to work as advisor to the Minister of Housing. His appointment appeared in *The Times* which made Miss Thomas at the junior school purse her lips when she referred to it. He was working for a Labour government and under a Minister of Housing called Richard Crossman, who was also a socialist. The school wasn't very Labour. Maybe he was responsible for some very bad '60s housing, but I was too young to be consulted.

My father was the only person in my whole world who I'd rather not have died and when he did it in front of me, before I was even a proper grown-up with an evolved brain, part of me changed forever and a new life began.

I began to seek out powerful and unattainable lovers. I didn't want boyfriends that I could feel superior to. I wanted amazing, powerful ones that I could look up to. I wasn't discriminating. As long as they were figures of authority, I was interested. One of my crushes was a lecturer and as long as he arrived with his briefcase, I could get aroused.

And then a very nice but posh friend of Tim's called Jules introduced me to Dave. He wasn't a student. He was a stained-glass artist who lived in some kind of funded commune for artists in Old Welwyn.

And he was the first person I can remember looking at and feeling immediately sick because he was so beautiful. This was very impractical. The sight of his Wolseley car made my stomach turn over with excitement. I was scared of his Dalmatian dog, but it didn't matter. Dave was a God. My friend Christine named him 'Pedestal'.

Soon after I met him, we got together. I never knew if I was allowed to say that we were having a thing because he was an artist and wasn't into commitment. I didn't even know if Dave thought we were having a thing. Did making love on the floor of his Georgian commune and listening to Van Morrison count as having a thing?

Arranging to meet in those days was difficult. There were no phones and, being an artist, Dave didn't seem to know when he'd be free. I would keep watch by the window in case he might drop by. And when he did, the sight of him parking the Wolseley and crossing the road in his faded jeans and perfect jumper would make me reel. I'd quickly put on the Joni Mitchell LP, douse myself with Chic by Yardley and close the Laura Ashleys. Sometimes he would play my guitar or use my ashtray. These were special times. I also knew I was the luckiest person in St Albans.

I can remember once rather rashly asking Dave, 'Do you think I'm beautiful?' And he replied thoughtfully, 'I'm an artist. I can see beauty in anything.'

I was grateful and insecure; he was beautiful with an unusually low voice. I had no rights on the relationship because we didn't speak about that kind of thing. And then came a cruel blow. He became dissatisfied with his life and wanted to find meaning.

Dave went off to France to find it, while I finished my final exams in the summer of 1978. We had a painful but knowing goodbye and I prayed we might marry in the near future – marriage was my top prayer. There was a party to celebrate the last exam and I ended up in Terry's tiny room in his hall of residence. Terry was one of the very few males in our year – one of two. To the best of my knowledge Terry didn't have a girlfriend.

I would never have considered Terry a plausible choice for sexual release if I hadn't been working so hard at getting over Dave. The euphoria over exams and the fear about leaving college forever had made me cling to anyone who'd have me. Terry seemed happy enough and, anyway, he had his own issues. Like being very fat, for instance.

I had a few more days rent paid at Marine Inn when I saw Dave and the Wolseley parking up outside. Life was suddenly good again. Dave possibly hadn't found meaning in France after all.

A week later I received Dave's letter.

'We have a sad malady,' he announced. What followed was a lot of prose about him not knowing about the future, particularly with all its 'twists and turns', which was understandable, and then at the very end of the letter, almost as a PS, he wrote, 'You had better go to the clinic and get yourself checked out.'

Clinic? What clinic?

But I knew enough to go straight to Terry to ask him if he could explain what had to be done in a clinic.

'Why?' asked Terry

'Dave has got this malady.'

'Where's he been?' asked Terry.

'France.'

'Then he must have got the malady from there.'

'But he says he got the malady from here. From me… from you?'

'I haven't got a malady. I've never had a malady,' Terry was outraged.

'Nor have I. Are you sure you haven't… been with anyone? I mean it's fine if you have, but have you?'

Terry promised on members of his family's lives that he hadn't been with anyone. And somehow, looking at his dejected, plump and rather kind face, I believed him. On the other hand, someone must have been fibbing. And it wasn't me…

We sat in miserable silence at the special clinic, feeling very sick about our symptomless, baffling malady that had no name.

Terry and I were given a pack of monstrously large penicillin pills 'to be on the safe side' and said goodbye to each other in a confused sort of way. There were no plans for a second date.

At least I was granted a last opportunity to see Dave in a pub. I had to share the information about Terry which would make him despise me even more than I despised myself. The shame felt avoidable and yet somehow very me. I prepared to beg.

'If I'd known you wanted to be with me, I would never have… done it.'

As bewildering as the phantom malady was, this was all my fault. If only I hadn't assumed Dave had gone off me, which he had, I might not have celebrated the end of exams in quite the same way with Terry, which I did. And this was only because I had no idea Dave was going to go on me again.

Dave's face remained expressionless. I asked if I could ever see him again. I may have said 'please'.

'I don't know, I just don't know,' he shook his head sadly.

Then he rode off on his bicycle and I knew that was what the end of a love affair felt like. The grief about my father was managed by not thinking about him, but this new heartbreak couldn't be managed in the same way. Our parting was my fault. The phantom malady, be it Terry's or Dave's – had exposed my stupidity. And my self-sabotage was to haunt me…

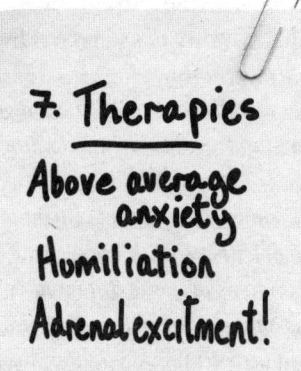

> **7. Therapies**
> Above average anxiety
> Humiliation
> Adrenal excitment!

I'm in St John's Avenue, Swiss Cottage, London. Most of the houses look like they belong to the Addams family. Gothic turrets and very small windows make a depressing sight in this road full of unusually tall trees.

I'm now waiting on a landing and wonder how many other quiet, sad people, willing to pay to be cheered up by a medical professional have sat on the same landing. There are no magazines. A door opens and a young woman emerges. I look to see if she's been crying but she scuttles past me and down the stairs.

I wait. There is silence.

Just when I start to think I've got the wrong day, the door opens. Slightly. A small woman in her 70s it seems to me (I am 27) stands in the doorway and nods at me. I already know it won't be long before I annoy her, but I follow her inside.

My therapist nips across the room to bagsy the large armchair and gestures for me to sit on the more junior one. I understand the therapeutic professionalism behind this gesture. What would have happened if I'd gone for her seat? Already she was saving me from myself. I sit where I am supposed to and nervously assess the woman opposite. She is my first therapist.

She is wearing a dirndl skirt with a cardigan. Not entirely Tyrolean but still a stand against adult clothing. No tights. And flat sandals.

There is a hint of a smile. She appears content to wait. Her hands are placed on her dirndl, palms up. More silence.

I look up at the hundreds of books displayed on her shelf directly opposite me. There is one especially big book labelled 'Suicide' which I try not to take as an instruction.

'So, why are you here?'

I wasn't sure. As a social worker (I became one of these after my mother suggested I might want to get a job, instead of mooching about her house and leaving coffee mugs everywhere when I left college), it wasn't considered unusual to see a therapist. The Dirndl was one of a few analysts who'd been recommended by someone in my team who knew about these sorts of things. Mind you, that person in my team may or may not have been having an affair with her therapist. At least that wasn't going to be an option here.

Dirndl is waiting, neutrally.

'Because... I don't feel I have a personality?'

She looks at the floor.

I hope that looking at the floor is her way of thinking about what to say next or else things will be very quiet.

Eventually she looks up.

'You don't feel you have a personality?'

'No,' I confirm.

* * *

I have a god-like trust that a good therapist has the potential to normalise inappropriate behaviour, rejection and sadness, and it's this optimism that keeps me paying for it. Over and over again. I wanted my need for laughter, boys, slimness and praying to be explained to me.

I saw Dirndl every week for six months.

It may have been the Jung in her, but Dirndl noticeably perked up with the words 'Jewish' and 'refugee'. She asked lots of questions about my family, particularly in the early days, when she said more words. I found myself describing what I'd been told about my father being sent to Margate on a boat in 1937.

'How old was your father?'

'Ten? Twelve? He didn't have the right uniform.'

Silence.

'He was very lonely,' I added.

I started to cry.

Dirndl looked at the floor again. To get her attention, I carried on.

'His parents were Czech, although Little Baba came from the bit that spoke German.'

'Little... Baba?'

'Little Baba's my grandmother,' I explained, in case she thought I was referring to a small baby.

'And your grandfather?'

'Big Baba.'

She may or may not have kicked herself for that question.

'Anyway,' I continue, 'they came over in '39 and I always felt they had a thing about the Germans, but it was never said. A lot was never said.'

'What was never said?'

I thought she should know this.

'Well, you know, the fact they killed my relatives. Some of them. Not all obviously... because I'm here.'

Dirndl nodded but said, 'It is time', which I found quite rude, until I learned this was always my cue to leave.

I had to give notice when I decided not to continue with Dirndl, which made the last four weeks rather awkward. But I'd found an alternative to therapy. I felt guilty about the (paid) rejection, but the course of diet injections from a clinic in Harley Street felt more exciting than sitting in the smaller chair, being quiet. To my surprise, Dirndl decided to pep up our last meeting with a positive spin on how far I had come and, also, where I was going.

According to Dirndl, the amphetamine injections were a sign that I was taking control of my life and doing something active to change it. I thanked her for this upbeat reassurance. At least I would remember what she said this time. Until now, I'd been paying for a mysterious landscape of nothingness and insights that I could never remember by the time I got home.

I wondered if it was worth asking if a Jungian like herself might consider injections to be a step towards a lifetime of addiction, but my time was up.

'It is time,' she said.

I said goodbye and wafted quietly, as always, down the stairs.

Seven years later I decided to have another go.

The second analyst was called Eleanor and lived in Notting Hill in a bohemian, but still posh, townhouse. I seemed to have a lot of jobs at this time, so I booked a therapy session very early in the morning. Eleanor thought nothing of taking her five-year-old out of her own bed to lie on a bundle of cushions on the floor during our sessions, which was interesting parenting for someone in the caring field. She spoke quietly. Maybe it was because she didn't want to wake up her sleeping child. I took to leaning forward to make sure I didn't miss anything and get my money's worth.

By now I had stopped worrying that I didn't have a personality because I had recently been ascribed personality traits such as 'neurotic' and 'eccentric'. Proof I was now part of the scene of women being judged for being funny in the '80s.

And by the late '80s, I'd developed a new problem that I felt could do with sorting. I wasn't happy.

It was becoming clear that my feeling of drowning into darkness and self-hatred before I stepped on stage may not be completely normal. Nobody else seemed to be nervous. They made jokes backstage.

I'd also developed a moustache, caused by the bursts of adrenalin, or possibly due to polycystic ovary syndrome. A kind comedian called John Sparkes had pointed out some bumps in my groin which led me to this diagnosis. My friend Helena pointed out the moustache, which was more than I would have done for anyone.

Eleanor (therapist with child on floor) was the first and only therapist to award me the helpful 'above average anxiety' score. Her rather pithy explanation of why I like to repeat pain has already been referenced in the introduction, but I repeat here again for ease.

'For someone who hates authority figures, failure and being humiliated in public, you've chosen the very career that would most likely offer all of these in one continued cycle of adrenal excitement,' she told me with a gentle smile.

It would have been nice to have been offered a solution, but I was relieved to have at least half an answer. Clearly, in her eyes, I was a masochist. I was getting somewhere. So shortly afterwards I stopped going. Maybe it was the saboteur in me, or the guilt about her sleeping child, or getting pregnant myself, or the hassle of schlepping across town and giving out cheques, but I'd done my time here.

My main take-away was that I liked pain.

* * *

There had to be a slight pause in one-on-one therapist action while

NOT THAT I'M BITTER

I got pregnant, married and separated – which took me 18 months, all in – but I was still game to have a joint go during the marriage. It wasn't just me now.

The first 'couples' therapist was a strict woman who invited us to her small but booky flat to make an 'assessment'. Within minutes of sitting at either end of her cream linen sofa (probably with some kind of throw since we were bordering on Kilburn), she got the measure of us.

'This is a very dangerous relationship.' She was looking directly at me as she said it. And we never saw her again. I made sure of it.

A few months later we progressed to 'couple therapy' with a couple who, unlike us, were happily married. They were also therapists. The sessions took place in Hampstead, in a cosy sitting room. We sat on one side of the coffee table, while they sat on the other. It felt like being part of a foursome on a bridge afternoon where no-one wanted to say anything mean.

The sessions ended with the woman suggesting I was treating the fate of the relationship as if I was about to amputate a limb. I suggested I would rather amputate a limb than be messed about. And assumed we were all talking metaphorically.

They were too nice to be helpful, and we stopped going.

A few years into single parenting, I tried the Group Analytic Practice in Montague Mansions. Group therapy was cheaper because everyone gets less attention, but the first group silence was harsh. It reminded me of having to hold the fort at a Lederer gathering while my father fetched in that ham to put on the hotplate in the dining room.

I didn't know how to let other people be quiet. Or cry. I wanted control, which isn't allowed in a group.

There was one client who started every single sentence with, 'I'm not being funny but…' and she was right, she wasn't. I ended up putting her character in my one-woman show, *Still Crazy After*

All These Years. I felt guilty about doing it and told the group not to come to the show. I confessed it was about group therapy and because there was so much trust between us, no-one came or maybe there were other reasons, like, they didn't want to.

I've spent years paying various people to explain why I am the way I am, and then not listening to what they say. The intention to be made better is there, but the palaver of deciphering what someone else who doesn't even know me tells me requires trust. Maybe I'd have to change?

This is when I decide it's not working and I can't afford it and leave. But, still, a new therapist offers new hope, like a new diet, or a new personal trainer or ordering a new dress online that you can't afford and know will pinch around the waist when it arrives.

> 8. **Drama School**
> Saucepan
>   Handle
> Up Jacksy

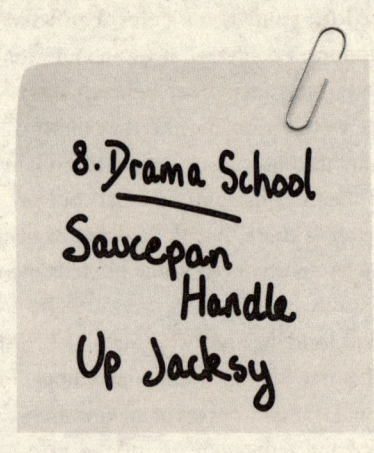

It's the early '80s. I'm at a drama school. Alison Steadman has appeared at the theatre across the road in Abigail's Party *and Jim Broadbent gave us a talk about improvisation with Mike Leigh.*

I'm on the phone to my drama tutor.

'Will you want anything to eat?' I ask, unsure of the etiquette for an out-of-hours psychodrama session.

'No. I'll bring a sandwich,' he says.

I wonder why he will bring a sandwich if he's not going to eat it.

'Have you got a tape recorder?' he suddenly asks.

'I do, yes. It's a Sony,' I reply with confidence. I may be in need of extra tuition, but at least I can furnish our session with a Sony cassette player.

I say goodbye and block out the afternoon to become more talented.

* * *

I always wanted to be an actor or do what my mother and my sister referred to as the 'showing off'.

The spare room became known as 'the piano room' when our English granny died and we inherited her piano, along with an item of furniture called a 'divan' (later covered with a Mexican bedspread). We stuck fablon roses all over the piano to turn it into a 1960s cocktail bar and used the 'divan' as a base for hospital games and later for somewhere to take boys and place them on it.

I wasn't given much opportunity to be creative at senior school because any kind of individuality was met with suspicion. Even a gentle jog in the corridor was seen as rebellious. Acting at home was my only outlet, especially as the teachers could only manage one theatre production every two years before exhaustion set in, and when they did, I was never cast in anything. My sister was given a speaking part in the *Insect Play*, which was a bitter pill. She didn't even want to be an ant.

The only time I got to be on stage in our 'new hall', with its 1970s trendy, striped curtains and pull-out raked seating, was when I played a cleaner in the end of year sixth form review and that was because I cast myself. So, by the time I'd got to Hatfield, the first thing I did was join the Drama Soc. At least I'd be allowed to get on a stage. Finally, I was in the right place at the right time.

It was the opening night of *Oh What A Lovely War*. I'd been given six different parts and this was my first scene. I'd just climbed up onto a wooden crate to begin my Sylvia Pankhurst when, out of the corner of my eye, I noticed a uniformed official making his way down the side of the audience. I knew this wasn't meant to happen, but my parents were in the audience, so I began my first line. But the man waving his hands had other ideas. He was from security, announcing there was a bomb scare and since it was during the time of the IRA bombings, people didn't waste any time getting out of the building. It was a nice opportunity for me to greet my parents on the forecourt and catch up, before we went our respective ways, but I didn't get to act at Hatfield again. And my father never heard my Sylvia.

I assumed the play would be cancelled. The bomb scare was on a Friday and I didn't go back to college until Monday. When I turned up at Drama Soc to talk about the cancelled show, I got a very frosty reception.

Eventually, David, the drama tutor, spoke to me, since no-one else would.

'Where were you? I mean... where were you?' David was baffled.

'When?' I asked. But the familiar feeling of dread washed over me.

'Last night?'

'You... you did the play last night? I assumed it was...'

Ridiculous, stupid. I'd wrongly concluded that a 'bomb scare' on one night would mean a cancelled show the next. But without a phone, no-one could get hold of me. We were only doing two nights. All my parts had to be divvied up at the last minute and a new Sylvia Pankhurst had to step onto the crate holding her script. I'd let everyone down, and for the next four years I had to walk past the Drama Soc studio with my head down.

Surprisingly, after leaving Hatfield I was accepted as a part-time social worker with Camden Council and part-time researcher at the same time. For the life of me I can't remember what the research was for, but when a full-time post became available, I decided to apply for that as well. By this time, I'd enrolled on an MA course in criminology at Middlesex to make up for my general loss of status, combined with a bit of interest in the subject. The shoplifting may have been an early sign. But I still needed to act. I had to keep trying. Even when I was trapped in my social work job, I wanted to find a way to do it.

One day, I suggested to my team leader that maybe I could teach young people 'some acting'. Amazingly, she agreed – possibly to get me out of the office so she could check my note keeping – and I set up some drama workshops with deprived youngsters, which I hoped would bring us all out of our shells. After three sessions, it felt sensible to stop. The lack of attendance helped this decision.

I started looking around for courses that had the word 'drama' in them and was pleased to find something called 'psychodrama' conveniently nearby. Perhaps I could still get to act but in a social-workery sort of way?

The psychodrama course took place in a small attic room of a building in Fitzjohn's Avenue. Not far from the Dirndl's premises. The group would start each session by sitting in a circle and talking. Mario, our 'enabler', would decide whose story to follow and although it wasn't always straightforward following his directions, without an interpreter, we knew he had a big following in Milan.

Once I lost a knuckle beating up a bean bag. It's still missing, but I managed to get angry in public which Mario was pleased about. We were an odd collection of people who couldn't act but were closet creatives in need of help. I met a future top literary agent there, before she became known as a ball breaker in her field, the usual way to describe successful women agents at the time, as well as the drama tutor who later gave me the extra tuition. It didn't take me long to realise the word drama meant 'acting out' and psycho meant 'unstable'.

I was still desperate to act and started buying *The Stage* newspaper to focus my search. When I saw an advert for new members to join the Open Link Community Theatre, I phoned up and was told to meet at a church hall in Crouch End.

I turned up in loose clothing as advised and met Ian Munday, a tall blond man wearing leggings, ankle warmers and a shawl. He was both an actor and founder of Open Link Theatre. Apparently, I was going to be cast in a play called *Dr Faustus*. I hadn't even auditioned and I was in. So was everyone else.

'No acting ability is required here,' asserted Ian. 'We are a community theatre; we are all equal.'

I found this very left wing and inclusive.

But a china cup would be thrown at the wall if people didn't understand his directions. This happened a lot, as people weren't always clear. I dared to assume I was one of the best actors since I never got the cup and also because the standard was so low. Graham was one of the worst. Cups often found their way towards Graham. Arnold Brown (the Scottish comedian né accountant) only slightly minded about these unorthodox methods of teaching but, like everyone else, gave himself wholeheartedly to Ian's production, performed in leotards and in the round. And even when Arnold was carried around on high during a workshop of the seven deadly sins (we were on 'lust'), he was perfectly fine with another actor smearing spittle on him.

I had been cast as the Good Angel, but to help people know this, I wafted a ripped-up tennis skirt that was attached to each wrist while I said my lines. These lines were 'repent Faustus, repent.' Unfortunately, the audience laughed. Ian wasn't happy, but as I said to him in the interval, I'd always done it that way in rehearsals. I loved Ian.

'Maybe it was the tennis skirt?' I suggested afterwards.

I was apprehensive about Little Baba, my mother and my sister seeing me. On the way out, Little Baba apparently said to my sister, 'Well, she won't be doing Shakespeare'.

But it was Little Baba who finally made my dream come true. In February, she died, leaving me enough money to give up social work and finally go to a drama school. And even though it was a bit of a weird course and I had to lie to get on to it, because everyone else was a teacher and I was a social worker with half an MA and Open Link Community membership, at least it was a proper drama school.

It made losing one knuckle as well as a beloved grandmother worth it.

I loved everything about drama school. I may have been on the weird course, but I could still revel in the parquet floors, the huge mirrors and actors wrapping themselves around each other in the coffee bar, wearing long scarves. Everything felt intense and physical.

This was 1981 when tutors could still put their hands up people's skirts and talk about being admirers of women without any comeback, because they had positions of power. The poet who taught us once a week about longing did this a lot. In fact, it was his thing.

This style of behaviour was accepted as bohemian and almost characterful. It wasn't particularly pleasant, but there it was. Only a few years before, a flasher in a plastic mac had got into our train carriage on the way home from school.

Flashers seemed to be everywhere in the '70s. Our one sat himself opposite my friend Fiona who must have been coming home with me for tea. If we didn't have tea together, she'd ring me at five (before Crossroads obviously) and then I'd ring her back again at eight o'clock in case we hadn't covered everything. Fiona went on to be the classical music critic for the *Observer* but at the time we mostly talked about clothes, where to get navy blue A-line skirts in particular (answer=Etams).

The Flasher began by staring at us. That's when we nudged each other. In a smiley way, he told us we were 'getting plump in the right places', which, I remember, we both took on board at the time. If you can't trust the judgement of a qualified flasher on a train home to Eltham, then who can you trust? But it didn't feel good. Then he flashed something else which wasn't a torch. So, I told my parents, they told the police and I had the embarrassment of having to use the word 'plump' in front of two police officers in my sitting room. Fiona didn't have to because she didn't tell her parents.

So, after my flasher whistle-blowing, I felt it was easier to just go along with things.

My own tutor, who I'd first met in the psychodrama group, was a funny little man called Gerry Christie, who we later referred to as 'Gerry Risky' in a complicit but semi-assertive, early 1980s, feminist-sort-of-way. This wouldn't happen now; we'd just report him and then wait 20 years to see who noticed. I've repeated this joke because I couldn't bring myself to take it out of the other section.

A few weeks into the first term, Gerry suggested coming round to my flat to do some extra 'opening up' exercises with me. I wasn't thrilled, but I knew I couldn't afford to be inhibited as an actress and really wanted to improve.

So, I accepted the offer.

When Gerry recovered his breath, after the communal stairs, he took my hand and told me how much he understood me. He especially understood my loneliness, he said, and showed me the cassette of music he'd made which was in his briefcase along with the home-made sandwich. He hoped it might speak to my 'lonely, middle European soul'. I hoped it would as well and placed his home-made tape inside my Sony cassette recorder. Once I'd pressed play, I went to join him on the sofa.

This was the same sofa my grandparents had managed to get sent over from Czechoslovakia during the war. I'd recovered it, rather inappropriately, in a fluorescent Designers Guild fabric. I used to tell boyfriends that refugees had been hidden inside as a way to escape Hitler. I didn't mention the refugees to Gerry. He wasn't a boyfriend.

The piece of music was a jazz number called *At the Window* by Jimmy Yancey.

'It's lovely' I said as he pressed start. Gerry held up his finger, which I took to mean I should listen to the whole thing, before commenting.

So, we sat together, listening to the instrumental jazz while I nodded appreciatively and tried to look less lonely.

Then the tape ended.

'Wow,' I said.

He raised an eyebrow at me.

'Yes,' I said. 'Really, like being at a window but… looking out…'

Gerry waited. 'And seeing things.'

Once the tape had been fully appreciated by both of us, it was time to warm-up. We both had to be in socks to make it feel equal, so we took off our shoes. Then he began by breathing loudly. I'd already done a lot of breathing work at the Open Link Community Theatre, so I felt on top of that side of things. But when it came to getting into 'character', I still struggled. I told Gerry I knew this was the thing I had to work on the most and shared his disappointment that I wasn't more 'open'. All was not lost though, because Gerry very swiftly started acting out things like 'space' and 'anger' and 'kittens licking things' to set a helpful example. This was where I had to be on my knees and be a cat on the carpet. Just when I was thinking, maybe if I act out licking my litter tray, he'll go soon, he decided to change tack.

I remember him asking if I had a saucepan with a smooth handle. I went off to get him one but wondered where this might be going. I didn't have to wait long to find out. Gerry was very deft with his pan work. The next thing I knew the handle ended up going boldly where no saucepan handle had ever been before. I remember keeping very still – just to be on the safe side. And then he left. I remember feeling a bit taken aback, because when my temporary flatmate let herself in, I was still on the sofa trying to work out if I'd become more talented or not.

'Do you know what happened today?' I asked my flatmate.

'No.'

'I just had a drama lesson with Gerry Christie.'

'Did it work?'

'Not necessarily. He used a saucepan.'

My flatmate looked at me suspiciously.

'A saucepan?'

'OK, not saucepan, more… handle.' I said.

'Why?'

'Why?' I repeated. 'Because the pan wouldn't fit, why do you think…'

'Which saucepan?' she asked, frowning.

'That one,' I said. And pointed at it.

Neither of us used it after that – not even for peas.

Spurred on, perhaps by my ability to remain very still, Gerry continued to find creative ways to try to 'open me up' to become the actress he believed I could be.

A woman who had been a student on his previous course was invited to join us both for another 'creative' afternoon at my flat. This mostly involved Gerry sitting on the psychedelic, originally Czech sofa and watching to see if we might become lesbians. I obliged as far as I could, to prove my creativity, but actually out of the two, I preferred the pan.

Gerry's 'central relationship', as he called his wife, was away on business when the next tutorial was offered.

'I'd like you to meet Kevin. He's a wonderful drama teacher.'

I can't remember being particularly keen on having to trek up to West London for another 'tutorial', but I had less than one year to improve, so…

Kevin turned out to be another ex-student but had allegedly been dismissed from his school for inappropriate behaviour, although I didn't know this at the time. We had to be blindfolded while Gerry, rather excitedly, suggested we 'explore' each other.

There was a slight awkwardness when we took our blindfolds off. Neither of us had been particularly engaged. Gerry had to admit defeat and offered us a tray of savoury home-made snacks, before we went home.

I'd like to blame the 1980s in general for my colluding behaviour with Gerry's 'creativity issues', but that doesn't explain my own accountability. Were other people as lacking in asking questions and as passive as I was? Did we all just keep quiet? Were we ashamed? Was 'creativity' Gerry's euphemism for knowingly crossing boundaries? Abuse? Or was Gerry genuinely attached to his teaching methods to facilitate creativity – just as the dodgy poetry tutor believed he was artistically imparting his craft and love of longing. If no-one challenged these men, then what did that say about us? I'd like to think I'd challenge this kind of initiative/abuse now if called upon, but there's evidence to suggest the middle-aged are less likely to be subject to wandering hands.

At the time, I really wanted to become a better actor and would have done anything to get there. If I needed to cast off any inhibitions – the same inhibitions that Gerry had identified – then I was in his hands. I don't remember feeling threatened. Just a bit depressed that out of the whole class, I was the one needing a saucepan to access my talent. And for a long time, I couldn't look at a Le Creuset pan without thinking that's my idea of an Oscar.

But since this was before the emergence of #MeToo, I simply filed all these encounters away under 'saucepan' and cracked on.

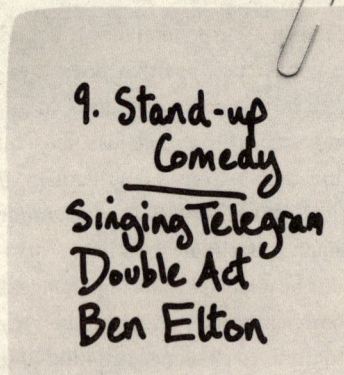

9. Stand-up Comedy
Singing Telegram Double Act
Ben Elton

It's 1982 and my first stand-up gig. I'm waiting to go on stage at Pentameters in Hampstead. It's a theatre club, and lucky for me, they don't hold stag nights in a theatre club. There are three of us in the Green Room. Me, John Hegley (very funny comic poet) and John Dowie (very funny comedian). Hegley has just come from another gig, Dowie is smoking. I'm writing lines on my hand.

There are no other women because this is 1982 and also because my female double act partner has bailed. I'm on my own for the first time.

'When do you want to go on?' Arnold Brown, comedian and compere, is in the doorway, waving a pencil.

'I don't mind.'

Arnold starts to write something.

'As long as it's not first.'

He nods.

'Or second.'

He nods again.

'Or just after the interval...'
Someone has dimmed the lights.
'Or wait, maybe that's ok?'
I'm still thinking when Arnold has started the show.
It's a comedy night, so people are drinking heavily.
Arnold's catchphrase is: 'Why not?' He says 'why not?' a lot during his set.

Luckily, Arnold thrives on silences. Even more fortunate is that John Hegley has offered to go on before me. This is kind. Dowie is last. Which is to be expected since he's performed with Victoria Wood. And is revered for doing so.

I've been gigging as half of a double act with the late Maggie Fox for about nine months, but tonight she's in Manchester with the original partner I stole her from. This is a landmark moment. Maggie and I have freed ourselves from our double act with grace (she left), but since I asked Arnold for this gig, there's no way I'm cancelling.

John Hegley has gone down a storm. I rate him. A lot. So does the audience. We've had a day out to St Albans and smoked a spliff on a hillock near the Roman remains. The first time I met John, we shook hands, and I received an electric shock. This may have been the static from his Breton tee, but I saw it as a sign. He is a little bit like Jesus. John/Jesus comes off and wishes me luck.

I launch myself out of the dressing room and prepare to walk on stage. Seconds later, I'm there. It's not far. Like walking from a hall into a kitchen.

A quietness descends while the audience adjusts to the fact that I'm not John Dowie. Worse, I'm a woman and I'm on my own. And even though Pentameters was in 'NW Twee', as Arnold described it, I can sense disappointment and surprise that a woman of 28, with a woollen singlet and clean hair, has the audacity to take up their evening.

'Good evening, ladies and gentlemen,' I begin. 'So, I'm not lonely... Well, not very lonely... Just a bit lonely...'

The truth might be a good starting point. Perhaps repeating a word would prove whether I had any timing...

I can hear the laughs starting. I carry on about how my partner is doing something else tonight but I'm fine about it. My semi-truthful existential material is causing a ripple...

I can do this. I'm here on stage, on my own, making people laugh. Tonight, I am a stand-up comedian.

* * *

The first step after leaving drama school in 1982 was to manage my mother's expectations about employment, in case I had to borrow some cash.

'But an acting job may not be… immediate,' I tell her.

'But aren't you trained now?'

'Sort of …' I replied.

Everyone needed an Equity card to get on TV and you needed six Equity contracts to be awarded a card. A six-month contract as a stripper would provide the necessary paperwork, as would joining the circus, but the third, more likely route was via a Theatre in Education (TIE) company.

I'd heard of an organisation called InterAction which had been set up by an American activist called Ed Berman who brought 'community action' to the people of Camden. More pertinent to me, was the fact that InterAction had their own TIE company, so I phoned up the switchboard to ask if there were any acting jobs going. There weren't, but there was a community job being advertised if I wanted to come in and chat about it. The prospect of having to live in a commune, share toilet rolls and be given helpful things to do for the community was not what I had in mind. I was an actor now, surely? But I went along for the chat anyway and since I didn't want the community worker job, I got it.

I was soon working in InterAction as some kind of community worker, buoyed up with my secret plan to infiltrate Dogg's Troupe (the in-house acting company) and be in pole position for when there was next a vacancy. It couldn't be that hard.

'Is it an acting job then?' asked my mother, already relieved I'd be getting paid.

'Almost. It's more community work.'

In between my community duties, which involved sitting at a desk doing nothing, I had plenty of time to bump into the actors accidentally on purpose whenever they came into the building. I formed an attachment to an actor called Chris Ellis who was already in Dogg's Troupe. He had been to Manchester University, knew Ben Elton and was very cool. A few months later he told me he was leaving. There was a vacancy. This was meant to be.

I put everything into my audition for Dogg's Troupe. I wrote a monologue which I performed 'in character'. Which particular character remained unclear, especially during the performance. I allowed myself to get put off by the 30 or so other desperate actors in the audience, all staring at me and all wanting the same job. At one point, I thought I recognised a pretty young woman who got up to sing *Only Women Bleed*. The fact that she could strum a guitar at the same time as being attractive gave her a huge advantage. Like everyone else, I felt obliged to be supportive and join in the chorus to sing 'only women bleed', over and over again – no matter that the target audience was probably meant to be pre-school.

We waited for the winner of the one place in Dogg's Troupe to be announced. I knew. I just knew. The pretty one, with the song about an abused woman in a marriage, was the new children's performer. Worse, she had been at Blackheath High School a few years below me. The school must have changed its tune to acting since I was there, which fitted the growing sense of doom about always being ahead of my time.

Something in my chest contracted and part of me died. My first big hope after drama school dashed. It was as if I was back in my leather jerkin being laughed at by the babysitter. Also, I had disappointed my friend Chris, who might now tell Ben Elton about my failure and since Ben was co-writing a TV pilot called *The Young Ones*, this wasn't ideal.

Feeling like this was not new: not getting enough marks to pass an exam, being sent outside a biology class for poking my friend Fiona Maddocks with a pencil through the hole in her lab stool (when she'd very possibly done it to me first), being called 'waggle bottom' in rounders – were easy truths to conjure up whenever I wanted to go on a bender of despair. But not being selected for Dogg's Troupe was the first big rejection on the ladder of my comedy career.

Not long after the women bleed rejection, I tried again. This time the audition was in Ipswich, would take all day and applicants had to be prepared to improvise. I was more hopeful about this. We were organised into pairs and asked to perform our 'scene' in front of all our competitors.

A tall, interesting looking woman had already stood out as being very funny, as we all trooped around the rehearsal room, being as creative as possible to catch the eye of the director. Everyone wanted to pair up with her, but I was too slow.

When I saw her waiting for the train back to London, I knew I had to speak to her. I certainly couldn't ignore the situation. I walked up to her and asked if she'd like to work with me. I think I told her I might need to work with her quite badly.

Then I took her name, Maggie Fox, and then I took her number. I felt empowered. I knew she was someone I had to see again. The better the partner, the more likely one is to shine. And I was lonely.

A few days later I followed up with a phone call and asked if she'd like to do some work with me. At this stage I wasn't sure how I was going to make this happen, but I knew I had to ask her first and then the rest would follow. Maggie hadn't got the TIE job either, which was handy. I was convinced she was the person to create the kind of comedy material I longed to do. I was ruthless. She said she'd like to work with me, but she'd have to ask Sue.

'Who's Sue?'

'My double act partner.'

'You're in a double act?'

'We're called LipService.'

'Oh ... and... would Sue mind if you... I borrowed you?'

'I'll ask.'

Sue Ryder generously agreed. I knew I had Maggie on loan, but I didn't care. All I wanted to do was write with someone I trusted and then after that, to laugh a lot and perform in public. It could change everything. This would be the key to unlocking my comedy. I was too excited to feel guilty.

Maggie came round to my flat in Finsbury Park and we started to write some sketches together. One of them was based on Joan, the bejewelled, tight-lipped treasurer in charge of a petty cash box at Kentish Town Social Services Area 8.

I was a very bad social worker. Sometimes I had to be 'on duty' and face people who'd come in without an appointment, who were often cross and always poor. My way of dealing with these encounters was to listen and nod, then race upstairs to beg Joan to give me some money which I would hand over to make the problem go away.

Joan would say, 'No Helen, you gave the Smith family their "section five" last week'. And I'd say, 'I know Joan, but they need more money now'. Joan would wave her bracelet at me and refuse. Then I'd have to go back downstairs empty-handed and try not to look too obvious about standing near the panic button.

I played the tight-lipped Joan, and Maggie played an eager

community worker. We loved it. In the end, Maggie offered to give teenagers in the community a second chance to be breastfed. This was of its time, I'd like to think.

Soon we had enough material to do a try-out set at Pentameters Theatre. Arnold Brown, who I'd met when we were both in leotards doing *Dr Faustus*, ran a weekly comedy night. The club was gaining momentum on the stand-up circuit and since Arnold was the most influential person I knew on the scene at that time, I asked him to give us a slot. He'd already toured with the *Comic Strip*; he knew Alexei Sayle, Tony Allen and Ben Elton. And the fact that he had supported Frank Sinatra and Steve Wright on tour put him in another league. Even more important, Arnold had seen me doing the 'Good Angel' with wings, so he knew I could be funny.

Arnold kindly booked us in, and we began performing every Thursday.

Maggie went on first with an ironing board under her arm. Then she would do the ironing board mime for a full-on five minutes, which was very physical. If the audience didn't laugh, it meant they would hate me too. The ironing board went everywhere with us, so we either borrowed a van or it went in my Renault 4, poking out of the back door.

When Maggie and the ironing board came off stage, I'd go on and do some of my own stand-up. Then we'd introduce each other. Then we'd do the community centre sketch. At some point in the routine, I went on with the same guitar I'd learned a section of Rodrigo for my classical guitar grade one, and sang a song called *Happy and Alone*. The first two lines were: 'I am happy, but I am alone. I would like someone to call my very own,' while strumming two chords. The words were sellotaped to the side of the guitar in the event of a memory lapse. I think the repetition of the two chords was supposed to be humorous.

There was also a Mastermind sketch, and a gag about Prince

Charles getting his middle names in the wrong order when he said his marriage vows, to demonstrate topicality. We wrote our own material and learnt it every week.

I was usually first up at the bar after we'd finished. This was where the other comics would come up and offer us advice. Sometimes the advice was offered before I'd had time to buy a wine. Maybe we looked scared, or grateful, or both. I'd end up buying drinks for other comedians to trash our looks, our chemistry, and our content. It was all very jolly. We were now part of the comedy scene, and our names were in *Time Out*.

From the regular gigs at Pentameters, we started to get booked at other clubs. But our dream was to perform at the Comedy Store. The venue had begun in 1979 above a strip club in Soho. The vibe felt edgy but, in our opinion, doable. Alexei Sayle, Rik Mayall, Adrian Edmondson and *French and Saunders* were already regulars. And we wanted to be there.

There's an entry in my diary in March 1982 saying, 'Ring Ben Elton'. This boldness shows how determined I was to infiltrate the system and risk having the phone put down on me. Luckily, he didn't.

Ben suggested we meet him at Pizza Express, where he would be having his mid-show dinner. He was very commanding and courteous. He was 23, five years younger than me, and already established and very sought after. Now Maggie and I were after him as well.

I decided that listing all my achievements while he got through his pizza would be the best way forward. Maggie had to watch in horror as I began sharing my list of accomplishments: my degree, the sorry but still amusing social worker bit, the drama school, half an MA, the Open Link Community thing with Arnold, the gigs, as well as our sketch set in a community centre which, I suggested, he might enjoy because it was a sort of social commentary? When

I finished my list, Ben said, 'Wow that's a lot of stuff. You must be about 50?'

I was attracted to Ben, partly because he reminded me of my junior school best friend's older brother, who'd moved to Jersey, but also, because he was so quick and funny; he'd make fun of everything. And I just wanted to be with funny people. He also made me feel that he liked me at some level, and even though I saw him do the same with others, I chose to see it as another sign.

We eventually got a gig at the Comedy Store, but before that we got one in Brighton where we all travelled down in the back of someone's van. Whoever's van it was, Ben and I were in the back. Maggie turned around a lot to check I was ok. I was.

Maggie and I looked very different from each other. She was tall, slim and sardonic. I was short, round and jumpy. It didn't help that I was also fiercely ambitious and very possibly highly sexed, in an erratic kind of way. Or maybe it was the 'above average anxiety', but being keen on a male comedian – or even a few at once – could get complicated, especially if Maggie knew the same one. We were not unlike the Siamese twins Chang and Eng, who, as previously referenced, I'd been mildly obsessed with, after stealing their autobiography from Eltham Library. The twins had to take it in turns to have sex with their wives. There was a sense we should clear it with the other before we snogged a fellow comedian.

Performing was an obsession. So, the friendships I made with John Hegley, John Dowie, Nick Revel, John Sparkes, Tony Slattery, Simon Brint and others, were intense. Simon had a flat in Upper Street which was particularly edgy because it was painted grey. We'd talk about comedy, listen to the Smiths and feel purposeful. It had been a lonely journey to be part of the scene, but I had found kindred spirits.

This was the behaviour. Everybody connected on a heightened level. If you had sex with someone you didn't necessarily think of them as your boyfriend. The hyped-up conditions of live performance meant that drinking and sleeping with people after a gig was often inevitable. It seemed best just to crack on with it. Combined with my middle-class upbringing of not knowing how to say no without appearing rude, it meant I may have had an overabundance of sex in a quiet sort of way.

If anyone got judgy, there was always a helpful range of positions of second wave feminism – from the radical feminists who stopped having sex with men, to others who chose to initiate it. Either way the main thing was not to get pregnant as this was a fate my mother feared more than me failing my O-levels or going to prison. She was prepared to dismiss a love bite when I was 15, but I'd been made well aware that becoming preggers was to be avoided.

Ben was living in a flat in Hampstead around the time of the Brighton gig and one night, after a drink in a pub, I drove him back to his flat in my Renault 4. If memory serves, we were parked on a steep gradient, and as we moved in to say our farewells and confirm that a relationship was off the cards, in a jolly sort of way, one of our legs or elbows may have dislodged the handbrake.

I'm not sure if Ben knew we were on the move, and I was too embarrassed to say anything, so we carried on rolling, quietly backwards before crashing into a parked car at the bottom of the hill.

This felt quite awkward. I'd taken up enough of Ben's valuable time and now he'd now have to walk back up the hill to his flat and nice girlfriend.

The drive home was quite draughty since the back door of my Renault had been smashed and wouldn't close. I had to ask a mechanic to get me another one from a scrapyard. My car was red. The one they found was blue, but at least it was the right size. I put the car bit of the story in my set as it seemed a shame to waste it. Years later at the Albert Hall, while I was backstage with Jimmy

Carr (who kindly remembered doing a gig with me) and Ben Elton waiting for Harry Enfield to finish, Ben whispered a reminder about the Renault mishap which took the edge off the nerves. Feelings were running a bit high because the gig was in front of HRH. And there was slight uncertainty about where I might be placed in the Royal 'meet and greet' queue afterwards, without looking like I minded. I wasn't the only one. Joan Rivers beat everyone to it and stood next to Miranda (which was clever). They featured on the front pages, but all was not lost. Some of my hair can still be identified on the official photo in the pics for *Hello* magazine.

Maggie and I did nearly a year together as a double act. I really enjoyed being in her company and we laughed a lot. Knowing that we would make each other laugh gave me a sense of security and a purpose which, in the scheme of things, was a precious and rare find.

But the comedy scene was changeable, competitive and harsh. We were only ever as good as our last gig. The pressure to achieve more was constant. I was always scouring the papers for auditions and opportunities. I made phone calls. I was rebuffed by secretaries. I was determined and single-minded. When Maggie returned to work with Sue and LipService, I could see why. Double acts are precious and complicated. Unless each person's dreams coincide at the same time, the connection is challenging. Best to shake hands and move on. I was only just beginning, while Maggie's path was with Sue.

According to *Spare Rib*, the 1980s was supposed to offer an era where feminist voices would be made welcome by both the establishment and each other. I never experienced much sisterhood on the comedy circuit. One woman comic used the exact same book I'd been using in my set, which can't have been easy to track down, since my copy had been left in my flat by an American visitor. It was called *For Men Against Sexism* by a Jon Snodgrass, and I made the joke that it wasn't *four* men against sexism, it was for *men*. Maybe it was a coincidence that out of all the books in the world the same one was chosen entirely independently. The male comic I was with in the audience gave me a look of sympathy when we clocked the book because he knew my act and could feel my pain, but no-one said anything. I was too feeble and he didn't want to get involved.

Around the same time, a female comedian allegedly decided my stand-up material was too 'vulnerable' to be feminist and may have mentioned this to other comedians, who may have mentioned it to me, in case I found it helpful. I had nothing but admiration (and a little jealousy) for said comedian's 'your willy's boiling in the kitchen' song, especially as an ice breaker. Guitar skills *and* a torch song? Hats off. Even so, I never found plagiarism or criticism to be that sisterly.

Apart from Maggie, I didn't have a woman friend from the circuit. There were other female stand-ups around, but they were still quite rare. Overloading the running order with more than one woman performer at a time was considered a waste.

Although I did meet the very funny Jenny Eclair downstairs at the Latchmere Theatre Club before we both went on, which led to a nice pairing later on. I remember she was wearing what seemed to be a white babygrow and seemed very, very tiny. Like a fragile bird. I was doing my 'four men against sexism' routine, and Jenny was doing comedy poetry. We were both nervous and didn't hide it, which felt unusual, and also friendly.

A few years after we met, Jenny suggested we do some gigs together. Since I never say no, and since I was lonely, it made sense to go to rehearse at her flat in South London, eat Ryvitas (no butter) for lunch and frighten each other into a shared gig. We found our ideas funny at the time of creation, but these same ideas felt rather different when we put them on stage. Particularly a sketch we wrote about baggage handlers.

I realised something was wrong as soon as we started the sketch, so I became very quiet, and Jenny got louder to compensate. At the end, we decided to leave over a roof, it was so bad. Jenny remembers putting coats over our heads.

But apart from Jenny, other women rarely spoke to me. We were all after the same jobs. And I sounded middle class, which was the worst class to be if you wanted to be comedically connectable and reflect back the pain of the ordinary people with any authenticity at that time. Instead, I did material about how my parents could talk about the weather (as long as it affected us emotionally) and sun beds. I often tell people that market forces kept us women apart, but that's not entirely true. Women had to be competitive and ambitious to get on.

In 1985, the TV slots were rare. And because there were so few women, we felt we were owed something as pioneering stand-up women who had 'come up' through the circuit.

A few years later, when brilliant female comedians like Jo Brand and Donna McPhail were being celebrated, it was hard not to feel supplanted. The established stars such as Dawn French who came before me, and who had already made it on TV, were so far ahead they befriended the new women coming through, without fear of overlap. And because they were generous, nice people. I felt stuck in the middle, sporadically employed and very much in my own category and era, which wasn't very attractive.

For every good gig there has to be a bad gig soon after, to prevent complacency. One of my best bad gigs took place in a basement on Highgate Hill called the Earth Exchange. This venue was quite famous in the '80s for its vegetarian meals and a noticeboard offering helpful information about bike shops, yoga classes and drop-in centres where you might get a free condom. There was no stage, so entrances had to be made from a set of stairs. The audience grouped themselves around the performers, who were expected to perform somewhere in the middle of the room, apart from the talented David Rappaport who chose to stand on an orange box for his set.

I'd been booked at the Earth Exchange on the same day as a singing telegram gig, offered to me by comedian Ivor Denbina who had a sideline in bespoke singing telegram management. The job turned out to be quite busy. I had to find the pub, change into a basque in the loo, identify the person whose birthday it was, sing a bespoke song to the tune of *Big John* – which I wasn't familiar with – hit the birthday person in the face with some shaving cream, which was pre-set on a paper plate, and then wait to get paid by someone who wouldn't be too disappointed to cough up on site. For some reason, my mother was visiting me that afternoon and I had to leave her outside waiting in the car while I concentrated on doing all of these things in the right order, before driving her back to Charing Cross station.

Once she was on the train to Chislehurst, I had to race home and get ready for the Earth Exchange. There may have been a mild form of PTSD from the basque, or maybe it was because I'd had a run of reasonable gigs, but I genuinely thought I could just talk about my relatively unusual day with the foam on the paper plate and the bad singing and be funny.

As I looked out at the sea of faces, many of them bike users, I sensed that telling my story about being a middle-class woman in a Basque, performing a singing telegram while her mother waits outside in the car wasn't going to connect. I was in too much of a panic to get the words 'Maggie Thatcher' in there which might have saved it, although unlikely. The longer I stood there, the more I created a distance between myself and the audience, even though most of them were up my nose along with the usual hint of stewed lentils.

After ten seconds, I said, 'Anyway… I think I'll leave now'. So I did and found John Hegley sitting on the stairs, as he was on after me.

'Could you go on now please, John?' I whispered.

'What happened?' John was scrambling to grab his mandolin.

'I'll just go on a bit later if I may…'

John whipped up the audience with a winning poem about his scoutmaster and I went back later to do the scripted stuff, but I wasn't forgiven. This was a lesson that what is funny in real life isn't necessarily funny on stage. Life imitates art, but only if you make it up. Whenever people say to me 'you couldn't make it up', I know with huge certainty that what they're about to tell me won't be funny.

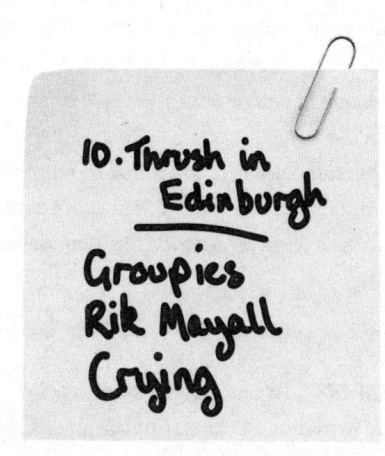

> 10. Thrush in Edinburgh
>
> Groupies
> Rik Mayall
> Crying

I'm in the Assembly Rooms in Edinburgh talking to a journalist called Martin. He's writing a piece about three women performers at the festival for Vanity Fair *magazine. I'm meeting him with the aim of getting free wine and compliments.*

'Were your parents funny? Did they tell jokes at home?'

'They were more… storytellers,' I say.

'Romanies?'

'No, Isle of Wight and Prague.'

'So why do you think you're funny?'

'I'm inappropriate. I find that funny.'

'What's funny about being inappropriate?' he asked.

I kept trying.

'Well, going to bed with someone when I was taking carotene pills to make me look brown and the soles of my feet went orange? That was funny. I had to lie about it.'

'Why?'

'Well, they were orange.'
I can tell Martin isn't connecting.
'And do people laugh at you or with you?'
Martin looks curious.
Later we do a photoshoot where I'm asked to jump up and down on a mattress. Jenny Lecoat and Meera Syal aren't asked to do this. In the published article Jenny is described as 'gamine' and 'mischievous'. I'm airborne.

* * *

By the summer of 1983, I'd been doing stand-up for more than a year. I'd chase the work but on the day of the gig, I'd have to take a lot of precautions.

As soon as I woke up, I'd need to know how many non-performing hours I had left until I was on stage – usually about 19 – and then move about my flat very carefully as if I were an old person. Sudden noises would make me jump. I couldn't speak to anyone after three o'clock. Or eat. Anything consumed after that time would repeat in the venue toilet, if not before.

But since the Old White Horse in Brixton put my name in *Time Out* magazine, my mother could officially tell her friends I did comedian work. Justifying my lack of solvency may have been hard with some of her colleagues at the Citizens Advice Bureau in Bromley. At one point my mother got so fed up with me asking for money I was advised to sell some of Little Baba's knives and forks at Sotheby's. Which I did. Before asking for another loan.

So, when Arnold Brown asked me to join him and Norman Lovett to do a show in Edinburgh, I knew it would bring in three weeks' worth of ticket sales. There'd be the usual unpleasantness in the daytime, but not being in Edinburgh at all would be far worse. By 1983 the Fringe was the only place to be for alternative comedians.

I'd gone up the year before in 1982 as part of a revue show. The job had been advertised in *The Stage* and I turned up for the audition, armed with my community worker monologue and a CV of stand-up gigs. I'd done the Earth Exchange, Lamb and Flag, Hemingford Arms, Camden Head, King's Head, Old White Horse and other clubs whose names I've blocked out, including a university somewhere, where I had to sit opposite Tony Allen on the train to get there. This proved the perfect opportunity for Tony to tell me all about anarcho-pacifism. The ebullient Ronnie Golden was doing the same gig and must have run out of matches, because he came to my hotel room, in search of a light. I didn't have one and said as much.

It was either my stand-up experience or the fact I had a car to drive their props up for free that got me the Edinburgh job. It was an intense three weeks. Two of the actors had met at Cambridge and had the confidence that went with it. Stand-up comedy at that time wasn't quite Cambridge.

Eddie, the director, used to go out with Emma Thompson who we bumped into in the Assembly Rooms, which was the place to be, so one could bump into people like her. I was given excellent eye contact and perfect manners. Unlike Eddie, it wasn't awkward for me, as I'd never been her boyfriend.

My revue group had set their sights on winning the Perrier Award. I hadn't heard of the Perrier Award in 1982, but I was assured it was up for grabs because Cambridge Footlights had won it the year before and Eddie the director had been to Cambridge. I was allowed to do my own stand-up material in the show which showed generosity, but I had to join in with the group singing.

On the night of the Perrier announcement, my group was furious. We'd only just missed winning, apparently. I didn't know how anyone could know we'd just missed winning, especially without any factual evidence, but I went along with being furious as it seemed right. Another revue show called Writers Inc were announced as the winner. To 'nearly have won' made us all quite cross with each other as we packed up to go home. In fact, I was more angry about being left without a car because Eddie's stage manager girlfriend had written off my Renault 4 on the way to get wine and crisps for the flat.

But by the following year, Edinburgh 'Revue shows' were out, and stand-up was in. This time I would get the train up. Arnold would open the show, I'd be next and Norman would finish with his unpredictable comedic flights of fantasy that were already popular with other comedians.

Arnold came up with some rather restrained looking posters to advertise the fact we were at the Masonic Lodge. We used passport-sized photos, with very few words from our CVs and absolutely no boasting. I don't think Arnold wanted us to look pushy.

All I had to do was my 20 minutes of stand-up and help Norman come to terms with the fact that a female member of the middle classes would now be working with him for three weeks.

Like most performers, I had to rent a small cupboard in a student house, where it is expected to take your own loo paper into the toilet and then out again. I'd wake with a hangover, queue for the shared bathroom, go through my 20 minutes of material three times, feel sick without throwing up, buy a can of Red Stripe on the way to the venue, perform my set on stage, drink the Red Stripe and then buy some more cans on the way home. I didn't question the loneliness. It was work. I was in Edinburgh. It mattered.

My material was about being single, self-help tapes, 'leave your partner at home' parties, answering lonely hearts adverts and a bit about being middle class in what I hoped was an ironic way. These were all things I had first-hand experience of, except for the 'leave your partner at home' party. That was made up. A lot of comedians came to see Norman. He'd suddenly go quiet on stage, if he felt like it, or just be strange. There was a mix of danger, innocence and authenticity to him that impressed and intrigued other performers. He became known as the comedian's comedian. Sometimes Norman would go over his allotted time and Arnold would have to placate the next lot of performers who complained they couldn't start their show on time and that it wasn't fair. Some of them had been to boarding school.

Not far from the Masonic Lodge venue, Ben Elton and Rik Mayall were doing their stand-up show with Andy de la Tour in the Assembly Rooms. One night they decided to walk over to Rose Street and see our show, but probably it was to see Norman. This gave us a bit of cachet with the boarding school people who had to wait for Norman to come off stage.

After the show we all ended up in the Assembly Rooms bar to drink as quickly as we could and talk about comedy. Ben and Rik were very focused on their show but would also ask me about my set. It felt good to be in their company. As we all continued drinking and talking, I noticed a tall blonde woman wander over and stand next to Rik without saying anything. I waited pleasantly for an introduction, but none came. The woman continued to stand by Rik and seemed content to just… be there.

It was later explained this person was a groupie. Comedy was the new darts. *The Young Ones* had elevated them to star status. They had a luxurious flat, a huge venue, queues around the block for every show and also an official groupie should one be required.

The same night as the groupie appearance, I went back to chat more with Ben at the luxury flat and shared my concerns about the 20 minutes of content and delivery. Before sharing more areas of commonality. This marked the end of me going back to my cupboard. Instead, I started going to the Assembly Rooms bar after each show. When the Flying Pickets, Cliffhanger or anyone from Pookiesnackenburger would drop in, everyone noticed and spoke louder. This was definitely the place to be and where I found out about a party in a flat in the middle of town and paid for by the BBC. The flat was packed with performers after jobs and three BBC producers on a three-week power trip because they could choose who they wanted for *Pick of the Fringe*.

One night, while I was waiting for more things like this to happen, Rik came over to have a chat and, while we were talking, he wondered if I'd ever considered crying on stage. I said I hadn't. He thought I should definitely consider it. I said I certainly would and then he suggested carrying on the discussion at the same luxury flat only in a different room from the one I'd stayed in before.

I was quite happy to be there and focused on the energy being offered up in an unquestioning manner. There was an agreeable amount of activity and would have been more, had a bee not decided to fly into the room, which brought matters to a close. So, we got up and ended up walking down Princes Street instead. We had reached the bit where all the big shops are when Rik asked me, 'Shall I buy you a dress?' I said, 'No, I think I'm okay thanks'.

Rik and Ben were both good friends and they were also having a great Edinburgh Festival. And even though I was doing my 20 minutes at the Masonic Lodge and they were doing their sell-out show at the Assembly Rooms, they were genuine in their offer of friendship.

It was clear that none of us were looking for an actual relationship together, and if I had been interested in anything of that nature, I doubt any connection would have been made. We were sharing the intensity of creating and performing new comedy that felt important during an exciting summer. We were on a similar path at the same time and they didn't patronise me. Respect with harmless benefits and connecting was just a bonus to the intensity that was Edinburgh.

A few nights after not needing to be bought a dress, Lenny Henry held a party for his 25th birthday at Bannerman's wine bar. I hadn't met the very brilliant Lenny at this point and wasn't invited to the party, so I'm not sure how I ended up there. Rik might have asked me to come along. Or maybe it was Norman Lovett, who was by now everyone's darling of the non-superstar kind.

Rik and I got drinking again, and since we had already connected, it didn't seem too odd that he might wish to continue the comedy conversation by whispering in my ear. The content was rude, strange and funny. James Hendrie, later scriptwriter for BBC1's *My Family*, was standing near us and I remember him saying, 'I just heard all that', adding that he 'thought I ought to know', in a kindly but serious manner. I felt it only right to thank him but wondered what this might mean.

I remember Lenny walking past me and thought I heard the words, 'There are some people at this party who were not invited'. Mortified, I decided this must be about me and might be my cue to leave. Outside, I found a taxi and jumped in. Just at that moment, a producer jumped in, but from the other side. At first, I assumed he hadn't realised I was already in it, since it was dark. But since I'd already met him and knew he worked in radio, and probably TV as well, it was tricky to get out the other side of the cab without appearing rude.

The producer asked the driver to take us both to the Caledonian Hotel which meant that it hadn't been a mistake. I didn't feel able to say, 'Oh just drop me off near my cupboard on the way', because he seemed very definite about including me in the trip to the Caledonian Hotel. So, we just bowled along, back to Princes Street, while he told me what he thought about our show. And, since I was keen to hear the feedback and work on any weaknesses (within reason, given the Red Stripe dependency, which I wasn't prepared to give up), the journey sped by quite quickly.

When we arrived outside the Caledonian, the producer asked

me to come inside the hotel with him. I didn't feel able to say, 'Actually, I've got to be back in my cupboard to start my rituals in a few hours' time', so I followed him inside. It was about 3am by now and the staff were laying the tables for breakfast. I wandered around, watching them smooth the tablecloths and eventually picked a table in the middle of the empty dining room and sat down. I wasn't sure where he had gone. Suddenly, he appeared from nowhere and said, 'What are you doing there?' (ie, among the cereal bowls), adding, 'Come up to my room'.

I couldn't quite work out how I'd got to be here. I'd been at the wrong party, I'd got in the wrong taxi, I'd sat at the wrong table and now I was in a possibly very important person's room, on a bed. As I found myself gliding downwards to the pillow, I remembered Rik's suggestion. I decided to cry. It was surprisingly easy, and I was soon sobbing. There was mascara everywhere. On me, on him, on the pillow... I think the sheer volume of tears surprised us both, and the producer and I finally agreed that it was probably best if I left.

The crying also saved me from disclosure about the slight case of thrush, which I'd like to put down to the yeast in the ten lagers a night I was drinking.

Sexual freedom was normal at this time. The height of the AIDS pandemic hadn't yet reached the media. I was on my own in Edinburgh and didn't really have anyone to compare notes with. I behaved the way the men did. I had no idea what Jenny Lecoat and Meera were up to. It would have been impertinent to ask Meera – soon to be a pioneering star of stage, screen and literature if there'd been any shagging to share about.

All those connections made in Edinburgh in 1983 felt natural and good. After that, the TV jobs started coming. I played a building society cashier in the second series of *The Young Ones* in 1984, got cast in the BBC Radio comedy *In One Ear* (directed by

Jamie Rix who won *Writers Inc* revue the year before), followed by *Happy Families* in 1985 where I played Flossie the maid with Dawn French who was the cook.

The next time I worked with Rik, I played a newsreader who trapped his tie in his briefcase in *The New Statesman*, then a Moldavian princess who may have been a prostitute in *Bottom*, and later in 2000 I played his wife in a BBC Radio play. By then, Rik had suffered a quad bike accident (in 1998) which affected his hearing, but he was charismatic and charming to everyone. The 1983 Edinburgh connection wasn't a secret and he would make jokes about it.

When I heard the news that Rik had died in 2014, I cried. I was asked to appear on GMTV to talk about working with Rik. I hoped Rik wouldn't mind. Maybe he would have found it funny or tease me that I might get a bit of TV exposure through his death. Rik's famous and very close friends and family didn't appear with me. But Rik was generous and I did it.

Rik used to say to people 'be careful with her' – I'm not sure if this was good or bad – but the crying tip still offers surprise, which is comedy at its best.

> 11. **Fat**
> Amphetamines
> Injections
> Cake

I'm in a dark Harley Street consulting room. Regency sideboards appear to be popular. I'm bending over a wing chair while a doctor is injecting my bottom with something or other. I have no idea what. And I don't think to ask. He is a doctor and I'm paying.

'So, that's you for the week then,' he says cheerfully, and washes his hands.

I pull up my jeans. Two weeks ago they were snug. This feels fantastic. I jig up and down slightly, admiring the loose feel around my stomach.

'Do you need any more sheets?' asks the nurse at reception, as she takes my money.

'For?'

I'm momentarily confused. Then I realise – diet sheets. My brain is not fully functioning. This is because I'm not sleeping. I don't mind not sleeping because I'm too excited about my loose jeans. I think I'll buy some in a size ten in two weeks' time so I can tell people…

'It's just chicken, isn't it?'

'No!' exclaims the nurse.

'Oh, yes. The apple at four o'clock.'

'Half.'

'Half. Got to dash, I've got a team meeting.'

'And five pints of water,' the nurse shouts after me, but I'm already inside the revolving doors and on my way out.

I literally run up Harley Street, across Regent's Park before I manage a half jog/half walk into Kentish Town.

I'm not even late for the meeting.

Doreen the social work admin assistant stares at me. I know she feels sorry for me because I'm middle class and we both know I can't change that.

'You all right, mate?'

'Why?'

'You seem a bit...?'

'I'm fine. I had to dash out for a birthday present.'

'Whose birthday?'

'A friend.'

'What did you get?' asks Doreen in her raspy voice. She's probably just put her 20th fag out.

'A vase.' I don't even falter.

'Show me.'

Very slight pause.

'I left it in the shop. God, how crazy. Maybe I'll just go back to the shop and see if I left it there and if I didn't, I might have to get another one – back in a minute.'

I run out of the office and down Kentish Town High Street in search of a vase to produce as evidence that I'm not lying. There's none to be had. Then I find one in the Oxfam shop. I run back.

'Here it is Doreen,' I say, brandishing the new second-hand vase out of a crumpled carrier.

No one looks.

The meeting has started. I put the vase under my desk.

I feel great in my jeans. The injections stop me from eating. But somehow people are against me. I wonder if the two things are linked.

It was around this time that Mary (the team leader) called me into her office. She begins with my name, 'Helen…'

'Yes?'

'Helen, you can either leave, or… you can leave immediately.'

She made this sound like an opportunity.

A Harley Street diet doctor had prescribed me a course of chemical injections, which meant I couldn't stop talking. Or folding things, or hoovering or thinking people were being hostile, which they were.

The weight dropped off which was exciting, but when people started telling me my head now looked too big for my body and my behaviour was getting alarming, I knew I had to stop taking them. Doreen was nice enough to buy me a leaving card.

* * *

I've always believed that if I could just have the perfect body, then the fear of failure would go away. A new diet offered hope, like getting a new agent or a new therapist. The dream of looking like somebody else sustained me. Or even a bit like me but with somebody else's thighs.

I've never been able to look myself up and down in the mirror and go 'phwoar! – you are stunning'. Who does this? Nor will I believe anyone who says, 'Curvy is nice', as they will most definitely be thinner than me. Or much, much larger.

I was an extraordinarily large baby. There's no getting around it. I weighed ten pounds. Perhaps that's why I was never picked up enough. Too large. And in the 1950s it was the fashion to leave babies in their prams to scream, at least that was what my mother

Parents' wedding My mother Jeanne met my father at a club in London where many Czech and Polish students gathered after the war

Grandparents Little Baba watching my mother doing something tricky *(right)*

Sisterhood Early uncertainty with Janet

1950s Smocking

1960s Somewhere in Austria before an asthma attack. I'm the only pupil with one ski, a runny nose and a wheeze

Early influence 1950s Magic show – about to volunteer *(above)*

Festive crafts 1970s Christmas card workshop with Fiona Maddocks. Curtains from Heals

Three generations Mother and Grandmother. Pinafore made by Christine's mum Pat

Birthday girl My 21st with Cousin Netty and G Plan corner unit. Largely empty

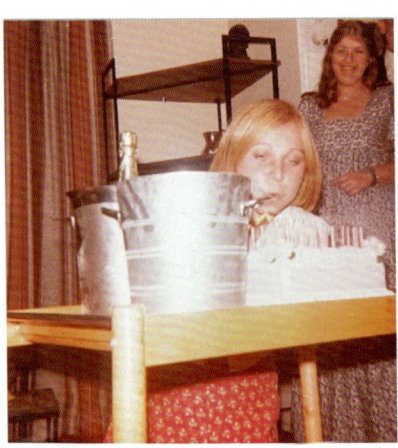

Throwback Permed hair, batik lampshade, G Plan shelving. Enough said

Early roles Drama school. Concealed hair in Sam Beckett mime *(above)*. *Dr Faustus* at Open Link Community Theatre. Tennis skirt as wings *(right)*

Work shopping Astride Arnold Brown in 1979 *(above)*

Improvising Clapham Bandstand. Arthur Smith, John Dowie, Justin Case, Peter Weir, Jim Sweeney, Sharon Landau, Maxine Oswald, me and Steve Steen in 1982 *(above)*

Best friends Fairisle singlet at party. With Christine and Jane

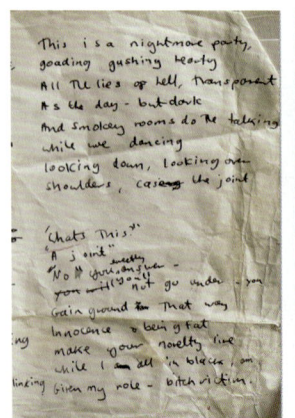

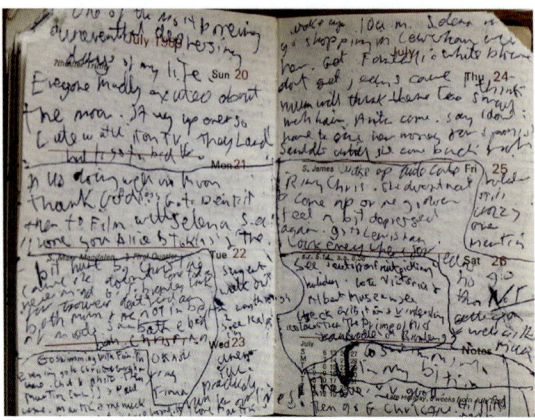

Melody Maker diary pages 'Everyone madly excited about the moon. Except me.'
Teen poem mentioning joint

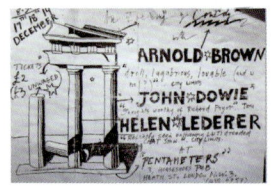

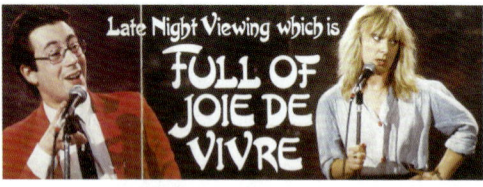

Scrapbook *(Clockwise from top left)* Poster by Liz Kneen; South of Watford documentary on comedy; Stand up poster. Restrained (1983); Our CV for sending out to people. A lot (1984)

Trevor Leighton / National Portrait Gallery, London

First Fringe *(Top row left to right)*
First Edinburgh Festival. People from Cambridge. Eddie, David Jackson Young, Robin; For some reason this was in the National Portrait Gallery. Nick Hancock, Neil Mullarkey, Stephen Fry, me, Jeremy Hardy

Happy Hour *(Second row left to right)*
Rehearsing *Happy Hour* in someone's loft with Nick Simmons and Sandi Toksvig. Tony Slattery taking pic; *Happy Families* BBC2 with Adrian Edmondson, Stephen Fry, Jennifer Saunders, Me, Dawn French

In a log *(left)* Thorpe Park. Filming *Happy Families*. Jennifer Saunders, Hugh Laurie, me, Dawn French

Shell suit showcase *(Top left)* Elaine C. Smith with me and some milk in 1986. *(Top right)* Wrap party. *Happy Families* with the ever-brilliant Jennifer Saunders

Cleverly insane apparently Poster from 1987 King's Head show

On air *(below)* BBC Radio 4 *In One Ear* doing a *Radio Times* photo with Nick Wilton, me, Steve Brown and Clive Mantle

Glasgow combo BBC *Naked Video* team, Gregor Fisher, Andy Gray, Elaine C. Smith, me, John Sparkes, Ron Bain, Jonathan Watson

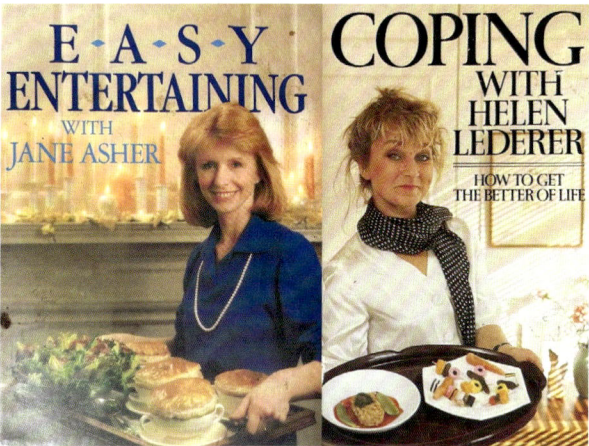

Early parody book Mentor Jane Asher and me smiling with a tray, published in 1987

West End while possibly post-natal. Me and David Ross (naked) in *Having a Ball* by Alan Bleasdale at the Comedy Theatre (now the Harold Pinter)

Pink ladies *Funny Women* gig arranged by Lynne Parker. Jenny Eclair and Vanessa Feltz

Scrapbook *(Below left to right)* Show at King's Head. Recent blow dry (1987); Warninks. Introducing the drinks to each other; My Where's Wally mention – Comedy Store (1990s)

cheerfully told me. I can't remember screaming back then, only as an adult.

But most babies aren't ten pounds. They might be in the region of eight, or sometimes nine, but ten is surely unusual. Especially if the weight is taken up in width. And I was always hungry. My mother stopped breastfeeding me at one point, saying, 'Enough is enough'. So, there I was, an overly round infant and wanting more milk than was deemed good for me before I could even walk. I must have been ravenous.

By the time I was ten, I was missing so much school from wheezing, I could hardly write my name properly. This was when Dr Ferguson first injected me with steroids. They did that to people in those days without asking. Mind you, I wouldn't have disagreed. As long as I had five bars of Nougat and a *Bunty* comic, I was happy to be pricked by anything.

The steroids reduced the wheezing but had the added effect of stunting my growth and giving me a moon face. So, each time the prick came, I got rounder and rounder, until eventually I looked like an emoji in a hair band. Not long after, I developed a longing for the perfect calf. My rough book in the lower third at Blackheath was filled with drawings of the perfect leg, the perfect thigh and the perfect calf. The disembodied legs floated about the page like a butcher's notebook.

Luckily for me, children in the 1960s weren't expected to be lookers. It's only now that children are all attractive and that's because of the abundance of dentists. By the late '90s it was becoming a rarity to find a child in East Dulwich who hadn't had their jawline improved or teeth wired. Every young person could be a model. When my daughter Hannah was 14, she was approached by a scout from Premiere model agency as she was coming out of Top Shop one Saturday morning with her friends and lots of tops. I was immediately wary, but Hannah was keen. I went to the agency's office and had to sit in a separate area while a tall, leggy, middle-aged blonde woman arranged a photoshoot to use for their catalogue. Hannah loved all the fuss that came with the camera crew and make-up people. She was signed for a few lucrative years before they got rid of her for no longer meeting their strictures. We were never sure what these strictures were, but without her mouth being wired together by our local child jaw specialist she might never have been recruited and rejected in the first place. And she wouldn't have had as much to put in her Building Society account. Or experienced sudden joy, followed by sudden rejection.

In the '60s, children came in all shapes and sizes with varying styles of teeth, hair and eye wear. No one expected anything else. But since I was a child who was fat, with a hair band, who wore jeans and lace-ups at the weekend and a home-made tent dress with a zip for parties, I may have fallen outside the range of normal.

Given there's normally one large person in every class in every school, it was unusual to find two bigs in the same year. Pamela Kemp and me. On the other hand, Pamela wasn't funny. And being large and funny at Blackheath Junior School in 1965 didn't feel too disadvantaged. It had a status of its own.

As time passed, I seemed to be getting wider and shorter. Apart from the steroid injections that were stunting my growth upwards, I was also eating a fair amount of carbs that no one seemed to be concerned about.

Food was a big thing in my family. Little Baba thought nothing of using lard in her pastry or producing at least three varieties of kuchen when we gathered for our formal Sunday teas. And even though my parents weren't large people, no one seemed to say anything about my size.

Most Sundays my father would drive us up from Eltham for tea with my grandparents. The card table would be moved into the middle of the sitting room to mark the occasion. A lace tablecloth would cover up the green felt and meringues (wedged together with cream), Gugelhupf, Nusstorte and cheese or plum cake would be laid out on beautiful little plates, and served by Little Baba with a silver slice. We'd use cake forks and napkins that had been placed in a silver napkin holder – all rather fine items that had been carefully smuggled out of Czechoslovakia by some kind friend or relative who wanted to make sure the Nazis didn't re-purpose them.

My mother Jeanne's baking was considered more modest compared with the nutty, cheesy, rather moist treats from the Czech side. There was either the Victoria sponge or the chocolate, which was the same as the Victoria, only with cocoa. Both delicious but lacked Little Baba's flavour and presentation.

When my sister and I got home from school each day, there would be a spread of bread and jam and cake laid out on my mother's orange seersucker tablecloth. After a sandwich, a bit of Swiss roll and maybe a slice of Battenberg, we might take a biscuit into the sitting room to watch *Crossroads*, making sure to leave enough room for supper at seven.

When my father got home from work, we'd all sit down to consume another meal with a main course and pudding. There'd be a different tablecloth which was more sophisticated, but more food. I thought this was normal until I had tea at my friend Fiona's house, where they had a slice of bread and jam with a cup of tea, followed by an egg salad and a slice of ham at five o'clock and, I assume, nothing more.

But because I needed to wear needlecords, my obsession with weight first reared its head when I was 15. Luckily, around this time, I also discovered *Limmits* biscuits which tasted half cardboard and half vanilla. I'd pack the biscuits in foil and take them out at lunch break when the teachers weren't looking. They were supposed to make you feel full, but since I was used to a lot of food it took quite a few. These worked for a while and soon I was able to squeeze into a maroon pair of needlecords to wear at the weekends when I would go bowling to worry the parents. I discovered *Stay-Blonde* shampoo around the same time, so my yellowed hair and snug needlecords were the first signs that I could do things to change myself, which was exciting.

For the next ten years or so, I was either quite plump or plump. And even though the first lot of diet injections made me nasty, lose friends and made my head look too large compared with the rest of me, getting into a pair of size ten jeans felt wonderful. Whenever I stopped, the lost weight soon found its way back on my body, which I was largely able to ignore until I got my first agent. The agent, Brian, arranged an audition for an advert. I had to walk into a room, say my name and then improvise seeing something unusual, like maybe a man washing a cup, and then scream. There was no acting required for these kinds of jobs, so understandably, they were quite sought after. There was a long queue of people in the corridor, patiently waiting to say their name and scream, all hoping they'd get lucky.

While I was waiting to be seen, I got chatting to an interesting looking woman in the queue who appeared to be slumped on the ground in a crumpled heap and looked so thin she could, as they say, have played hide and seek behind a standard lamp.

'Wow you look great,' I said enthusiastically, 'what's your secret?'

'Put that Cornish pasty down and I'll tell you,' she said.

I got rid of the pasty and wrote down the name of her slimming pills. They were called Tenuate Dospan and instead of me thinking, 'But you're a really teeny tiny, crumpled and sparrow type person who can't stop talking and who's so weak you can't even stand, so why would I listen to you?' I said, 'Great!' and headed off to my Greek doctor in Finsbury Park to get six months' worth so I could start talking fast, and be teeny, tiny and crumpled as well.

Interestingly, I next saw her presenting a travel programme and she looked really great on camera with the pyramids behind her and her tiny shorts.

So, once I started taking these pills, and managed to reach what might be described as a 'Norfolk farmer's' idea of svelte, I began to get cast in TV jobs, knowing I could fit into the costumes at the same time, which took the pressure off. Particularly helpful for doing *The Young Ones* when I had to play a bank clerk and was given a skirt with a zip. Or the Moldavian princess in *Bottom*, where the bodice of the frock had to be tight enough to display some kind of waist. In my view both these jobs could not have been done fatly.

I knew television put on half a stone, which meant there was always an extra amount to shift. Having lunch in the canteen on the day of a recording was unthinkable, even a Diet Coke could bloat. These were tense times, but at least when I was actually acting, I forgot what I looked like.

But after five years of habitual amphetamine pills, bad breath, heart palpitations and extreme housework, I knew I had to go it alone. Lying in bed at night with my heart racing was becoming a concern. My father had died of a heart attack. I didn't want to go the same way before I'd had the chance to be happy or normal.

Maybe it was time to be fat again. Until I got another idea…

12. Doing 80s Comedy

Young Ones
Dawn French
Happy Families

'You're only one part away from stardom,' said the first acting agent.

It was the 'away' bit that troubled me. How would this work?

I'm answering the front door of a stately home in my pinny and flats. A lamp deliverer is on the front step with a lamp. Hugh Laurie is directly in my eyeline and it's really putting me off, he's not even in this scene.

'Can I help you, sir?' I say – not to Hugh, but to the actor who is playing the lamp deliverer with the lamp.

The lamp deliverer says his line.

Then I say another line.

And then the scene is wrapped.

The lamp deliverer, myself and Hugh are in Happy Families written by Ben Elton. Everyone (apart from the lamp deliverer who turns out to be the future husband of Maggie Fox) is very famous. Me, less so. But my hotel room is next to Dawn French's one.

I start walking back to the main set. Hugh is going the same way.

I assume he's been sent by the equally talented Stephen Fry to see if the new girl is any good.

'Was that all right?' I asked, since I may need to tell my friends and family about him being in my eyeline if it wasn't.

'You were...' Hugh makes a face and waves his hands as if searching for the right word.

I keep walking. I can see the catering truck ahead.

'...brilliant,' he says.

I am elated. Just a few steps more of small talk, then I can sheer off for a coffee before we both drown in my eagerness.

I ask how he's getting along playing a doctor.

'Quite well,' he replies. He tells me his father was a doctor.

'And was your mother a nurse?' I ask.

This conversation is not quite singing. We are both aware of this.

* * *

The rewards from doing Edinburgh '83 continued because, by 1984, the jobs were still coming in. I could now contribute to the new world of '80s iconic comedy instead of 20 minutes of stand-up, sandwiched between the men. I was in *The Young Ones*, I was on the radio and I was also on diet pills. If anyone suggested meeting for lunch, I'd look at them as if they were mad. Why waste my time with a meal?

When I got sent the script to play 'medieval game show hostess' in *The Young Ones*, I was beside myself. This was the only show to be on. I took time to consider my role. Who was this medieval game show hostess I wondered? And what might motivate her to host a game in medieval times? I suggested, ahead of rehearsals, that it could work if I played her with an Essex accent. When this was agreed, I enunciated my Essex vowels with such a wide mouth, you could even see my teeth. And when I spun the wheel of fortune, I think I managed to make it look quite sporty.

I didn't trouble Alexi Sayle with conversation in between takes. I sensed a middle-class comedian in a wimple, who'd just got lucky in TV, shouldn't push her luck with a member of the alternatives. Especially one I hadn't slept with.

I may have spoken to Steve Frost and Mark Arden from the Oblivion Boys because we'd all done Pentameters which was a leveller. And they were reliably funny and excitable.

When I caught sight of Lise Mayer, girlfriend of Rik and co-creator of *The Young Ones*, I may have bowed slightly. She was known to be the brains behind it all, particularly the more surreal elements, and when Amazulu played their single live in the studio, I absolutely knew I was witness to greatness. Their single *Cairo* was played by John Peel on Radio One shortly afterwards.

* * *

I was asked back for another episode. This time I was held up at gunpoint in the Fascist Pig Bank by Rik Mayall. I played a smiley bank cashier and had to say, 'Good morning sir', over and over again, without stopping. The real Woolwich Building Society advert had a cashier doing the same thing, but she only said the line once. Repeating it made it funny. In fact, the repetition of lines in a comedy was something I would revisit a few years later at Watford Rep, playing Mrs Smith in Ionesco's *The Bald Prima Donna*. On the opening night, I thought I heard the pitter patter of gentle rain on the roof. In fact, it was the tipping up of theatre seats as the audience got up to leave. In the bar afterwards one of them said to me, 'That was the worst play I've ever seen'. I said, 'Be happy. You don't have to be in it'.

Before *The Young Ones*, the only TV I had done was a monologue for the *Janet Street-Porter Chat* show for LWT in 1982. The H had been cut out of the word 'CHAT', suggesting that women could now be CATTY as well as politically correct and that Janet Street-

Porter was leading the way in this area.

My debut was as a 'plant' in the audience. On a cue from the floor manager, but unannounced by Janet, I was to stand-up and deliver an entirely prepared comic monologue for a full five minutes. By the time my cue came, a couple in the row in front twisted round in concern, to see if they should get me removed. Five minutes is a long time to be a plant.

Two years later in 1984, I'd progressed from being a plant, to not only entering a stage on purpose but to rapturous applause as well. Radio audiences were known for their appreciation and generous clapping, although cheering if anyone dropped their script or made a fluff took a bit of getting used to. Nick Wilton, Clive Mantle, Steve Brown and I were recording *In One Ear* at the BBC Paris Studios. Being the only woman felt very different from a stand-up gig, where I could see people in the front row look at their watches when I came on.

Barry Took, in *the Radio Times*, thought the show was 'anarchic', which we decided was a positive, especially as *In One Ear* had to compete with *Saturday Night Live* on LWT for an audience. I had a regular slot of reading out a 'pen pal' letter in a child's voice, aimed at political leaders of the time. This was my idea, but mostly written by other people, including Paul Merton and his then double act partner John Irwin. After a few weeks, it dawned on me that there might be more jobs like this that I could do. This is what actors did. Actors turned up, got handed a script that other people had written, and people laughed.

In 1985 we won the Sony Radio Award for best comedy, which meant going along to the Dorchester to collect it and eating a lot of bridge rolls while we waited for the wine to be opened. Annoyingly, there was an alleged fallout between our very fine producer Jamie Rix and someone else higher up, who was also very important inside the BBC. This disagreement, whatever it was, caused the

In One Ear cast photograph to be removed from the walls of the Paris Studio, which also happened to be the venue for the coveted BBC Light Entertainment Christmas party. Everyone wanted to be invited to the Light Entertainment Christmas party to get jobs, but now there'd be no proof I'd ever been in a Sony Award-winning radio series between the years of 1984 and 1986.

This wasn't the first time I was airbrushed. Either it was personal or the male archivists were more interested in listing the funny men, and because there were fewer funny women around to distract them. Although it helped if you were quite large, quite thin or quite gangly (or in my case, quite short). Funny, *odd-looking* women tended to be sought out by producers to drive the comedy. And funny *pretty* women were more likely to be sought out to serve the jokes. Madeline Smith said of her time in *The Two Ronnies*, 'I found myself typecast. I was a couple of breasts with a face above them and a squeaky voice'. Janette Cranky and Bella Emberg were seen as funny individuals, without having their breasts referred to.

I fell between both of these categories. Not gangly or massive, thanks to the Tenuate Dospan, and while I wasn't a conventional beauty, for a time, I was young. And I was intense. This afforded me being known as 'The Girl at the Bar/Girl in the Team'. So not entirely invisible.

And I was ambitious, so in spite of the untimely removal of the cast photo, I turned up at the Light Entertainment Christmas party after 1986, along with other hopefuls, to mill about on stage with a free glass of wine, hit on a producer and then get a commission or a job.

I could see producer Bill Dare talking to another writer. This looked promising. Bill's father was a fine actor called Peter Jones who I remembered offering me a nip from his hip flask on the way from the Green Room, for my first and rather rare appearance on *Just a Minute*. The following exchange may have been slightly altered.

'Hi Bill Dare.'

Bill didn't move away, which I took as a welcome.

'Yes... I was wondering why you haven't put me in any of your shows?'

Stupidly, I forgot to temper the exchange with the nice reportage about Bill's nice father.

'I've sent some ideas in,' I said, in case he might like to know I could write as well. Perhaps he hadn't seen them? I offered a prompt to start us off.

'What do you think of me?'

Bill thinks for a minute,

'That you're high maintenance?'

This was the exact moment I really could have done with that photo. I could have said: 'But Bill, if you'd like to look on the wall up there, you can see a photo of me with Jamie Rix when we got the Sony Award for Best Light Entertainment 1985.' But I couldn't since it was no longer there.

In the '80s, a woman could be considered 'high maintenance' if she sent in original scripts. And spoke to producers at the same party.

So, when I was invited to a read-through of *Happy Families* written by Ben Elton, for the part of Flossie, the worry of being high maintenance became less vexing. I didn't have to audition, go to a party, speak, write a treatment, show off, network or pay for stamps. This was an offer.

Flossie was a flirtatious, but dim, possibly pansexual, chambermaid and Cook was a cheery, sadistic powerhouse played by the utterly excellent Dawn French. Dawn would whack me on the head with a saucepan and I would submit to it. It felt so right. We got the train to the location in York together, went through our respective life stories and laughed.

'Helen, do you ever eat?' Dawn asked curiously one day while we were sitting on the top deck of the catering bus.

'Of course I do… this is yum,' I replied and tapped some radishes to prove it.

The best way to avoid scrutiny was to ask Dawn lots of questions about her life so she wouldn't notice my secret, speedy condition. Luckily, Dawn had been the head of her debating society at school and was very good at offering different viewpoints. Perfect for distracting from an empty plate. We got to know each other with me on speed and her excellent debating skills. I rewarded her by asking her to be godmother to Hannah. She rewarded me by saying yes and asking me to her tennis party. And being very kind.

Everyone else in *Happy Families* got their own series, except me, so I had plenty of time to be pleased for them. I was probably even less than close to being 'one part away from stardom' by now.

13. From Stand-up to TV

Sit down comedy
'Pajamarama'
Sexual Overload
Audition for Blackadder

I'm turning up to audition for Elizabeth I in Blackadder *series two, clutching the now crumpled few pages of script and wondering why I didn't learn it properly beforehand. I decided to keep the pages in my lap and glance down if I needed to, but in a queenly way. Ben Elton's Elizabeth was going to be a bit mad and neurotic, which I assume is why he thought of me.*

The producer, John Lloyd, greets me as if I'm the only queen in the room. Which I am. The other queens are outside, waiting. I already know John is a Cambridge person. Not only will I have to become obsequious with him, due to not going to Cambridge; I'll also be struggling for lines...

'In your own time,' John encourages me and sits back to watch.

This instruction is always quite pressurising. It means you have one chance.

I try not to look at the script as this would be annoying, so I go for delivery of Glenda Jackson mixed with 'The Girl at the Bar' in

Naked Video, *throwing in a few pained expressions to help it all along.*

John doesn't appear to flinch, which may be because he'd been in Footlights and already done some acting under pressure, in his own time. We both talk about Ben Elton and Happy Families *before he charmingly shows me the door.*

The nicer the producer is, the more they want you to leave the room. It may have been just me of course but, I sensed John really wanted me to leave the room. I soon find out that Miranda Richardson had already been seen for the part, and the rest is Elizabethan history.

* * *

The television jobs were still coming in. I might not have my own series, but I was happy to be included in anything and everything.

Soon after *The Young Ones*, I got a part in a strange series called *Little Armadillos* for Channel 4. Like *The Young Ones*, there were absurdist sketches, but based in a nightclub instead of a student hovel. And it was tucked away, quite late at night, so people didn't know it was on. Bob Spiers directed it, who I met again eight years later when he directed *Absolutely Fabulous*. Bob also directed *Faulty Towers* and *Are You Being Served?*, so we had great hopes that someone with such pedigree could change the scheduling. He couldn't.

When *Little Armadillos* failed to get a second series, possibly because no one had seen it, I was reminded, yet again, how I was still one part away from stardom. Maybe this was going to be my normal.

The writers of *Little Armadillos* decided my 'stand-up persona' could be plundered to create another entirely different character who was also single, sloaney and looking for a relationship. The character was given a wig, a frumpy blouse and the name Amanda (in case a small minority of my audience who'd seen me on the circuit might think it was me and get confused). The very funny Steve Steen and Jim Sweeney played the brothers who ran the nightclub.

When filming ended, we all got very sad and panicky, so I decided to knock on Jim's door in case I never got the chance to work with actors again. Even I was baffled by how much needless shame I could conjure. I may have been ahead of my time in taking the sexual initiative, and though I may have considered this feminist in its inception, there was still an anomaly, that when I liked someone, I sometimes forgot to check if they liked me back.

And this kept happening. When I was in Egypt filming a strand for *This Morning* with Tony Slattery, I decided there was a shared frisson between myself and the cameraman without checking. On the last night, I called his hotel room, and he replied with a slightly alarmed, 'What's up?' which wasn't the kind of reply that meant, 'Yes please, what took you so long?' I was mortified and Tony had to give me his last valium for the flight home. At least the humiliation was included in my Edinburgh show, since humiliation is funny. I met the cameraman a year or so later on another job strand for *This Morning* and he told me he'd got married. I felt I'd helped somehow.

Around this time, stand-up comedy was being given a platform on TV which was particularly exciting for someone like me who was passionate about doing a minority job and desperate to be included.

LWT came up with a comedy series called *Pyjamarama* which ran for six episodes, hosted by Arthur Smith with comedians including John Dowie, Clive Anderson, Mark Steel and me doing sets.

As soon as I heard I was in, I bought my outfit. I believed a grey and rather stiff cotton parachute suit would work well on camera as there'd be no risk of a camel toe or need for tights. I looked casual, in a starched sort of way.

On the night, I was introduced as a 'sit-down' comedian by

Arthur and had to be given a stool so I could half perch on it, which made me look as if I wasn't staying for long. In the end, I did ten minutes, so this was true.

I was on the same show as John Hegley, his group the Popticians and Mark Steel, and out of six episodes myself and Jenny Lecoat were the only women comedians.

These were the early days when TV was experimenting with stand-up but there was always a live gig to do, or other people's gigs to see, and in between, I'd spend some of my time with John Hegley being creative and thinking about new material

I'd drive to meet him in the Old Red Lion in Islington, park up a side road and join John at the bar. Once we'd ordered, I'd tell the barman rather importantly that we'd have to go and 'check on the car' so I could share a puff on John's spliff outside. Then we'd return to the pub and laugh hysterically for the rest of the evening. It all felt very heightened and illegal.

Sometimes John would write a poem on a bar mat. These were great times. Sometimes we'd meet to be creative in my flat or his room and I'd play one of the chords I knew, while he improvised with a song. On these occasions I would sometimes hum and we'd tape the results onto a cassette in case we ever wanted to play it back one day.

John was always so encouraging to me and other performers and so sure about the work we were doing. Performers came to see John as the good shepherd of the comedy circuit. He was kind to everyone, original, and could work any audience under any circumstances. Russell Brand was one of many performers to watch his show at the Bloomsbury Theatre London.

Even though everything was intense, I never felt I belonged on the circuit as well as John did. I still wanted to act. I felt the gigs were there to lead to something else.

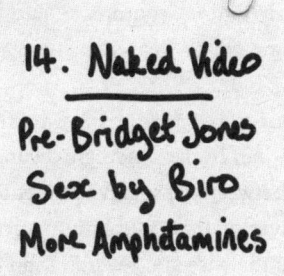

> 14. Naked Video
> Pre-Bridget Jones
> Sex by Biro
> More Amphetamines

I'm looking up Elaine C Smith's vagina. I've known her for a few weeks and I am telling her to push. Then we break for special effects to reset the blood.

We resume, until a baby flies from between Elaine's legs and around the studio, like a balloon. Seconds later, the floor manager faints.

The floor manager insists the flying baby and the fainting are not related.

This is Scotland, so it's best not to fuss.

I'm on the set of Naked Video, *a Scottish comedy sketch series for BBC. I go back to wardrobe and take off my nurse's uniform and prepare for a sketch about the Freemasons. An episode without a nurse or a Freemason joke in it was rare in 1985.*

* * *

I was the new girl. Again. I'd just finished filming *Happy Families* which may have earned me some wary respect from the Scottish cast, but only because it was written by Ben Elton and they'd heard of him. I was still on the diet pills which allowed me the important freedom to go for high-waisted trousers that stopped above the ankle. And while my bottom contours would have to be visible for rehearsals, I knew not to wear a skirt in case I had to dance suddenly.

Most of the cast of *Naked Video* had come from *Naked Radio*, although the word 'naked' was never explained. The only cast member I'd seen naked was the very talented John Sparkes and we'd stopped going out by the time filming began.

Colin Gilbert was the wise and revered head of comedy for the BBC in Glasgow but had come down to London to scout some non-Scottish comedians from the circuit for his new TV series.

John Sparkes and I provided an insurance policy in case the Scottish actors were deemed too Scottish by the English commissioners. John was Welsh and I was Southeast London, so we got the job. John was to write his own monologue in his Shadwell character, while I was to write and perform a monologue as 'me', sitting at a bar with a glass of pretend wine.

The character had a job, used a Filofax and wanted sex. She was also single and drank wine. But 'The Girl at the Bar' was ahead of her time in the '80s. By the time *Bridget Jones* appeared in *The Independent* in 1995, I'd been doing my 'singleton' for ten years. But, in 1985, the world didn't seem ready to empathise with the fact that women had jobs and sex outside marriage.

Colin called me a few weeks before I moved to Glasgow.

'I'm wondering how you'd like to write for us,' he began.

'I've got an Amstrad,' I was pleased to tell him. Not everyone had a word processor in the 80s and I wanted him to know I had one.

'Would you like to write with Spike?' he asked.

'Spike?' I repeated.

'Spike Mullins. He writes Ronnie Corbett's monologues.'

Colin's investment was overwhelming. Ronnie Corbett, and now me. I wondered if Spike had written for *Dad's Army* as well. I had been gifted an establishment writer. This more than made up for having to miss Jeremy Hardy's wedding to Kit Hollerbach, or saying goodbye to Harry Enfield for three months. Harry had offered to be my boyfriend the summer before and, eventually, after being reluctant and a bit mean, I succumbed to being temporarily adored.

My first digs in Glasgow were in a basement flat off Byres Road. An actor called Freddie Boardley was my landlord. Freddie didn't believe in knocking before he came into my room to light my fire. But since Glasgow is mostly cold, and Londoners like me didn't do well with an empty grate, I saw the benefit.

On my first night, as Freddie lay close to the leaping flames, keen to bring me up to speed about the *Naked Video* cast (since everyone knew everyone), I couldn't help wondering if his tight, leather trousers were fireproof.

As I didn't really eat in the daytime, I was kept alive by calories absorbed at the BBC club at night. I often left the club in tears, which wasn't just because I was being fast-tracked into learning how the English had been very cruel to Scotland, but also because my stomach was empty and it only took a few glasses to set me off.

At the end of a read through of an episode, Colin would cast us in the sketches. Most of us wanted to be in everything, but camaraderie was highly valued and no one sulked if they weren't cast. Not openly anyway. Gregor Fisher was given the most demanding parts. His round face was perfect for the 'baldy man' character who became known for combing one hair across his head. This was picked up by an advertising agency and, a few weeks into filming, Gregor became the mascot for Hamlet cigars. This sealed his status as an untouchable star, because the BBC allowed him to advertise.

Elaine C Smith was a wonderfully throaty, talented actress and singer, with great warmth who knew a lot about everyone. And she was kind to me. Tony Roper, Andy Gray, Johnny Watson and Ron Bain took all the other parts, including female ones, while Elaine and I would take it in turns to be the nurse, housewife or cleaner.

After a week of filming and dealing with Freddie lighting my fire unannounced, it was time to record the first episode in front of a live studio audience. John arrived from London to do his Shadwell the poet monologues and everyone assembled in the studio to do the tech run.

I decided the best way to deal with the John arrival situation was to pretend our relationship had never happened. So, I was cool. The evening before, in the BBC club while drinking on an empty stomach, I let slip that I'd had a thing with John but wasn't going to tell anyone, except the one person I was telling. This information spread like wildfire and I was viewed as untrustworthy.

This method of being cool and then oversharing about the John situation was just the beginning of my self-sabotage. My next own goal was forming an intense, sexually-charged connection with one of *Naked Video*'s highly prized writers, Ian Pattison, who later went on to create one of Scotland's proudest exports – Rab C Nesbitt played by Gregor.

I first met the very brilliant writer Ian on the BBC coach in the middle of a field in the Scottish rain. I'd been playing a conservative MP and was still in my headscarf and Barbour when I climbed on to the coach to get dry. I had no idea who he was apart from someone who appeared to be watching the actors through the window with a notepad. I offered a polite greeting and was about to ignore him when he began to ask me interesting questions which, as we continued, felt surprisingly arousing. At first, I put this down to me being lonely, misunderstood and untrustworthy. But as we talked, I began to sense how much he knew about comedy and how easy it was to laugh with him.

He had also been sending Colin scripts, for some time, and Colin liked his work. In the read-throughs, the cast would laugh more at Ian's sketches than anyone else's. They were quite filthy. Colin would chuckle quietly into his beard at Ian's descriptions of body parts and various fluids. These early sketches were a contrast to the alternative comedy I was used to and they were rudely funny.

After my request to personally re-write the first Spike Mullins monologue, Colin suggested Ian work with me instead. Also, Spike was pricey. Ian was just starting out and hungry.

We were given a basement room to write together. Ian had since made it known that he was interested in me. I hadn't seen it coming, but Harry was getting very famous with his 'Loadsamoney' character, which I was finding difficult.

At first the main attraction took place in my brain. But after a few sessions, the 'word play' between us became quite charged in other areas as well. We would sit opposite each other, separated by a desk and a typewriter and we'd start talking about the week's monologue. Everything we said would become charged with innuendo. One look from Ian, twiddling his biro, would make me lose my train of thought. The act of sitting opposite someone in an empty room with just a desk and a biro, especially when we were supposed to be writing, became deeply erotic. Steve McQueen and Faye Dunaway had food in *The Thomas Crown Affair*. For us, it was the biros.

I was determined that nothing should happen. And it didn't. At least not at first. I knew I would be giving my power away; the cast would not approve, and I wouldn't blame them.

The third incident in my 'How to Become Unpopular When Working Away' self-sabotage guide happened when I was messing about in the coach with Gregor one day on the way back from filming. We sat in the back and began improvising a couple called *Bernard and Miriam*. The couple were based on the parents of a college friend whose father had been a local mayor and his wife, who liked to display her collection of porcelain hands in a glass cupboard. This amused us a lot. So much so, we would drop into our *Bernard and Miriam* voices and disappear into a *Bernard and Miriam* fantasy world whenever we bumped into each other.

Ian wrote several 'B and M' sketches for the show, and the characters became regulars. None of this was very team friendly. The cost of initiating new fun with one person meant that other people were left out. This reminded me of being in the playground at school and not knowing who to play with at break time because, for everyone I had to choose, I had to reject others. Standing out from the crowd never ends well for me.

But the very, *very* bad thing finally happened in the second series of *Naked Video* in 1987. By now I had a recognised agent who was more familiar dealing with people above my level. He was very connected and used to doing deals.

'Why don't you just fly up to Glasgow and back again?' he said.

'I'm planning to. A train would take forever.'

'Just fly up for your monologues as a one-off for each episode. Then you wouldn't have to turn down other work.'

I decided this must be what his other clients would do, or else he wouldn't have suggested it. So I turned up on the day for the recording of the second series without doing any of the group filming beforehand or rehearsing any sketches to do live in the studio. It didn't take too long to note a slightly frosty atmosphere.

Embarrassingly late, the penny finally dropped. I had declared myself too grand to be in the team. I had changed the dynamic of the cast, and now they had to replace me with another actress for the sketches. The atmosphere was not the same. Worse, I missed doing all the sketches. My time in Glasgow was the perfect lesson in how not to gain respect and influence people.

By the final series, Colin was considering making a *Bernard and Miriam* pilot, which may well have been developed, except the character of Rab C Nesbitt had taken off and consumed BBC Scotland's comedy department. A brilliant new sitcom had come out of *Naked Video* and I wasn't in it.

I was too early for *Bridget Jones* and too late with *Bernard and Miriam*. I was also too grand to join in the sketch acting, and possibly worst of all, I had the audacity to steal their own home-grown writer to share a unique, weird, literary, respectful, erotica-biro-based connection that endured the next 30 years. My affection for Glasgow remains huge, even if this may be one-sided.

> **15. Two Timing**
> Regrettable
> Pickle
> Error

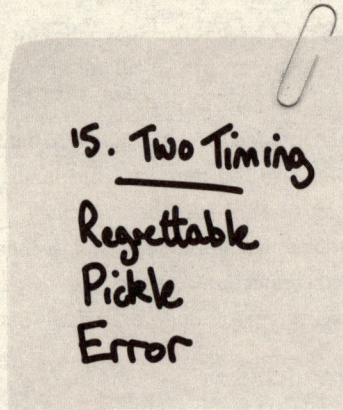

It's August, 1985, and I'm in the Botanic Gardens during the Edinburgh Festival. I've met John Sparkes for a secret rendezvous among the palms. We don't say much. We care about each other, but it's all hopeless. I've started going out with Harry Enfield, who I also care about, but seemingly not enough to prevent a polite snog with John.

This would have passed off without incident had Harry not been watching through a palm tree, if indeed he was. The snog does not look good for any of us. Except maybe John who, as the more cuckolded party, conducted himself well.

Earlier that year, as I'm taking down a card from John and replacing it with a card from Harry, the doorbell rings. I panic.

Who gave me the perfume? Was it John or Harry?

There's a receipt from Pizza Express. I can't remember who I was with. No clues. I put the receipt in my chest of drawers. There's a pair of new knickers in there. Who were they from? John or Harry? My mother?

Doorbell.

I put the card, receipt, and knickers in the kitchen utensils drawer. Baking is unlikely this evening.

Doorbell again.

I'm not ready. Two timing is scary. Being found out is the worst thing that could happen. The worst. It will cause pain. I'll be hated. Not being found out means I can just hate myself.

I open the door and pretend I'm not a bad person.

* * *

I was rarely in my flat unless it was to rinse my pants or have a bath. Every so often I'd have to lug my washing past the flat below to go to the launderette. Neighbour Bob was almost normal, except for the floor to ceiling mountain of newspapers he kept in his kitchen. Previously, we'd enjoyed a system of avoiding each other, but now I was on Radio Four...

'Is Clive Mantle really that tall?' He'd ask, jumping out of his flat to catch me on the stairs.

'Yes,' I'd say, and hurry away with my bin bag of dirty blouses.

The busier I became, the more interest I got from men. Getting the gigs, going to the gigs and doing the gigs required a lot of stamina. I was so focused I wasn't even looking for compliments, but if they came, I succumbed easily. In any case, rejecting people meant I had to face them and be mean, so it was easier to say yes.

I first met Harry Enfield when he was doing his double act with his university friend Bryan Elsey. Their 'Dusty and Dick' characters spoke in clipped 1940s English accents and were getting quite the following as a satirical sketch duo. I only knew about them because John Sparkes – a nice satirical Welsh poet who wore an anorak – was occasionally booked on the same bill, and since I was going out with John, I decided to see them both in the one outing. Or maybe I was invited to go, I can't remember.

At first, I assumed Dusty and Dick were just another pair of graduate comedians who were clever, ambitious, agreeable, and loved what they were doing. Their act was definitely classed as 'character comedy', but since I was already going out with a poet in a parka, this may have been my chance to embrace costumes and accents.

After the Dusty and Dick gig, Harry (either Dusty or Dick) invited me to be part of their Edinburgh sketch show called *Mouthing Off*. I wasn't keen. I knew Edinburgh was a slog. Also, I'd been around longer, so who would be helping who?

But as I never turned anything down, I found myself agreeing to do another Edinburgh and the three of us began rehearsing in my flat. Impressionist Steve Nallon was already booked to do his Margaret Thatcher for the second half of the show, which left the three of us to come up with the rest. Half a show couldn't be that hard.

One day, during rehearsals, Harry stroked my leg while I was being Meryl Streep. I looked guiltily at Bryan to check if he had seen, which wouldn't have been hard, given the proximity of rehearsing round a small coffee table.

We were parodying a scene from the film *Falling in Love* where Robert De Niro and Meryl bump into each other while carrying a brown paper bag of groceries. I had made it very clear that the brown bags had to have a stick of celery and French bread poking out of the top or I wouldn't do it. Thankfully, Harry liked the grocery idea as much as I did, which may well have been the catalyst of our affair.

I must have swapped allegiances during the cut and thrust of being Meryl Streep with a bag of celery, which was all very careless. How could I possibly have got myself into this? Now the offstage was going to be as stressful as on. Bryan didn't let on if he had seen the stroking of the leg and, even if he had, he managed to outwit us both by becoming a highly successful writer, producer and creator of *Skins* on Channel 4.

I was seven years older and more established, whereas Harry

hadn't yet hit the big time. This imbalance was short-lived but may have shaped Harry's decision to buy a white minivan to drive me around in, which felt quite racy. Especially if you sat in the front seat and avoided the van bit. As he got more famous, I became more invisible.

For a time, Harry and I were actually a pretty good team, especially in the practical sort of way. He generously wrote and helped me record a lot of my material for my voiceover tape. I could do Cockney, northern, rural and Greek, while Harry could do all those and everything else as well. He was very, very good.

My Greek accent was based on the accent of journalist and presenter Arianna Stassinopoulos which amused us both. Meanwhile Harry was creating Stavros 'Loadsamoney' with a mix of Cockney and Greek that soon became the iconic symbol of yuppie-dom.

We went to Taormina in Sicily which is where I discovered other middle-class people go for their holidays. Englishmen strolled around the town square in Panama hats while their wives did the shopping. The cracks may have begun to show here as I resolutely refused to get a grip on how many lira there might be to the pound. I lived in a dream world and tended to get by with other people doing things for me, particularly when it came to foreign currency or booking tickets for things. I was very, very annoying.

I remember being on the set of something – possibly *Happy Families* or a *French and Saunders* – and worrying about Harry, when I remember Jennifer Saunders said to me, 'Oh, just give him a snog', which I've found is the best advice for most issues to do with relationships. Simple but powerful.

While we were doing *Mouthing Off* in Edinburgh, I'd foolishly, weakly, guiltily (but also on purpose) arranged to meet John Sparkes in the Botanic Gardens for a secret rendezvous. How this Botanic meeting could have been known about, without the assistance of a private detective, remains a mystery, but the illicit sighting was revealed to me back in London when Harry arrived at my flat with a perfume named *Poison*, which was particularly generous, if apt, given my earlier betrayal amongst the palms. I felt sick, ashamed and horribly rumbled. This was low behaviour from me. The lowest. But my final comeuppance came during the second series of *Naked Video* when I was well and deservedly chucked.

I was sitting in the makeup room next to the studio floor, about to record a monologue and sobbing. I had just received Harry's chucking letter and hadn't stopped crying. Sheila, the kind makeup girl, was wiping my mascara off to start all over again as I let out another howl. We both knew there was a fair way to go before I could compose myself without risk of a relapse. The floor manager was hovering around the door looking tense. 'No rush Helen,' he said before dashing back to the studio floor to tell the warmup man to keep going. But there's only so much a warm-up person can do to cover a sobbing actress. The tears kept coming. In the end Sheila put her face very close to mine and told me to pull myself together. So I did, as I respond well to strictness. I did the monologue. But the chucking was deserved.

Harry was going places. He told me he knew he could get other girlfriends, but none who were like me. By this, I assumed he meant someone who was into self-sabotage and slimming pills with a thing about bags of groceries in American films.

I'd forgotten how I must have hurt Harry when I went back to John. And how I must have hurt John when I went off with Harry. And how John's nice girlfriend must have been hurt when John took up with me. At the time the easiest way to avoid hurting either of them was to just crack on with both at the same time. It seemed to be the less vexing solution. I hate hurting people, so it was unfortunate that I seemed to be so good at it. And they were both so nice.

Thankfully, we all moved on. A few years later, Harry generously cast me in *The Harry Enfield Show* to play a sex worker. Harry played a punter while I leaned, in a sultry manner, against a wall. Harry, the punter, walked up to me and asked, 'How much do I get for tuppence?' I gave him the once over, paused, looked to my left, and said, 'Mum.' An older version of me was clearly cheaper.

We met again at Jeremy Hardy's memorial in Battersea Art's Centre in 2019. The hall was packed with producers, politicians and mostly male comedians – apart from the brilliant Barb Jungr and Francesca Martinez – doing bits of their sets. I felt a surge of not belonging and, for a few mad seconds, wanted to reveal some of Jeremy's last messages on my phone as proof I knew him. This was as impractical as it was ugly, shameful and competitive – especially at a time of shared grief – which might have been funny, but only if woven into a set by a very practiced comedian.

Instead, I settled on memories. In particular, Jeremy's kindness at remembering my birthday, his early love and his constant reminders about my lapses of dignity, especially when he lent me his bed one night after a curry.

Lavatorial anecdotes would not have stood up well compared with the sharply curated citations from John McDonald and Jack Dee. And although Jeremy had been in touch a few months before (enabled by close friend and writer Paul B Davies), I really knew him best when he began gigging at 23. He would think nothing of waking me at two in the morning to tell me how his gig had or hadn't gone down.

He cast me in his TV series, *Jack and Jeremy's Real Lives* in 1996 for Channel 4. He visited me at King's College Hospital when I had Hannah and we arranged a few outings with his daughter Betty. There was an unfortunate episode of Radio 4's *News Quiz* when I wasn't very funny and we avoided each other in the pub afterwards. But when Jeremy came round to my house in 2018 to do a podcast, he was as dangerous and delicious as ever. We sat on my sofa and ate sausages while he made outrageous comments about people we knew.

And as more people spoke at the memorial, it became clear how many others had seen this side, and so much more. People he had helped, comedians he had supported, political leaders he believed in and then came the special words from his devoted wife Katie.

Harry and I smiled at each other, because it was impossible for us both to pretend we hadn't seen each other. I filled the subdued silence with some words and Harry nodded at them respectfully. I hope Jeremy would have found it funny that we both shared the same respectful impulse to go back to our seats.

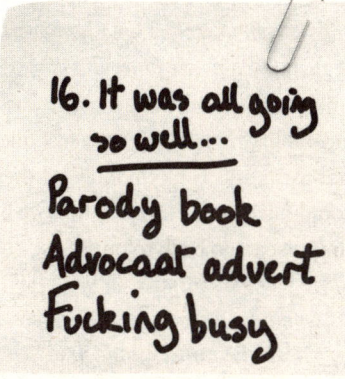

> **16. It was all going so well...**
>
> Parody book
> Advocaat advert
> Fucking busy

I'm in a third-floor flat at the end of Old Compton Street. Roger Planer (brother of Nigel Planer aka Neil in The Young Ones) *is looking out of the window.*

'What are you doing?'

'I'm thinking,' says Roger.

'You're not,' I say

'I am.'

'You're looking out of the window,' I say accusingly.

I go to the window. There's nothing to see. The ladies of the night opposite have gone for a sandwich. A man is sweeping the road, but I know Roger can't see that from his chair. Roger tears his gaze away from the window and looks surprised.

'I can do both.'

'We need a title,' I say, tapping his empty notepad.

We are writing a book and there's a deadline.

'Coping with Helen Lederer?' he suggests.

Myself, Roger Planer and Richard McBrien are writing a parody of a self-help book. It is a spoof guide to life, offering helpful hints that we all hoped would be seen as ironic. Jonathan Swift may have been mentioned in the pitch by someone other than me.

The chapters were quite instructive.

Holidays: 'It might not be too late to cancel your caravan holiday. If you rush.'

Men: 'Do not go on holiday with them to Greece.'

Parties : 'If your home is really ugly, try turning out all the lights.'

The photo on the cover was inspired by Jane Asher's Easy Entertaining *cookbook, where Jane smiles at the camera while holding a tray of her canapés. I do the same, although my canapés are made from Weetabix with a ketchup jus and Liquorice All Sorts. There must have been a draft to my left when the photo was taken because a nipple is sticking out from my blouse, which no one thought to airbrush at the time of going to print. I can't have been sexually aroused because it was only on one side. Readers who buy it from second-hand book outlets may still have sight of it.*

***

In 1988 if someone had a bad TV idea, no matter how awful, money was found to make it happen. I was 33, no longer wheezy and free of facial hair thanks to half my mortgage being spent on electrolysis which could pock mark if the practitioner decided to go in hard. And given my ease at climbing the stairs to get to my flat, I may have even been in my prime.

I was forever getting the train to take part in a highly paid, non-transmissible pre-pilot pilot, recorded at Television South in Southampton. These usually consisted of some kind of guessing game involving Roy Hattersley, Yvette Fielding and Fred Dinenage. Even Janet Street-Porter was known to turn up to guess the price of a house in Barnsley. On one occasion, in the Green Room, Roy asked me to tea at the House of Commons, which was kind, but we never fixed a date because I was always working. And possibly because I didn't want to go. The wonderfully sharp Tony Slattery hosted a music-based panel game called *Cue the Music* where we had to guess which song was being played on an electronic keyboard by his talented friend and comedic musician Richard Vranch.

The vibe for all these shows was jolly because all we had to do was guess things. And when Tony locked himself in his dressing room to take drugs, no one seemed to mind at all.

I had already fallen in love spiritually with Tony while doing a sketch show called *Happy Hour* in 1983. I'd been talent spotted at the Finborough Arms by Sandi Toksvig who invited me to join Tony and another Cambridge colleague Nick Simmonds. It was a modest tour. We had to cancel in Guildford because there were more of us on stage than in the audience, which was an equity rule apparently, but one we were happy to adhere to.

Needless to say, I preferred the acting jobs. When Anna Ford said she couldn't do *The New Statesman* with Rik Mayall, I was thrilled. I was offered her part of newsreader and had to slam Rik's privates into a briefcase. During the rehearsal, I sat in the canteen with the writers Marks and Gran and, as was everyone's habit at the time, we shared our passions about comedy. When they mentioned, in passing, that they'd been thinking of writing a comedy with me in it, but decided Rik Mayall was more of a safe bet, I sighed inwardly but agreed that he was.

At this time, women-led comedies were more likely to be hosted by women impressionists rather than women writers. The talented Janet Brown, Karen Kay, Kate Robbins and Marti Caine all had their own series. And while Victoria Wood wrote *Wood and Walters*, and Emma Thompson could invite whoever she wanted to write for her sketch show, that was it. Victoria Wood came into TV after winning an open talent show and Emma Thompson as part of the Cambridge Footlights. These two great talents were representing all of womankind in a male-dominated comedy canvas, and no one thought this was particularly strange.

I was starting to get the message. Jon Plowman loved *French and Saunders* and he loved Ruby Wax. And while he was always polite to me and even took time to read my scripts, these were the women he championed. I was alternating between wanting to be a comedian and wanting to act and write. But I was three years behind the Comic Strip who already had their own series on Channel 4. I wasn't pushy at parties yet, I hadn't won a talent contest, my piano playing was limited to one hand and I wasn't Oxbridge. And while my comedy was in the same ballpark, my delivery could alarm people and was inconsistent. It was best to give up on my own ambition and be grateful for the jobs that came my way.

Being cast to play Baby Sue in a *French and Saunders* episode was one of these jobs. I positively skipped into my gingham pinafore dress to play the little sister to their Farton Sisters. I was always happy to be with the 'girls', as Jon liked to call them, because they were fun and jolly.

There was an increasing divide between the people on the circuit and the people who were now on television. While these comedians had gone mainstream, replacing Monty Python as the new TV darlings of wit, those left on the circuit kept going, hoping for different nuggets of notoriety. So, when Roger Planer suggested writing a funny self-help book with a clever writer pal of his called Richard, I jumped at the opportunity. The fact that neither of them appeared to be famous was a bonus. Even better, Roger was one of the few people I knew with a literary agent. The chances of getting it finished looked promising. As far as we knew, no one else had done a parody of a self-help book before. It turned out that writing a self-help book about 'living a better life' led to living a better life when we landed a publishing deal.

Sometimes we all met to write. Sometimes we did it in pairs. Sometimes I did stuff on my own, and sometimes I went to Roger's flat and watched him look out of his window to think. And it was while we were writing about stencilling house plants and commissioning my sister to bake her first (and I suspect only) Tampax cake for *Coping* that I got the news that *In One Ear* was to be made into a BBC TV series called *Hello Mum*. I was once again the only woman in a team of men, but this time it was on TV.

Saturday Night Live was just taking off as a showcase for stand-up comedians on ITV, but the sketch show format of *Hello Mum* didn't appeal to the more edgy comedians. Since I got jobs on both programmes, it was best to keep quiet about it. I wore a blue patchwork jumper for *Saturday Night Live* that was far too hot but unique, and a puff ball skirt for *Hello Mum* that was gathered at the hem like a toadstool.

At least Roger and I had some success to sustain us during the silences. The people at Grey's Advertising had liked a monologue we wrote for *In One Ear* and thought there was a fit between my party hostess monologue and a drink that was used to make 'snowballs' at Christmas. For a short period of time, I became the face of Warninks Advocaat.

The character manically introduces her guests to each other before introducing the guests to the food, and then the food to each other. The last line is a rather desperate, 'So, has anyone not met French bread and pâté?'

This was how I would behave at parties in real life, influenced by the Sunday morning drinks gatherings at Ryefield Road. I'd hand round the peanuts while keeping my eye on who was saying what to keep the conversation flowing. The fear of being with people who might stop speaking at any moment led to my controlling introduction compulsion, which led to the monologue.

I filmed several versions of being keen on Advocaat – one was where I was skiing, one playing tennis and one at a cocktail party with loads of extras. Then I forgot about it. That Christmas I was seated near the front row in the Streatham Odeon to see *Fatal Attraction*, when I saw myself loom out of the screen, weaving my way between the extras, brandishing an unopened bottle of Warninks Advocaat. Even though I was still pill-popping like crazy and wearing a size ten polka dot taffeta cocktail wear, my face looked far too big for the cinema.

The clever, yet wise Stephen Fry gave the voiceover its credibility, which was a bit like Mr Kipling, but with more irony to work with the alcoholic element. Jeremy Hardy wrote me a very worried letter warning me about doing the advert. 'Did I realise I might be selling out,' he wondered? I thanked him for his concern and did it anyway.

I knew I still wanted to be an actress. And then it happened.

The call came that made me really, really, properly happy. I wasn't as happy as that again for another 20 years when I fell in love and was able to stop eating food without the help of drugs for the first time.

I was asked to audition for the part of Bunny opposite Denis Quilley in *The House of Blue Leaves*, at The Lilian Baylis theatre. The venue was described as 'off West End' as opposed to 'fringe'. Until then, I'd only done fringe theatres, including one a few hundred yards further up Upper Street at the King's Head where I'd done my one-woman show.

Nick Hamm appeared to be a very strict director who I immediately wanted to please and do literally anything that he asked me to do, except maybe crash my car on purpose. He was assisted by the very kind and knowledgeable Elinor Day. They worked well together. Nick made me cry, Elinor made me tea and explained things so, between them, they got me ready for the first night. Apart from freezing on my very first line, which Michael Billington tolerantly noted down as a 'rocky start' in *the Guardian*, I managed fine.

Being kept behind during rehearsals to find the 'something' they thought was there in the audition was worth it. There were no saucepan handles to be wary of, no dodgy drama games. I liked being pushed. I knew I had to be. I learned not to get involved in dressing room issues when Kelly Hunter and Nichola McAuliffe had a miscommunication over a small towel.

Since I had to kiss Denis Quilley, I decided to practise a few times so it wouldn't come as a shock to either of us in rehearsal. I practised in various ways on my hand in my sitting room in Brixton, sometimes leaning against the wall. When it came to the moment in rehearsal, I drew on all my hours of practice and afterwards Denis went a bit quiet. Kelly took me aside to demonstrate the kind of lip brushing used at the *National Theatre*. No one in the rehearsal room referred to this again, although they might have mentioned it in the pub.

I loved the feeling of community that came with being in a play. The visits to the pub, the phone calls to cast members, the common purpose, the pep talks. We supported each other on stage which felt very new. It was like being with Maggie again when we had to rely on each other to sink or swim at each gig. And the fear was different from doing stand-up. This time the cast shared the fear, but the actors didn't call it fear. They called it acting and they relished it. It made me see how it could be different.

17. And then I met a man...

Bald
Paris
Pregnant

I'm in the Groucho Club for my book launch and I'm wondering what kind of guests would be up for a wedge of salmon so early in the day. I've barely brushed my teeth, yet here I am, staring at canapés and waiting for the launch to start. The autumn sun is streaming through the window. The Groucho is too cool for curtains, making the room so bright that I'm suddenly worried that it resembles a Sunday School meeting.

The publicist and I continue to lay out copies of 'Coping with Helen Lederer' and hope some guests will start to arrive. According to Charlotte, it's better to host a book launch early in the working day, so journalists can 'drop in' before going on to another event.

'Like back to bed?' I want to ask, but I don't, because I have another event to go to as well.

I'm in 'The House of Blue Leaves' and it's advisable to be at the theatre an hour before it starts. I also need to allow a few hours for the psyching up ritual inside my flat. By these calculations, I might have half an hour to give to my launch before I must leave. I've got a book out and I'm in a play with a famous actor. I'm living the dream. And then I met a man...

* * *

I was loving being in the play, my parody self-help book was nearing publication, and I was still single after a year of involuntary celibacy. I had just bought Gregor Fisher's house in Brixton, my fridge was always empty except for wine and that was how I liked it. Being independent – apart from fantasising about falling in love so I wouldn't have to be alone – felt natural and comfortable.

I was filming the fourth series of *Naked Video* when Gregor jokingly, but not really, suggested I buy his house in Brixton. He was moving back to Scotland. I was still in my flat in Finsbury Park with Bob the newspaper hoarder living downstairs, but I had been to a party at Gregor's house and thought it was perfect. I later realised I'd only ever seen the house when it was full of people dancing, with someone plonking out a tune on a grand piano, which may have influenced my urgent need to move in.

When the Fishers moved out, they took the piano with them, and the house looked very small without it. But I was determined to buy it. I sold my flat to a photographer and, as I was so keen to sell, I offered to throw in Little Baba's sofa as part of the deal, as well as the orange boxes on the wall that my friend Helena had erected for me when I moved in. The walls might have come down if we tried to dismantle anything, and I needed the deal to go through.

The photographer was the last of my dalliances. I pursued him and he reluctantly agreed to a few dates. As a punishment, I was to meet him again five years later when Cheryl Baker and I were both up for a SlimFast campaign. We had to be photographed with some 'before' photos. As soon as I walked into the studio for my 'before' I recognised him. The last time I'd seen him was in my old flat smooching on Little Baba's sofa, listening to *Purple Rain*. Five years later I was facing him in a dressing gown, about to be snapped in a swimming costume, three stone heavier, divorced and a single parent.

At this time, I was resolutely single and ready to launch *Coping* before getting myself on stage to lightly brush lips with Denis eight times a week. I don't know who'd been invited to the launch, but my co-writers and I were encouraged to add any likely media people to the guest list. None of us could think of anyone, until I remembered the name of a journalist called Roger Alton. I'd been tipped off by renowned journalist Carol Sarler that a Mr Alton, who was high up in a broadsheet newspaper, had a crush on me, so the name was framed in a positive manner. Anyone with a declared crush should definitely be on the guest list. If only I knew more people who had one of those. Another journalist called Paul Webster offered a bit more background. Apparently, Roger liked climbing and may have had a nanny. So, Roger liked climbing, may have had a nanny (he didn't) and was known to like me, according to two newspaper people which made it true.

I was holding a glass of wine when our editor began a nice speech about the largely positive experience of working with the three of us, what lovely photos had been taken and how she hoped the highly successful actress and wonderful cake maker Jane Asher would take it all in good heart, when in walked the journalist with the alleged crush – Roger Alton. As soon as I saw him, I thought, I am going to marry that man... And divorce him.

The divorce part I knew about already, because in junior school, my friend Mary James had looked at the number of creases in my thumb and confirmed I would both marry and divorce the same man when I grew up. The lay out of my creases were very reliable, she told me, so at least I was braced for heartache from an early age. All our friends were well aware of my marital destiny and knew what I would have to go through in my adult years.

After meeting Roger at the book launch, he came to see me in *The House of Blue Leaves*, and although we went out for dinner with the cast a few times, I felt too busy with the play and my new acting friends to respond in the way I sensed he might like. In other words, I wasn't looking for a relationship, which is probably why I ended up in one.

Apart from the three date fling with the photographer, I hadn't had a boyfriend for nearly a year. I'd decided to be clear of men. In the back of my mind, I was wanting to clean myself up for the next chapter, which was obviously supposed to be meeting a nice man, ideally, and having a child, definitely. I was very focused. I prayed at night that I would have a child – I didn't know when, or who with, but I was aware my 34-year-old clock was ticking and needed to believe that something would happen along those lines. Also, if I prayed enough, it would stop me from getting off with anyone too silly, like a reluctant photographer who bought my old flat.

During the run of the play, Roger was kind enough to leave some perishables on my doorstep. He had clearly been badly shaken by the state of my single person fridge. I had wine. And butter. But instead of gratitude, I felt under siege with these groceries. I liked my empty fridge and my independence and my dreams and my work. I was in the right place, I was on the cusp, and I had proven I could be in a play.

He wasn't my usual type at all, but when he asked me to go to Paris, I faltered. If I agreed to go, we'd have to pack passports and night wear. I wasn't sure about making such a commitment so soon, so I phoned my mother.

'God, it's really weird,' I said. 'There's this bloke and he's really keen.'

'Oh, yes?' I could hear my mother's voice perking up.

'Yes. And he's very bald, which is new.'

'Not necessarily. Uncle Frank was bald. Go on.'

Uncle Frank was my mother's uncle from the Isle of Wight who came to stay with us, the same weekend I'd been given a facts of life pamphlet to read. The pamphlet was very clearly labelled 'The Facts Of Life' and I took it into the sitting room so I could ask any questions while my father read the Sunday papers. When I got to the chapter on 'hair' he sharply told me to read it to myself. Uncle Frank was eighty. Roger was forty.

'He wants me to go to Paris with him.'

At this point, my mother thought I was either a lesbian, or difficult, or both. At best I'd have to wait to meet a widower on the rebound or maybe, she had suggested, it would just 'happen'. For instance, I might meet someone in a queue of some kind, or maybe while being saved from a house fire while staying with friends…

She said 'Oh, go! Just go! What have you got to lose?'

'Are you sure?' I asked my mother again.

'Oh, give it a whirl,' she said cheerily.

I wasn't sure, so I did.

I remember a photograph of me in a vintage nightie, staring out of a window with a view of Paris, hoping I looked very French. I may have been smoking. It felt as though Roger liked all the things I represented and, as we know, I liked being chased.

After a few months we tried for a baby which felt very dramatic. Ever since I'd read the 'Facts of Life' pamphlet, my mother had drilled into me how disastrous it would be if my sister or I got pregnant before it was the 'right time'. Her generation had dealt with unwanted pregnancies more painfully than my generation would ever have to and she didn't want the same for us. She did such a good job on caution, that when I was in the Lower Sixth, I remember being convinced I could be pregnant. The fact that I was still a virgin didn't stop me worrying.

For the first time in my life, I was in a place where everything and everyone seemed aligned. The pills were left in the drawer.

Six months later we were in Barts Hospital to see if my polycystic ovaries were delaying the arrival of the wanted baby. The doctor came back into the room having done some tests and looked at us oddly.

'You're pregnant,' said the doctor.

I called my mother.

'Are you sitting down?' I asked.

I'd been told that's what you say when you're imparting important news.

By December I'm in a velvet smock, five months pregnant and getting married. Tony Slattery makes a funny speech, and we all eat a cake made of profiteroles spun with honey.

> 18. West End
> Stage Penis
> Post-natal

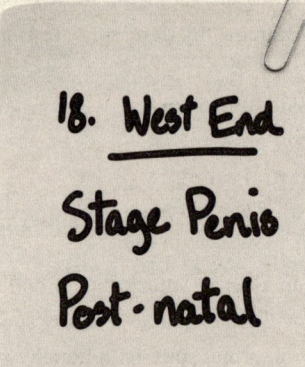

Gregor Fisher has dropped in to see his old house and my new one. There is no grand piano any more to make the house look big, and the carpet is covered with toys.

'Cup of tea?' I want to add, 'would be nice' but this would mean saying more words and I'm not quite up to it.

I'm not sure how Gregor got inside his old house, as I seemed to be still slumped on the sofa. Had I stood up at all?

'That would be great,' says Gregor, eyeing up the different wall colour which I'd painted from their clever green to my more bachelorette 'tea rose.' I may have confided in Gregor that I can't remember where the kettle is, since Gregor has disappeared into the kitchen. Luckily, he knows his way around.

I can't remember what happens next. Gregor may have found a kettle. I do remember wearing a scrunchy and not being quite on my game. As far as I know, I am a mother. I think.

* * *

Roger carried the baby basket into the house and set it down in the sitting room. The baby was in it. So far, so good. We looked at her carefully. Then she sneezed. All of our nightmares came true at once. Our child was ill. We would have to go back to the hospital. Hannah had an illness.

I phoned my mother.

'Oh my god, I'm really sorry to tell you this, but she's just… Oh God.'

I broke off to look at my sickly child.

'What?' shouted my mother.

I almost hear her grabbing car keys. Chislehurst could be half an hour away from Brixton with her foot down.

'She's just sneezed.'

'Sneezing is normal.'

'Yes, but this was twice.'

'Yes.'

'How do you know it's normal?'

'It's what babies do.'

I was still huge. I could feel my necklace cutting into the layers of added fat around my neck. Looking in the mirror was out of the question. I looked at Hannah instead. I did this a lot. It was as if we had a new Christmas present to look at whenever we wanted to.

Our first outing as a threesome was to a gift shop called Tessa Fantoni on Abbeville Road. The plan was to select a 'new baby has arrived!' card and maybe put the body stats on it, as people had been wanting to know size. I looked at the rack of stationery options and picked out a packet announcing, 'It's a girl', before handing them to Tessa.

'Er, no,' she said, gently taking the packet away from me. 'You only send these out when you've HAD the baby and… oh.' Tessa caught sight of the pram outside on the pavement with Roger.

An easy mistake to make. I was massive. Even more joy, the Caesarean section had gifted me with what was known by male doctors as an 'apron'. The NCT teacher had not mentioned aprons.

'Ask your visitors to make their own cups of tea and get your mothers to bring you casseroles,' she had advised, assuming correctly that we all had casserole support systems. My mother drove over with a few stews, and we got quite good at turning on the oven. The NCT teacher also wouldn't be doing her job properly, she had said more ominously, if she didn't tell us all about expressing milk. One would need a breast pump.

In spite of six preparatory sessions for 'the birth', held in a semi-detached house in Clapham, I managed to zone out with complete success about anything physical. The baby was in there and would have to come out at some point. Then it would be alright again. Although being sent a yellow dotted nappy bag by Elaine C Smith did bring reality closer. There would be nappies. At least I had a bag to put them in now. Sent by an actress. Showbiz was not entirely over.

The breast pump was a farmyard-y type of instrument which I would have preferred to keep in the shed, but was more useful in the hall if I wanted to get out of the house without carrying a milk pail.

My opportunity to use it came a few weeks after Hannah was born. If I'd been sensible, I would have thanked Jenny Eclair and Julie Balloo for their kindness and generosity in inviting me to be part of their new excellent BBC radio series, and regretfully declined as alas, I had just discovered I was one of those new types of mothers who had temporarily (one hoped) forgotten how to be civil. But, pride and my reluctance to allow anyone else to be cast in their series instead, got the better of me. So, I turned up at the Paris Studio in a tent dress, with an industrial breast pump and no baby. In between rehearsing, I would take myself off to the Green Room, attach the nozzle and go over my lines while the pump whirred into life. If Nicholas Parsons came in to look for his glasses, I told myself, I'd just pretend to be asleep.

The series was a success, but I left under a cloud because of my bad behaviour. This was their moment. They had worked hard and been rewarded with a series. I didn't know how to break out of my fog of chaos and be me again. Even if I was jealous, which I was – I would have been a fun team player if this had happened a year before. But it hadn't. I had spoiled what should have been their celebratory moment in radio. Poor Nicholas was very confused. Whenever I saw him, I always wanted to apologise and say, 'Remember me and my breast milk and my slight strop?' I would have added 'and the 'post-natal depression' but I didn't want to over aggrandize my behaviour.

I have been forgiven by Jenny. Hormones, a floundering relationship, and a new baby were my excuses. Feeling sorry for myself and missing out while others thrived may have been the reason. One moment I'm on stage brushing discreet lips with Denis Quilley, less than a year later I'm sulking on stage with Nicholas Parsons and a leaky duct.

But Hannah smiled a lot and so did Roger and I, and even if our smiles weren't always for each other – we both loved our baby, and we cracked on in the chaos.

When Hannah was four months old, Roger suggested we go to see a play at the theatre. This was normal for him, less so for me, but I accepted any lifeline to be who we used to be.

While I was getting ready, my agent rang. I was keen to sound normal for him. Our relationship had been really good before the baby. Paul had even come up to Newcastle just before I got pregnant to see me in *Educating Rita* and had been very forgiving about my unusual accent which I told him was 'Liverpool-based'. Now Paul wanted to know if I'd like to do a play in the West End called *Having a Ball*, written by Alan Bleasdale with a first run in Liverpool.

I looked around at the mountain of clothes piled up on the floor. Some of them were mine and the rest were Hannah's. I wasn't dressed. Hannah would wake up shortly needing to be changed and, for the first time in my life, I didn't want to be in a play.

'When is it?'

The play had been written for Julie Walters, but the part was now vacant. I was thinking of costumes.

'Do they know I've just had a baby?' I ask carefully.

'Yes. It's set in a vasectomy clinic.'

'Funny,' I said.

We talked a little more and I told him about the play I was going to see that evening to demonstrate how non-motherly and vibrant I really was. I'd wanted to be in a play in the West End all my life. I wasn't even fully dressed and now the baby was awake.

We watched the first half of the play, although I was more relaxed propping up the theatre bar in the interval than I was watching the actors onstage. Suddenly two men in raincoats burst through the rotating doors and headed straight for me. At first, I assumed this was a mistake, but when they introduced themselves as Bill Kenwright and Alan Bleasdale, I knew something difficult was about to happen.

Even with my baby fog, I'd made the connection. Paul must have told them which theatre I was in. They needed me to play Doreen, they said. And they needed an answer by the end of the week if that would be alright. And the play required the main actor to be naked at all times, if I'd be alright with that as well? The main character had to have a small penis 'for the plot', they explained, as if that might speed up my commitment.

The more I got to grips with the concept, the more I realised I would have to do it. No one turns down Alan Bleasdale and Bill Kenwright. Having a baby who was a few months old and being unsure about the state of my relationship weren't valid reasons to refuse. As the bell went for the second half, one of them suggested I get a live-in nanny which was something I hadn't thought of.

They must want me. And I always go where I'm wanted. I had forgotten this situation was dangerously similar to the radio series, because I couldn't say no.

But, before I formally agreed, I wrote a list of painful questions. Would I be told off by my agent if I didn't do this? Would saying yes be as problematic as saying no? Was I showing myself to be feeble and work shy? Had everything I wanted so badly been for nothing? Had I let down those who'd worked hard for me, only to bail when the going got a bit tough? Would they find out that I was a mess? Maybe I could fake it? I erred on habit and said yes.

I did the play. Six months later, the stage manager made a grave announcement to all the actors that sadly, very sadly the play had to come off. The investment was just not there for another six months. I arranged my face to look as sad as everyone else's and returned to a life where I didn't have to do eight shows a week and the live-in nanny went back to Wales.

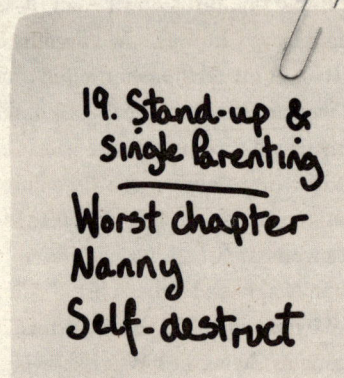

> 19. Stand-up &
> Single Parenting
> ——————
> Worst chapter
> Nanny
> Self-destruct

I'm holding the phone with one hand and Hannah with the other. I need to get a rather crucial point across to the agent.

'It's just that I didn't know that I was being picked up later, Paul.'

I move the phone to the other ear and place Hannah on the bed.

'Because now I'll have to book more childcare...'

I stick my leg out to stop Hannah rolling.

'And also, there's not much acting required?'

There's a small thud as I lose my balance. I use the f-word.

'Do you want me to get you out of it?' he asks.

I pick up some tension on the other end.

'I'm not saying that,' I say. 'I mean it's really not working, is it? Any of it... And I don't know why there's this constant miscommunication about pick-up times, do you? I mean, did you tell them I needed collecting earlier?'

It dawns on me that Paul may have wanted to say something.

Hannah has rolled off the bed.

'Paul?'

The agent has hung up. I've gone too far. Something bad is going to happen.

Thirty minutes later there's a knock at the door. A man in a helmet is handing me a posh envelope. The agent has biked round a chucking letter. He must have written it while I was still on the phone.

I have rendered myself chucked by one of the biggest and best agencies in London. And I liked him. We had been together for seven years…

I'm doing a TV job. It is called Ps and Qs *written by Victor Lewis-Smith. Victor, I later learn, is also a reviewer for the Evening Standard. A few years later, in 1996, Victor wrote about my American accent in* Murder Most Horrid *with Dawn French. He found it to be quite poor apparently, before adding in some bonus non-acting information as background. 'Helen has recently had all her money stolen by her agent – deservedly so.' Jack Dee allegedly hit him in the Groucho Club once, but I can't take any credit. My accent was indeed very poor. RIP Victor.*

* * *

I hadn't predicted that I would be single and a mother at the same time. If I'd known then what I know now, I might have asked myself more questions about what I really wanted and how I could be more self-aware. But at the time, being angry and feeling sorry for myself seemed the best way to go, so I got by with those emotions instead. Being a mother was good.

I watched myself allow my work and relationship to disappear without knowing how to say or do anything to make it better. And I was also angry in traffic.

Soon after this own goal of professional suicide regarding my agent, a producer called Paul Z Jackson contacted me out of the blue. He had read *Coping* and wondered if I'd like to write a radio series that was similar.

I would like this very much, I tell him. Even better, I could write it while Hannah was asleep and manage without a nanny for a while. I didn't mention that aspect, as no one seemed to speak about childcare issues in 1990, or use the word 'nanny' in public for fear of reprisals.

But paid childcare was necessary, which meant I began a partnership with a series of young women who adored Hannah and resented me. If they weren't dysfunctional in some way or other, then they didn't get the job. My interview skills were a bit lacking, so I tended to choose the most forceful, mistaking that for commitment. One stole a few of my clothes as a leaving gift. Another one charged me damages for a scrunchie.

Then I got used to it. Young women who had problems would now be part of my life until Hannah was ten. Except for Vanessa, who started innocently enough as a babysitter, but was persuaded to upgrade, resulting in Hannah ending up as godmother to her daughter, most were tricky. But if I wanted to work, the nannies were an essential part of single parenting. My child would grow up with a pretend paid mother who smoked, rummaged through my wardrobe and drove my car.

I wanted to use some of my nanny-disaster-single-parent material on stage, because the awkwardness of the whole thing was funny. And no one else seemed to be doing it. Few female comedians who were single parents had broken through to TV. Men were expected to talk about Thatcher in the 90s, and simply none appeared to be talking about breastfeeding, let alone the word 'nanny.'

'Could I be in the radio series as well as write it?' I asked.

'That's the plan,' Paul replied, and we began a remarkably straightforward system where I wrote the scripts, travelled into

Broadcasting House, read them out loud in a studio and joined in with proper actors who did the other parts.

Life with Lederer scripts were slightly escapist vignettes where I made things happen. One week I'd set up a company, another I would go on a cruise. I'd explore a new culture, a hobby, a career, or a relationship. Each episode, I became empowered in a different way. It was so empowering I didn't even have to worry about a nanny going through my chest of drawers while I was out.

It was almost too easy, but I got a second series. If I hadn't been so busy being disappointed about my home life, I might have allowed myself some pleasure in the fact that I now had a producer, a studio and three brilliant actors to act my words with commitment and verve.

Hannah and I would picnic on the floor in front of the TV to watch *Spot the Dog* and make our own fun. I may not have had time for best friends, second-best friends, or boyfriends, but the love for Hannah made up for that. And even though this was the loneliest I'd ever been as a grown-up, *Life with Lederer* was a nice surprise, especially coming from the BBC.

But the anger was still a problem. I couldn't get closure in my marriage. I wanted to understand what had gone wrong but wasn't quite able to.

My mother had remarked on our separation with a thoughtful but relatively non-judgemental 'mm, it's a pity for Hannah', but I knew she was sad. Since I had no idea what family life was, it felt perfectly natural to invite my mother to make up our team. We worked well together. She said no to Disney in Florida as she said it wasn't her thing, but agreed to Malta for a package holiday. When we watched Hannah push her buggy into the lift and disappear up to the fifth floor on her own, at least I had someone to share the panic with. My mother shared it by telling me off.

When Roger finally left after Hannah's first birthday, I knew I had to get back to stand-up. My hopes for an acting career had been interrupted and I had to get back to my earlier risk-taking and start finding myself some gigs. At least I'd be in control of that. Even better, I was now even more angry and sad, which had to be the perfect ingredients for a new show.

In June 1991, *Hysteria* was being performed at the London Palladium and I had to bring Hannah with me to the rehearsal. It was a weekend, so the nanny would have been off smoking somewhere with a bloke. My mother offered to pick her up later leaving me to do the gig in the evening. It was very odd having a one-year-old in an environment that had previously felt starkly competitive and ambitious. The producer wasn't interested in a toddler, nor was anyone else.

The show was an opportunity to own who I was now and do some new material about 'having it all' and being 'happy'.

'Hi, it's great to be here, particularly in my condition. I am, of course, nine months pregnant – or as Judge Pickles would say – guilty. Now, one of the interesting things about being pregnant is...? (Pause while I consider) No, it's gone! There isn't one.

And then I went on a birthing course. Just to learn the ropes. You have to take your partner with you. Preferably the one that got you pregnant in the first place. But I don't think they check up.'

The material got laughs. I could have been sharper, and it would have been nice to have looked less bloated, but a large tent dress would have to do. A few months later I was invited onto BBC's *Paramount City*, a stand-up comedy series presented by Arthur Smith, Curtis Walker, and Ishmael Thomas.

The audience sat around at cabaret tables while I performed material about breastfeeding and being resigned to a non-fulfilled life. Ian Pattison had written some of this for the monologues in *Naked Video* and my show in Edinburgh. Abbie Grant, a sparky young writer with pink hair and white trousers, wrote some great material as well. People who laugh easily, especially at me, are highly prized and Abbie was one of these. She was also clever and fiercely loyal, which was handy.

Last time I did a gig I'd just had the baby and I'll admit I had a touch of the old post-natal depression, but thankfully the baby's turning out to be very special. She's very bright. She said her first words the other day which were 'that's it, I'm leaving', which made us very proud.

And I tried to do everything right. Breast fed. In public. Covent Garden, actually. Drew quite a crowd. Got heckled twice. Mind you, 'show us your tits' was a bit superfluous...

Of course, the focus of your life does tend to change when you've had a baby. I mean, when I was single, I used to go out on my own and have fun. Now I just go out on my own. In fact, the only thing my husband and I do together is... lead separate lives. Which is why we went for marital therapy. Which is lovely. And expensive. The first time we went along the therapist said to us: 'What do you like about your partner?' Then, to break the silence, she said: 'What don't you like?' Well, we only had an hour, but I managed to slip in a few minor points about dress sense, friends, family and personal hygiene. Obviously, I had to wait till the next session to open up more fully.

But the therapy has been useful. We're learning new things all the time. Like not saying the N-word in public. NANNY. There, I said it. Sorry to be offensive. But I can put my hand up now and say, 'Yes, I have got a nanny and I'm proud of it.' It took a while. But I'm there now.

But anyway, a nanny is also a person you pay to look after your child so you can work in order to pay for the nanny and have a bit of spare for the luxuries in life. Such as a car you can call your own. But now that we've worked out an appointment system it's fine. I ask her if I can use it and she says 'no'. And she's a very caring person. Especially about my clothes. Now she's had them altered to fit her. In fact, she's a real gem. And people are always saying to me, 'Where did you find her?' and I say, 'Easy, it was one of those little cards in my local telephone box.' It said: 'Spankingly good nanny, satisfaction guaranteed, good hourly rates,' and she had great references. I think her last job was with David Mellor.

In between gigs, the birth and the divorce, a nice man called Peter invited me out on a few dates. This required the hiring of a babysitter and a lot of effort all round, but I was up for it. We were having dinner when I allowed a large yawn. 'Hope I'm not keeping you up,' he quipped, and I realised what new dating would involve. I had no spare energy apart from contacting Ian Pattison who, by now, was having a passionate affair with Kirsty Young. My timing was out.

Which, if nothing else, was consistent.

> 20. Divorce on stage
>
> Oddity...
> Mental Health or
> Comedy Section

It's 1995 at the Pebble Mill TV Studios, Birmingham. I am sitting on the sofa and smiling at the very kind and very lovely Alan Titchmarsh.

'So...' Alan is considering his words carefully. 'Why get married in the first place?' he asks.

I have just finished speaking about being a single parent, and sounding extra jaunty to sell the book, and learning that marriage and motherhood is a serious subject for some people. As luck would have it, Alan may just be one of these people. Jauntiness may not be the right way to go. The pill was invented in 1960 but single parenting is still awkward to talk about. The words 'sanitary towel' may have received a better response than 'single' and 'parent'.

'Well, we are both parents of a lovely child,' I say.

'But this book is about you being a "Single parent."' Alan inquires intelligently..

I was commissioned to be funny about a thing that isn't. Always.

Instead, I say, 'Correct Alan. It's a humorous book about the reality of single parenting... to lessen the taboo about it, and connect with people who...'

I look at the blurb on the back of the book for inspiration...

'... who feel that to be "dumped with offspring" is a new beginning, rather than a failure in life?'

Because Alan always does his research, he Alan continues with his inquiry.

'So, why bother with a marriage if you were going to do it on your own?'

But I didn't know that when the sperm was placed, did I Alan?

Instead, I say ...

'I just wanted to write a book... to show that it's not all bad and that lone parenting is normal, not uncommon, and a lot nicer than being stuck in a lift?'

This is also written in the blurb.

The interview didn't happen quite like that, and it might not have been in Pebble Mill, or even with the very fabulous Alan Titchmarsh. It could have been another radio DJ with big hair, but I can't remember.

Was the chasm between me and society or just me and Alan? Or indeed the person who could have been Alan?

Turns out the chasm was universal. While promoting the book, I found myself having to big up single parenting as a life choice, in order to make jokes about it, or else I sounded bitter – which I was. There were no role models sending up single parenting at this time, and since male journalists had only just got used to the idea of there being women comedians at all, making jokes about dating with a nappy bag was a stretch.

High street bookshops didn't know whether to put Single Minding *in the humour section or the family health section. Was I funny? Or a mental health expert? They didn't have a section for 'angry'.*

* * *

The book came after the show. I would write a show for Edinburgh and set it in my therapy group. I decided that group sessions where people tried to solve each other's problems were probably funny. And surely my divorce was funny? And my relationship with the agent was funny? The hopeful meetings with producers and trying to get a date with a child were funny… I could write a show with monologues as well as stand-up. Pain is funny. If I made my pain recognisable, might allow other people to feel better about themselves but mostly, I might get laughs.

But I couldn't write it without jokes. The only person who knew me and who could, in my view, write the best jokes for me was Ian. He agreed to look over what I'd written and make it funny. I began a script. Elinor Day, who'd directed me in *The House of Blue Leaves*, agreed to direct it and, slowly but surely, we created pages that Elinor put in a neat green folder. She refused all payment and said she was doing it as a friend. The only way I could think of repaying her was by arranging for a floor tiler to be let into her flat when she was out, and re-tile her kitchen floor. She told me she was utterly and totally surprised.

The green file was soon full of group therapy sessions, dating, being a single mother at the school gates, and being on and mostly off TV. This was the show. Apart from two people who left very early on the opening night, the audience remained in their seats and sold out for the whole run. This wasn't too difficult because the Wildman Room was quite small. I remember the moment the couple walked out. They were seated in the middle of a row and the exit door was at the back of the room. Their determination to leave helped them find the door relatively quickly, with only a bit of noise from people at the end of the row. They left at exactly the moment I was talking about having a child. In the back of my mind, I worried they were going through IVF or adoption. In fact, I worried about this for the next 50 minutes while continuing with the show.

This is some of the material from the show (although it's helpful to have been there).

MARRIAGE

One thing led to another and before we knew it, we had settled down into the sort of relationship where we'd sit in a pub without a single thing left of interest to say to one another. I said to my mother, 'Look, we bore each other silly, take each other for granted, what shall I do?' She said, 'Book the church, it's time to get married.'

MARITAL THERAPY

In the end the therapist suggested we go for a trial separation and, in fact, it went so well we decided to go full steam ahead and make it a fully blown estrangement, so at least we ended on a high.

GROUP THERAPY

I've just done tele and I'm understandably drained. It's called a non-transmittable pilot, Barbara, so no, your kids can't watch it. No, I'm not being negative, Maureen, that's what you do in showbiz. I see it as a privilege, actually.

NANNY

The other place to get a good nanny is to buy a newspaper called 'The Lady' – that's a real paper for the people. At least I think they're people. It has articles on how to steam clean your tapestry and renovate your ball room. Really whiles away the time while you're queuing for your oven chips in Safeway.

OUTSIDE THE SCHOOL GATES

The child is supposed to isolate and then identify its parents. My child sometimes claims other people's parents just to show me up, which I tend to laugh off in a weak sort of way, then I try to pal up with the full-time mothers, most of whom are nannies in disguise just to trick you…

The show ends with everyone leaving the group, including me. The fear of missing out, the trying not to be awkward about initiating sex and the jealousy of other funny women were all themes that echoed my own life.

The rebuff from the cameraman on that TV trip to Egypt was turned into a monologue about a man called Derek. Being a mother while wanting sex was more of a taboo in 1995 so I did material on it. The lunch with the producer showed how I tried to be pleased for another woman who got the job I was hoping for. I wanted to reflect the jealousy of being set against other women for the few jobs going. Taken as a whole, it is a small wonder that anyone found anything to laugh at, such was my misery bowl, but the show was picked up for the Perrier Pick of the Fringe and transferred to the Donmar in London. This was where I spotted my mother and sister sitting in the audience halfway through the run and I froze as soon as I came on stage. The first awkward silence in the therapy group wasn't supposed to be that long, but how dare they get themselves tickets? I didn't want them seeing me like this. My secrets with the public are not supposed to be overheard by my family.

Glynis Henderson toured the show and paid for me to get driven around the UK by a wonderful woman called Linda. She'd pick me up from Brixton and we'd start off in good cheer. By the end of the tour, she'd be luring me into each theatre with the promise of a bottle of wine and cheesy cheddars for the way home. I put on a stone.

Paul Jackson, the producer, came to see the show in Edinburgh and set up a meeting at Carlton Television. They'd just been sent a pilot show called *Ellen* and he was wondering if I'd like to do a similar kind of show. I said I would *like this a lot*. Inconveniently, Paul left not long after and the new ITV controller Nick Simmonds (who'd been in the show in Guildford with Sandi Toksvig) understandably wasn't interested in Paul Jackson's cast-offs. Or indeed me. But I had hopes when my script about being a single parent *Onwards and Upwards* was optioned by Zenith South. Less so when it didn't get commissioned.

The same night my mother, brother-in-law and sister snuck in to see me at The Donmar, a nice publisher from Hodder and Stoughton was also in the audience. She told me she was interested in the single parenting angle and commissioned me to write a 'humorous' guide.

I wrote the book in six months. I'd fax material across to Elinor who'd send them back, adding the occasional 'too bitter' in the margin.

Coping was written before motherhood when I felt laid back about being funny on the page. *Single Minding* was written while I felt angry, rejected, and bitter. But it might be useful to read if one finds schadenfreude in any way cheering. And I manage to end on a note of optimism.

'The important thing is forgiveness. Forgive yourself. Forgive the bastard who got you into this mess. Forgive your lovely child who one day might forgive you – with any luck.'

I think she has... but I'm not complacent.

In *Still Crazy*, I addressed the audience, and talked about being single and having sex. It was 16 years before *Miranda*, 23 years before *Fleabag*, and 27 years before single motherhood appeared in the sitcom *The Duchess*. Not that I'm bitter...

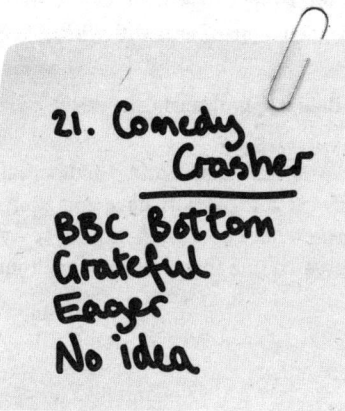

> 21. Comedy Crasher
> BBC Bottom
> Grateful
> Eager
> No idea

We are in Studio 2 at White City. I've got a part in Bottom with the two greats of alternative comedy. I'm hovering around hoping to go through my lines with Rik Mayall one last time before we face the eager audience.

There's a lot of exuberance from Rik and stillness required from me. We take a moment to run the lines.

Just before we start, 'Don't crash the laughs...' he says in my ear.

Crash his laughs? I would rather die than crash his laughs, even though I'm crashing their limelight. I would never crash the laughs. I nod and prepare to say my lines.

* * *

Whoever got the part of Lady Natasha Letitia Sarah Jane Wellesley Obstromsky Ponsonsky Smythe Smythe Smythe Smythe Oblomov Boblomov Dob, 3rd Viscomptress of Moldavia would have to own a pair of 'wazzo jugs' in order to serve the plot. It helped that the head of costume was as excited as I was about disguising myself as some kind of Moldavian aristocrat with visible jugs. I was happy to be in her hands.

The episode, called 'Digger', starts like this:

> Eddie (Adrian Edmondson) and Richie (Rik) go to a dating agency to find a rich date for Rich. The date must own large jugs. The dating expert (played by Lisa Maxwell) is given a line to query their jug request.

> **Lily:** ...fun to be with... and a wazzo pair of jugs?
> **Eddie:** That's right.
> **Richie:** But obviously we're flexible.
> **Eddie:** Ah, but not about the jugs.
> **Richie:** No, we have to be firm on the jugs.
> **Eddie:** And the jugs have to be very firm. **[gesture]**
> **Richie:** We--ah, come off it Eddie! I mean, there must be more to life than jugs.

> **[Eddie shakes his head and looks questioningly at Richie. Richie thinks.]**

> **Richie:** Well... You're right, a wazzo pair of jugs it is.

I wanted to be the best Moldavian aristocrat possible, and if earrings, lipstick, false eyelashes, and a revealing of bosoms were needed, then so be it. I wanted to be professional but not pushy. Someone they wanted to work with, who wouldn't want their limelight. A mate who did their own thing, who wanted to serve their script with dedication, respect and without being seen to be jealous or bitter in any way.

The costume turned out to be a massive, sticky-out, soft furnishings sort of frock with layers of net and a velvet trim brocade – but with a low-cut bodice, which was never intended to contain any breast material. The result was a large expanse of bosom with a frock somewhere underneath.

I took the costume lady's number because I loved her enthusiasm. Which came in handy for my second wedding outfit, since I wasn't pregnant for that one and there was more scope for couture. She made me a tight skirt out of net and a jacket that did up tightly.

In rehearsals, Rik and Ade enjoyed messing about with each other, which made the atmosphere upbeat for everyone else present, but it was obvious they knew what they wanted from each scene. There was a sense of having to get it right while also having fun.

Somewhere between the tea urn and the script table, Rik made a cheery reference to the night in Edinburgh, which was both clever and respectful. No need to dwell, no need to deny. Heartening and classy, I decided.

At one stage in the recording, some mashed potato became attached to Adrian's spoon and we had to stop filming. I can be seen looking very serious as we re-set. It would have been unheard of at the time to even consider making an off-the-cuff remark to the audience while the props were re-set. Women comedy guest artists didn't do that in the 90s. Or if they did, they had to be family… The clip got shown on *It'll Be Alright on the Night*, and I can be seen sitting reverently and quietly while the potato got sorted.

This was the scene:

> **Natasha:** That was delicious.
> **Richie:** Oh, you've eaten -- everything. Well done. That's very brave. In that case it's time to... Oh, Natasha. That is your name, isn't it?
> **Natasha:** Yes.
> **Richie:** Oh, right. Oh, Natasha. I know it's a bit sudden but... I love you. I love you with all my heart, and all

my soul, and all my... **[looks down]** you know. I know it's mad, and I know it's crazy, and I know it's wild even but... **[kneels]** Will you marry me?
Natasha: Yes.
Richie: You don't have to be like that – pardon?
Natasha: I said yes, of course I will marry you, but not because all of my family's assets have been wiped out in the civil war in Moldavia and we are now penniless.
Richie: No, no, d-d-d-d-d-d-d-d, never mind about all that now! Did you just say "yes?"
Natasha: Yes.
Richie: Hah, ahhh-haaahhh! Er, Natasha, do you believe in sex before marriage?
Natasha: Yes.
Richie: Would you, would you... practise it?
Natasha: Yes, I would.
Richie: [panting] Would you mind signing something to that effect? You know, just an informal agreement between the two of us – just legally binding, obviously!
Natasha: Sure.

On the one hand, I got recognition from the cameo slots, but I didn't feel I deserved the praise for being part of a hit comedy when I had nothing to do with creating it. It was a case of being genuinely grateful to be included even though I hadn't given up on devising my own TV series. There was a thin line between delusion and fawning, so I straddled both to be on the safe side.

Bottom and *Ab Fab* went out at the same time. And even though I didn't deserve notoriety through association, there it was. I became less of a new girl as highly prized actors lined up to join the cast for guest episodes, and they were in awe. Even the wonderful

Lindsay Duncan's hand shook slightly in the read through for *Ab Fab*, which shows how even the most accomplished actors reacted in the face of the *Ab Fab* phenomenon of the 90s.

Dawn and Jennifer's rise was steady and consistent. I was three years behind them and I didn't have a rise. I'd started in stand-up, remained in stand-up for as long as was bearable, and jumped at the acting jobs when they came along. I didn't want to be the comedy guest who stays too long, sleeps with the host, and doesn't bring anything new to the party...

The public thought I was besties with the whole of alternative comedy. To explain the real pecking order would have disappointed them. So, I didn't.

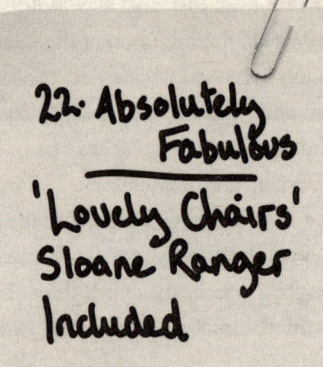

22. Absolutely Fabulous
'Lovely Chairs' Sloane Ranger Included

It's 1992 and I'm driving to the BBC rehearsal rooms in Acton for my first day on Absolutely Fabulous. *I'm belting out 'Born in the USA' as the A40 flyover takes me up towards the sky. It is a moment of complete happiness. The prospect of a job, Bruce Springsteen, and driving on a gradient turns out to be an intoxicating mix.*

The man at the desk ticks my name off a list, offering even more positivity. The rehearsal room is full of people, one of them has a clipboard. I have a handbag. I decide to do something with my bag, so I put it on the table and look at it.

'Hi, I'm Janice, assistant production manager,' says Janice with the clipboard. I'm overwhelmingly grateful to her for speaking to me. It means I don't have to look at my bag. 'And you are...?'

It takes me a few seconds. Does she mean my character name or my real name? The part I have just been given has a name – 'Catriona', which is an upgrade from 'Medieval chat show Hostess' and 'Cashier' but I don't want to appear over invested or too actressy.

'Helen.'

'Wonderful,' says Janice, and she points at two big urns of boiling water. 'Help yourself.'

I make a coffee. This doesn't take very long.

I eat a custard cream. Then, once I've done that, I take out my script and look at all the places it says 'Catriona'.

I start mouthing my lines. I stop when I realise I've been doing that.

I'm aware there are a lot of important people in the room engaging with each other. The very impressive Joanna Lumley, Jennifer Saunders, Julia Sawalha, June Whitfield, Jane Horrocks, a man whose name I soon learn also begins with a J... I wonder if I should tell anyone my sister is called Janet.

I remind myself of what we were taught at drama school: 'No one likes chatty on the first morning.'

After what seems like a very long time of other people talking to each other, the man called Jon suggests we take our seats around a big table. There are about 30 people in the room and not enough chairs to go round. The people round the edges are make-up and costume people. We are actors and producer people. We get the table.

Jon makes a genial introduction and invites everyone to go round and say their name. He suggests Jennifer begins. Everyone laughs. We know who Jennifer is. She is the supreme talent who has written the series and will star as PR guru Edina, as well as a global comedy icon of all our tomorrows. When it comes to my turn, I hear myself say my name 'I'm Helen?' and force some eye contact, mostly with people whose names begin with J.

People with other initials are the very excellent Harriet Thorpe and Chris Ryan. I know Harriet from Girls on Top and she is also very good at acting, and Chris Ryan who played the 'cool person' in The Young Ones. Chris tells me he is feeling nervous. He is also the same height as me. I decide I will talk to him a lot.

Jon reads out the description of the first scene and anyone who *needs glasses puts them on. This is a sign we are ready. Julia, Jane, Jennifer, June and Joanna get into their roles and sound perfect.*

Once we start blocking my scene, Harriet and I stand on an area marked out on the floor with masking tape. There's a lot of tape depicting different rooms. I hope I'm in the right section. It is soon very clear that Harriet knows what she's doing. She did the acting course at Central. I can't concentrate. Very soon, I'm going to have to say my lines in front of everyone. This will be expected. I have no idea where my character is from or who I am. Would it be unsophisticated to ask Jennifer if Catriona has an accent? I might ask her for a bit of background.

I wait for my turn to speak to Jennifer as she is talking to Jon. He is the show's producer and seems to be guarding Jennifer. But I urgently need to ask about my character, because I need to know how to say the lines.

'Sorry Jennifer, just to check, so what kind of person am I? Am I posh or Northern, or …?'

Jennifer cheerily waves her hands around. 'Oh, you know the kind of person. Doesn't really have to work. Cardigans. Quite benign, just turns up for things. You know?'

I do know. Airhead. Benign. Just turns up. Got it.

Catriona is born.

* * *

When I was cast as Catriona in *Absolutely Fabulous* in 1992, I had no idea the series would become such a hit or be part of my life for the next 20 years. Or that it would offer such joy and happiness to so many people, particularly to those in rehab and a large percentage of male cabin crew.

Every comedian, actor, pop star and newsreader wanted to be in *Ab Fab*. Even the chocolates on the set were real. No expense was spared.

The excitement about the PR woman who wore slightly too tight slacks was massive. Drink, drugs, falling out of taxis with Elton John playing himself, proved that *Ab Fab* could do anything.

Harriet and I were cast as rather thick Sloane Rangers (a person from Chelsea who wears flats and does gallery work), who somehow managed to be given jobs as editors on the magazine where Patsy had some kind of job. We weren't family, but our characters were often found sitting in front of the designer distressed dresser in Eddie's kitchen. We were rarely needed for plot reasons but were somehow always part of the action. And always on standby.

Although on one occasion, in the third series episode 'Fear', Catriona was offered Bubbles' job, and I got to do some filming in the Conran Shop with Edina on my own. There was much awe from passersby as we were filmed crossing the street with large carrier bags. Back in the studio, Jane and I received a few laughs while we were waiting for a shot to be set up. If one of us said, 'Which camera?' the audience would literally heave.

The rest of the time, Catriona and Fleur generally tried to join in, being pointless, but keen to be helpful to Edina and Patsy, and generally getting in the way, as time wasters on the magazine. The more hanger-on-like our characters were, the more known we became. A fan club in the States even threw 'Fleur and Catriona' parties in homage to our strange characters who managed to get jobs without really doing much.

I'd get picked up in a car from Brixton, driven to Harvey Nichols, where Rebecca, the costume person, would be waiting for me in 'personal shopping' with some unusual clothing combinations. The stranger the jacket, the happier she became. I didn't mind. If odd, large, incongruous collars were considered suitable, I wore them.

The 'hanger-on theme' was close to how I saw myself at the time, especially if I caught myself making comparisons. Most of the cast appeared to have stable home lives which made me keen to hide my own early, single parenting set-up. The first time Roger came to Brixton to collect Hannah for an overnight, I remember, rather determinedly, pouring a gin and tonic at 11 in the morning to make it feel festive for us all. So it was a relief to leave the sense of failure at home and concentrate on all the new people in my work life.

I liked Joanna Lumley immediately. She made everyone feel valued and told witty stories with excellent and profound punchlines. And, just like Emma Thompson, there was also great eye contact. On one occasion, after a rather interesting conversation about our preferred scents, Joanna very kindly brought me in a bottle of perfume called 'Happy'. Or maybe it was called 'Sunflower'… I didn't know whether or not to declare it to other cast members as I didn't want to step out of line. Or be seen to be sucking up. These kinds of thoughts could preoccupy a whole morning.

June Whitfield spoke to everybody. There was a kind motherliness about her, but not totally, because she was also great with props and a lot of mothers aren't. She would sit and do her crossword while she waited for her scene. Occasionally, she'd ask other people for clues or talk about the sandwich choices for that day. And then in a blink of an eye, she would be ready and completely in character to do her scene.

Sometimes June would ask Jennifer what her motivation might be if the script required her to move from one side of the set to the other. I enjoyed these exchanges. Jennifer always had a good answer. Sometimes it involved not having one.

With familiarity came my urge to be funny and mess about. I began to offer up a slightly scared stream of consciousness commentary of what was in my head while we sat in outer rooms, waiting to be called. I was always looking for approval but was ready to shut down quickly if it wasn't forthcoming. I might start with an incident that had actually happened recently (usually disastrous) and see what kind of response I'd get.

Julia Sawalha was always happy to listen. Jane Horrocks would sometimes ask questions to make sure she'd got the story clear in her mind and then be very funny herself. If Jennifer didn't move away, I'd take it as my cue to go bigger in a panicked sort of way and the story would get heightened. And if, on occasion, she responded with a laugh, I'd feel validated. Jennifer has a very authentic laugh, which spurred me on. If, on the other hand, the interest wasn't there, I would know to be quiet. The role of 'storyteller' was nerve wracking but thrilling. If it went wrong, or if the story got interrupted as we got called away, I'd worry that I'd be seen as a disrupting influence which would not appear becoming for a 'hanger-on' with an unstable home life.

In the early episodes, Jennifer cast a lot of performers she'd known from the comedy circuit, but as the series continued, more established stars would appear. Actors would often say to me, 'I couldn't do what you do,' about my stand-up comedy. I'd reply, 'Well I couldn't do what you do,' even though this was a lie, since I was doing it with them.

In 2003 I sat in the rehearsal rooms along with Baby Spice, Baby Spice's manager person, and possibly Baby Spice's hairdresser – I can't remember – while Harriet and I regaled them all with insider anecdotes of what had gone on in series one and two.

If I'd been a guest celebrity or highly prized actress, I'm not sure I'd have been drawn to my slightly hysterical, handing-around-the-Wagon-Wheels-to-put-people-at-ease action. But it was my way of dealing with the fear as much as wanting to put people at ease.

Sometimes I did get too excited. I once invited everyone in the rehearsal room to a party at my house. Julia Sawalha very thoughtfully sent flowers. I'd gone too far. But at the time I must have thought the nation's top comedy people and heads of departments would quite like to be invited to venture south to an unknown house in Brixton on a night off. This was me being the wheezy hysterical ten-year-old who spilt my milk as a child and got told off for showing off, when I knew I should have calmed down, but couldn't.

The episodes were filmed at TV Centre in front of a live audience. Jon would come out to warm up the audience before anything was recorded. When he introduced Jennifer and Joanna the audience would be beside themselves with excitement. Sometimes they had to be told very firmly to be quiet.

On one occasion, my job was to walk on set, then through a door and into another room. After 'action', I began walking and the audience broke into hysterical laughter. I thought, 'What did I do? All I've done is almost walk into a room. And I'm not even Jennifer.'

As the series continued, Jennifer might say to Harriet and me, 'I haven't written these lines yet, but you'll say something like...' and then she would ad lib something that got written down by someone else and put into the script. These lines would then be divvied up between me and Harriet, so that it was fair.

In the first episode of the second series in 1994, Fleur and Catriona visit Patsy and Edina in hospital. They talk through some ideas for the magazine.

> **Catriona:** CHAIRS. I thought it might be quite interesting. I've got a friend who's got a shop with some lovely CHAIRS in it.
> **Fleur:** Jocasta?
> **Catriona:** Yes. And she believes CHAIRS are as important to civilisation as a masterpiece. Or something. I wrote it down somewhere. So, we could print that up and do some lovely photos.
> **Patsy (to nurse):** Oi, more champagne.
> **Catriona:** Can mine be a Bucks Fizz?

I became known as a person who said 'lovely chairs' while Harriet was known for saying 'words du jour'. And while those words are so slight, they still offer recognition to something much bigger.

I wrote this into my stand-up material. 'Anyway, hands up, anyone seen me in *Absolutely Fabulous*. Back in the 90s I was one of the journalists who had to say "lovely chairs". In fact, they were my only lines, so I just repeated them a lot. I got asked to give a motivational speech and say "lovely chairs" at a correctional institute in Colorado. I said, "What do you want me to do?" They said, "Say 'lovely chairs'." I said, "But aren't you all on death row?" They said, "Yes." I said, "Couldn't I just talk about myself for an hour?" They said, "No. They'd been punished enough..."'

At one point around 2002, when there was a gap between one of the series being made, I wrote to Jennifer to say I hoped she would consider placing me in the next *Ab Fab* series, were it to happen. These are not easy letters to write. I had, as gracefully as possible, accepted that I was not to be cast in Jennifer's *Jam and Jerusalem* comedy. But I couldn't be sure about *Ab Fab*, and I would have to come up with a good lie that was full of grace, to tell people why I wasn't in it.

Thankfully, this never came to pass. And if it does, I am genuinely full of grace already.

As the series continued, the fans of *Ab Fab* wanted to know if we all got on in real life as well. They saw a camaraderie and it was important to them to feel that this was true. People would say, 'I bet you all get on, don't you? You all look like you have such fun. Do you go round to each other's houses?' And I'd reply, 'Yes, all the time. Not when they're in, obviously... Cos that'd be stalking.'

Looking back at times like that, I realise what an extraordinary thing it was to have been a part of. It's on my gratitude list.

23. June Whitfield

Accidental PA
Restricted View
Joanna Lumley

I'm at the BBC studios rehearsing for the 2011 Absolutely Fabulous Christmas special. As usual, June Whitfield is doing the crossword, waiting for her scene. She's 85. I go over and say hello because June always speaks to me, and I also don't want to sit on my own. This is when June tells me she might buy a sandwich from the canteen for lunch and would I come too. I probably say something like, 'Carbs! Yes, please,' because that's both polite and friendly.

During our chat over lunch, we discuss the play that Joanna Lumley is due to appear in at the West End. It's The Lion in Winter *at the Theatre Royal in Haymarket, and Robert Lindsay is due to star too.*

'I'd love to see it,' says June.

'Gosh, so would I,' I add, excited, flattered, overwhelmed and then very frightened that I seem to have included myself in June's theatre trip. Maybe June has mistaken me for one of the Js?

But June hasn't mistaken me for one of the Js, because she's looking at me as if I'm a legitimate theatre going pal and is now planning when would be best for us to both go.

I can't help but feel involved.

'I'll get the tickets,' I say before I can stop myself.

'Perfect,' June nods with satisfaction, adding, 'Actually, get three, can you? I'll bring my daughter.'

'Three tickets. Sure.'

'Lovely!' says June. 'I'll look forward to that.'

I make a note of June's phone number and the day she wants to go, and panic. I'm now a PA to a star. It's official. Bubbles could do this better than me.

* * *

June was both a national treasure and a very senior citizen who deserved the highest level of VIP treatment. I'd never even been to her house. How much work would it take to make this trip really happen? If only I hadn't got involved in the sandwich lunch burst of enthusiasm.

I think June mistakenly assumed I knew all the right people and would pull strings to get the best seats in the house. Or maybe she didn't think about it at all.

One thing was obvious. If June had known me better, she would never have placed herself in such jeopardy. But now I had a duty of care. I couldn't break it to her that I didn't have practical skills.

A normal person might have asked Joanna if she could arrange for some tickets to be made available as these would have guaranteed a good seat and some comfort for June. But I was too embarrassed to ask for such a favour. I hate to be seen as an enthusiast. Or a fan. Or out of control. Or random.

Instead, I called the box office like any normal customer. At least I knew not to ask for a box. Even June would have thought that was too much.

'We don't have any stall seats left on that day,' said the theatre booker. 'The only seats we have left are in the upper circle.'

'Great, I'll have those please.' I said, now anxious to please the booker as well. She could have been an out of work actress and might have recognised my voice. I needed her to find me courteous. She sounded like she had calls waiting. Everyone wants to see Joanna in *The Lion in Winter*.

'Have you got three together?'

Another agonising wait, while the booker checked her database.

'You're in luck,' she said. 'We've got three together. Oh, but…'

'What?' My heart sinks. My reputation is riding on this call.

'They're at a reduced rate.'

'Why reduced?' I asked. 'They're for … June Whitfield.'

The possible out of work actress ticket booker ignores this extra information.

'They're restricted view.'

I booked the tickets and tried not to think about it.

The day of the show came and we found each other outside the theatre. June's lovely daughter Susie was with her. It was all smiles and laughs as the three of us stepped inside.

'Have you got the tickets?' June asked cheerfully.

'Indeed, I have,' I smiled.

Then we began our long climb to the upper circle.

On the grand circle landing, June was still smiling.

The next set of stairs gradually got narrower and narrower until we reached the Gods. June was a bit puffed by now, but still had a smile on her face.

Eventually we found our seats, which were in the middle of a row, so the people already seated had to stand up to let us through. There's no doubt that they were all thinking, 'What is June Whitfield, one of the most famous faces in Britain, doing in the worst seats in the house?'

The seats were tiny and hard. There was barely room to open the programme without feeling pulled towards the edge and certain death. The lights dimmed and the wonderfully poised Joanna entered for her first scene. At least we sensed she had. We couldn't see anything, but there was a gasp of appreciation. June (five foot two) discreetly raised herself forward to peer over the railings. I prayed she wouldn't sneeze.

Egged on by this success, June took the coat she had placed on the back of her chair and folded it to serve as a booster cushion. From this elevated and slightly precarious position she was able to enjoy the rest of *The Lion in Winter*.

After the play (and the long climb back down), we were invited to have tea with Joanna in her dressing room. Joanna immediately made a fuss of us in her charming way, having no idea I'd single-handedly masterminded the enormous hike for an 85-year-old up to the Gods and back. I wasn't going to mention it if no one else did. We were all over Joanna because she was excellent, and she was all over us. Just as it should be. And it is to June's immense credit, and reflection of what a consummate star she was, that nothing was ever said to me about the disaster of the theatre seats.

'What a lovely time we've had,' she said, as we parted outside. 'Thank you, Helen, for organising such a wonderful trip.'

I may have shaken my head modestly.

June died in 2018, aged 93. A comedy legend who appeared to lack any bitterness about feeding punchlines to a host of male stars with such grace, wit and professionalism. She was warm to others while taking the world of comedy seriously. Working with her, in my small way, was special. She had a motherly warmth without being motherly. A bit like my own mother. RIP June and Jeanne.

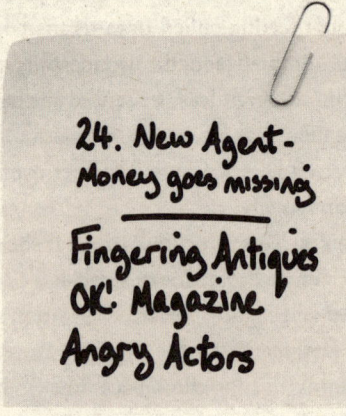

> 24. New Agent –
> Money goes missing
> ──────────
> Fingering Antiques
> OK! Magazine
> Angry Actors

I'm in my newly converted attic in Brixton, staring at my word processor. The ceiling is quite low, but as long as I don't jump up and down, I can avoid direct contact. A teacher has just called me to tell me that my five-year-old daughter has called another girl's painting 'rubbish' and could I apologise as there has been a complaint.

'From the mother or the child?' I ask.

'Both.'

This is particularly bad. I feel sick. The mother is not in my circle. I don't know which circle she is in. My own circle is quite small. It consists of one couple who, I later learn, are Conservatives. But they are the only parents who are prepared to ask me to their house for supper with other couples at the same time, so I like them. They call me a 'thespian' if I ever have to disagree with anything, which is kind.

I'm frantically looking for the slighted mother's phone number on the crumpled list of other parents' addresses that I also don't know when the phone rings.

'0208 697 5341,' I say (it is 1995 so you have to say the number).
'Is that Helen Lederer?'
'Yes.'
'I'm afraid I have some bad news.'
'Could there be more bad news?' I'm thinking.
'And you are?'
'The accountant for...'
The voice rattles off the name of a firm – something like 'Gregory and Telford,' but not that.
'Oh, yes?'
'There's been an issue about the client account.'
I wonder why this is any business of mine, but I say, 'I'm sorry to hear that.'
'And I'm sorry to tell you that £30,000 of your earnings are not in the account...'
Beat.
This money is what I have just earned from a TV job requiring a lot of social engagement with antique dealers and interaction with Michael Parkinson.
I now feel sicker than I did about Hannah's art critique.
'Oh, noooo.'
My 'no' is very drawn out... as is my money. From my agent's client's bank account. Without me knowing. If she'd asked, I might have been flattered, before saying no.
Thankfully, it wasn't just my money that was nicked. The agent stole from other clients as well, so at least I didn't feel picked upon. In fact, if she hadn't stolen from me, I'd have insisted she did, just to prove I was working. I was bottom of the 'top' earners apparently, which should have been more of a comfort than it felt. Caroline Quentin was missing £250,000, which put my paltry £30,000 in perspective.
Even in theft, I was bottom of the top.

* * *

I'd recently been taken on by an acting agent who was known for her largesse and networking skills. I heard she'd arranged cars to take casting people to see a client in a play which sounded impressive. I had great hopes about getting some acting work and so did she. Soon after I signed up, she called me.

'Great news,' she said. 'You're going to be a team captain and alternate with Tony Slattery.'

'Wow, is it improv?' I asked excitedly.

'Not entirely,' she said.

I was being offered the role as team captain for *Going for a Song* for the BBC. Although I hadn't expressed a passion for antiques on TV at my first meeting with the agent, I said yes.

Mariella Frostrup was the other team captain and Michael Parkinson was the chair. It took a few episodes to get good at guessing the price of old fish knives, or a spoon with a windmill on it (especially without any training in cutlery), but after 20 episodes, I started to get some right. Valuing artefacts became quite compelling.

Tony made headlines early on in the series when he was handed a Ming vase by someone who very possibly didn't know Tony's character that well. Shortly after it was handed to him by a man in a brown overall, Tony promptly dropped it. We were told to be very careful after that.

'Remember the Ming,' warned the floor manager, without laughing.

At the end of a recording, Mariella and I would have to point at each featured antique with our fingers for the cameraman to get his close-up shots. Sometimes we'd have to stroke the items which could start to feel a bit sexual if we did it for long enough. A few episodes in, Mariella asked for us both to be offered a manicure.

This was of less use to me as I was an adult nail biter, but we were refused anyway, and we had to crack on without one.

There was a lot of filming to get through in one day. It was a case of, 'Which show are we doing now? Is it three or four?' Whenever I got distracted by thoughts of Hannah at home being looked after by a nanny, I'd think of the money I was earning to pay her, just for touching an old cup. I was happy to watch Michael and Mariella wander off round the grounds while I made small talk with the odd expert who'd been directed into the canteen because they'd arrived early.

For three months I would travel to Bristol, talk about spoons with Michael and Mariella, bond with an expert, guess the value of a few old ink pots or a teapot, maybe, do a bit of fingering for the camera, before getting the train home again.

So, when I heard all my fees had been 'reappropriated' by my agent, I felt the injustice. Then I felt a helplessness, followed by a sense of violation.

The story was headline news for a while. There was a particular interest in the very talented and successful Caroline Quentin's rather large, missing fee, along with some speculation as to how she hadn't noticed it was gone. Possibly, the journalist didn't understand that actors don't look at their bank statements.

The same accountant for 'Godfrey Bingham, etc' rang me a few days after I'd been told about the missing fee.

'How are you?' She asked.

'Quite poor, actually.'

I didn't say that. I said, 'I'm really upset,' as I'd had a bit of time to process my feelings.

'Yes! Anyway, I'm just telling you there's a requirement for all the acting clients to be at the White House Hotel next week. It's near Regent's Park.'

'Why?'

'It's part of the bankruptcy proceedings. She will be there as well.'

'Really?' I asked. 'Isn't she somewhere else? Like a prison?'

'No, she's in the Mendips.'

This appearance was brave. If I'd misappropriated a load of money from my clients, the last thing I'd want to do is sit and face them in a hotel lobby. Actors can be very unforgiving when they get roused, especially if they feel they have been wronged.

'It's all part of the legal procedure,' soothed the representative from 'Godfrey etc.'

'Won't it be weird?'

'It won't take longer than the morning.'

'And will it be weird?'

'Probably,' she said and hung up.

So I set off to the White House Hotel as instructed. The chairs had all been set out neatly as if laid out for a humanist service or adult baptism. We took our seats and the people who knew each other well enough did some nudging. I didn't have anyone to nudge, although I recognised a few faces. Someone from *Casualty*, Shaw Taylor from *Police Five*, and Craig McLachlan. There was a feeling of repressed hysteria. Of not wanting to laugh at a funeral. But I was also baffled. The money had been taken and I didn't know why. My upset wasn't against the agent personally; I even liked the woman.

It became clear there was to be a pecking order about who should be seen to look the most cross. The top earners didn't turn up. Maybe they were too famous. And the actors who were too poor to have any money nicked didn't want to show too much outrage, out of respect for the middle people.

I was one of the middle people, but only because of the *Going for a Song* wages. Without those, I'd be one of the 'respectful nudgers'. As it was, I was an 'authentic outraged'.

It was down to me and a few others to express our pique. I could understand how a lot of 'nudgers' expected some kind of spectacle to unfold, as opposed to people like myself who were after a reasoned explanation and some kind of plan to get my money back.

Sharon sat behind a table looking a bit sheepish. She was flanked on either side by nervous looking men in suits. There was a carafe of water on the table, which wasn't quite big enough for her to hide behind. After a few coughs from all of them, the man with owl glasses invited us to ask questions. This invitation was met with an awkward silence. It was all too formal. Like being an extra in Crown Court.

After more coughing, Craig stood up and spoke quite forcefully for 20 minutes. I think a finger may have been pointed. There was clapping. Then Shaw stood up to ask a catalogue of tough questions. The gist of these being 'Why?' 'How?' 'We trusted you,' and again, 'Why?' Then he sat down.

There was more silence. Shaw was very good. His naturally authoritative outrage had cast a bit of a spell and the atmosphere began to turn more hostile. This had to be my cue. I could now step into space created by Craig and Sean. I stood up. I didn't know what I was going to say but I felt compelled to say something. My sense of outrage of doing a paid job that kept me away from Hannah, only to find the money gone, would be the gist.

But I surprised myself. Finding a grown-up and rather cross voice isn't often required in showbiz. Normally I hear myself sounding like a kindly onlooker who happens to be at the same party. Today I wasn't kindly.

I echoed Sean's main line of questioning which was 'Why?' I might have said 'It's not fair,' ending with a feeble, 'Can you just explain why you did it?' I might have mentioned the words 'single parent' a few times which may or may not have influenced Sharon to stare at the carafe of water in front of her. It must have been hard. If I were in her shoes, I'd have slipped myself a few Valiums to get through it.

No one quite knew what to do or say. The owl man closed the meeting, declaring some future plans that no one understood, and we all shuffled out, entirely unclear about what we had just witnessed and why we all had to be there.

Apparently, the agency owed over £480,000 to 150 actors.

I went home. Others may have gone to the bar in the hotel. None of us now had agents. Well, agents that didn't steal.

A few agents got in touch with me directly after the meeting and were all very quick to point out that they, personally, had never knowingly stolen from any of their clients. One of these agents introduced me to a journalist who, he told me, was experienced at brokering deals with *OK! Magazine*. The idea was I could recoup some of the money with a magazine deal. The more I revealed, the bigger the fee, as long as I agreed to have my house photographed.

I was slightly surprised that anyone would want to see inside my house, but the journalist told me they could bring flowers to cheer it up, and she could get me five grand in return for her having control over the copy. I said yes immediately.

A stylist and photographer arrived with flowers and coffee which I thought was generous, until I realised the coffee was for them. Perhaps they'd been told I might be too poor to own a kettle.

I was asked to sit in the middle of the kitchen table with Hannah, and since I was getting five grand, we did.

The first headline was bad.

"MY AGENT HAS RUINED ME, SAYS HELEN LEDERER."

The next caption was also quite bad.

'The TV star made millions laugh, and she thought security was part of the deal. But her agent's bankruptcy means the single mum must now watch every penny. You might think such a star would live in relative luxury on the back of her successful career. Instead, despite years of hard work, Helen is currently flat broke and faces a daily struggle to make ends meet.'

And in case my destitution hadn't quite landed for the reader, my tragic explanation continued…

'Helen is the first of Sharon's clients to speak openly about the trauma she has been through.'

"My life has suddenly been turned upside down, and I don't know how to cope...Everything is in doubt now. I have no money in the bank and face the very real fear of losing my home. I've had to re-evaluate everything and everyone in my life. All this has left me scarred and vulnerable."

'The episode has triggered a deep depression, and Helen has started seeing a therapist to help her cope with her feelings.'

This wasn't a complete lie. I'd been seeing the odd counsellor off and on since I was 27, after all. Thankfully, the journalist decided to include some heart into the piece at the very end.

'Despite her experience, Helen is not bitter, and she hopes that, whatever the outcome, Sharon will get professional help.'

This was true. I'd never wanted to see the agent or anyone else go to prison, even if it was an open one where she could offer inmates advice about how to put on a play.

Not long after the magazine was out, I received a phone call from one of the other agents in her office who had since set up on his own. Perhaps I'd be offered a place in their new agency?

He said, 'I don't think you've done yourself any favours, Helen.'

'Really?' I asked. At this stage, I was still telling myself that five grand off the 30 grand shortfall brought the loss down significantly. Especially as all I had to do was be photographed sitting on top of a table.

'Really,' he confirmed.

I re-read the article…

'I am now very nervous about anyone who has my money. I feel like the only solution is to keep it under my mattress now. I don't have another agent yet because I'm having trouble trusting people after this.'

I could see his point. What agent would ever trust me now?

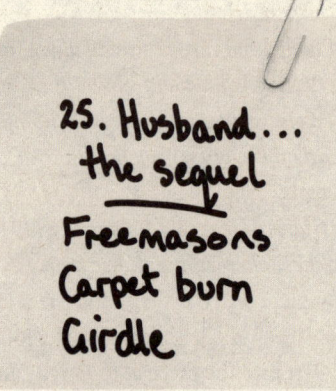

> 25. Husband...
> the sequel
> Freemasons
> Carpet burn
> Girdle

'I know I will never marry again and I'm at peace with that,' I tell Christine.

It's 1999 and I'm in the garden of my second-best friend from school. I don't have a best one due to my commitment issues. We are in Wiltshire. Whenever I meet Christine in Wiltshire, I cry. It's quickly dealt with.

Christine looks at her watch and pours us another gin.

'I'm happy with Hannah, and I absolutely know this is me and my life, and that's how it's going to be,' I announce after my release of tears.

Hannah is nine. I've had two boyfriends since the divorce but currently there are none, nor are there likely to be.

I blame myself. I bit the first boyfriend and, on the whole, once you've bitten a boyfriend, you can't go back. I blamed the antidepressants and wine in my 'Whoops, so sorry I slightly bit you,' Notelet.

At least the second boyfriend was happy to give our kittens a *loving home, having been chucked by me in a cowardly letter. This made him a saint, which was not my usual type. The kitten's mother had been gifted to me by the very brainy Emma Freud along with a helpful instruction letter. Perhaps she sensed I had no idea about pet care, which was perceptive, although some additional specifics in cat contraception would have gone a long way.*

Hannah chose Daisy, who was the only one of the litter who scratched her and didn't have a tail. It was clear we had to have her. Our new cat scratches and I bite and chuck people by post. I'm 44 and single.

* * *

My need to surrender to spinsterhood was confirmed at a 'mind and body workshop' weekend called the 'Mastery' in Hampstead a few weeks before. For two days I'd been indoctrinated by an immaculately coiffed Australian, who incited 40 hopeful but lost people to pair up and open up to mood-altering music. Some people left in the first hour. I stayed till the end. For the final ceremony, we read out our affirmations on a card while someone took a polaroid. This was to be our keepsake.

My affirmation was: 'I am an intelligent, lovable woman ready to share my talents with the world.' I started out with, 'I want to be an intelligent actress comedian,' but the charismatic leader said this was too specific. The affirmation had to be in the present tense and more general for it to have a fighting chance of coming true.

That's what affirmations are. They are lies to trick you into a better place. She made me say 'lovable' and 'ready to share my talents'. I would never have thought of being 'lovable' and I certainly wasn't keen on 'sharing my talents' as I hate being ripped off. But when I read them out loud, everyone whooped and cheered (as instructed), and we all tumbled out into the pub on a high of hope and arousal.

I also had arousal and hopes about a short drummer who was a bit famous and who I'd managed to get paired up with, but he didn't call me. So, I could have been crying about that in the garden. I was neither lovable nor intelligent as a potential partner. But I did have a child, which was nice.

I could also have been crying about my career. I'd just filmed the 'Titanic' episode with *French and Saunders* who were now working with a talented but teenage looking director called Edgar Wright. The confidence of young people was a marker of time passing. We'd all grown older, but I was still the oldest with the least work.

Christine had noticed my new staring thing. I explained, the mind and body weekend had made me very open, and I now had to look people directly in the eye. It was one of the pairing exercises. Each person had to stare at a stranger for five minutes with minimal blinking. The idea was to be open and face who you are. In my case, unlovable and single.

Christine and I were due at the Freemasons Ladies Night Dinner Dance, which wasn't something I'd been invited to before. The only way I would normally agree to attending a branch of possible devil worshipers and their associates in Wiltshire, was if I could write it up for *Woman's Hour* as a quirky monologue. Luckily my loyal BBC producer, Sarah Taylor, had already given her blessing for the 'dinner dance' to be an audio piece, even allowing the use of the word 'stiffy' in reference to the posh invitation already on my mantelpiece. And if I could even disguise the same material for my column in *Woman and Home* magazine to recycle it – at least I'd be working.

'I'll be alright,' I say.

'We don't have to go.'

I know she doesn't mean this.

'It's fine. I'll do it, it's fine.'

I sigh and hoist my girdle up, ready for the off.

Christine and I both failed our fire lighting badge at the same time in the Girl Guides. A few years later we managed to avoid sex with a French farmer while hitchhiking around Brittany – which took a certain trust.

The suggestion to join her table at a dinner dance was out of character, but since she'd mentioned it several times, I felt obliged to go. Apparently, there'd be a 'divorced friend' on our table who played tennis with the local butcher who was also a doctor, as it turned out. I irrationally hoped this didn't mean he was a chiropodist. She described the friend as a gentleman, which immediately made me think of a short person in a tweed jacket who'd most likely be bald with glasses. I wasn't thrilled. Someone else to be polite to.

I was still feeling begrudging when we walked through a car park and into what looked like a temporary building.

'Is this where it's supposed to be?' I asked, to be mean.

Within minutes of handing our coats over to a Masonic wife with a coat hanger, I saw the room spring into life. Women in long dresses and men with black ties appeared from nowhere and surged towards a trestle table to be ticked off a list. We were surrounded by pashminas.

The idea behind the event was for the Wiltshire Freemasons to thank their 'ladies' for being their wives, although a lot of these wives seemed too busy with coat hangers and ticking people off to appreciate being thanked.

One thing that struck me was how quiet everyone seemed. On the other hand, I was fresh from my Mastery Mind and Body weekend with a famous drummer who didn't want to go out with me, and a lot of shouting and clapping, so it wasn't a fair comparison.

And then I saw him. I could hear Christine saying, 'And this is Chris,' so I braced myself to greet the small, bald man who was to join the table. Instead, I looked up to see a tall man with brown hair. My first thought was, 'Oh,' followed by a cautionary, 'I'd better behave.' What a difference an hour makes.

The combination of being so recently opened up and actually meeting a man who didn't seem to have a partner in tow was interesting. Made more so by the rather shameful fact that I hadn't had sex in about five or six years. Our eyes met. This may have prompted Christine to step away and adjust her pashmina. For a moment it seemed like there were only the two of us in a sea of bow ties and shawls.

We soon got stuck in over the melon balls where I asked him lots of questions about his life. I didn't want to talk about me. He had a quiet authority. He wasn't remote nor was he pushy. Then we danced. I instigated some interesting palm to palm hand moves I'd be doing at my salsa evenings in Brixton which, I noted, were not being rejected. I was going for it, basically. I forgot that being a doctor in a small town might pique some interest, particularly if the GP in question was spotted doing some weird hand moves with a semi well-known face from the telly. Our table of guests went back to Christine's house. Then people disappeared, leaving the two of us alone. That's when I grabbed him. There's an area in front of Christine's fireplace which has become known as the 'carpet moment'.

On the way to the station, I suggested to Christine that she give him my number. She later told me she'd given him my address, postcode and fax number, 'just to be sure.' Two days later, he called.

On the one hand, I couldn't quite believe all this had happened. But on the other hand, I could. Everyone gets a chance at happiness. The call began well. We were both bashful but acknowledging. Then it went a bit dark. I heard the words 'someone else'. Frankly, why wouldn't he have a someone else? Perhaps I could have had one as well, if only I hadn't gone round biting people. (Note: The adult biting was just the once, and through a highly textured jacket and, I'd like to think, maybe more of a nibble? I was too tanked on Prozac with wine to recall the details. Maybe I've made it into a bigger clamp-down than really occurred. The receiver was very understanding. And I know that doesn't make it alright. Ever.)

But the 'someone else' was a blow. I admired him for being so honest and there was relief in that, as well as the disappointment.

'How about you?' he asked casually, as if it was the most natural thing in the world to have sex on a carpet with somebody who was already romantically entangled. 'Is there anyone?'

'No, I haven't got a someone, actually,' I said as cheerfully as I could.

I wasn't sure what to do. But I knew something significant had happened. I needed counselling so booked a session with my hairdresser.

'What should I do?'

'What do you mean?' Malcom asked. He seemed puzzled. 'You had fun, right?'

'Well...'

'And you like him?'

'God, yes.'

'So just go for it. See what happens. Chillax! Don't get heavy.'

I would never have thought of doing that had Malcom not suggested it. It was the first time I'd ever done 'chillaxed' and it felt liberating. Six months later we got married. Two weeks before the wedding, my mother died.

This was the fear that I had carried around with me all my life, and particularly as a single mother. What would I do if my mother went? We were a team. When it happened, it was as bad as I thought it was going to be. Worse. We'd already been shopping together to choose her wedding outfit. I remember her having to sit down in the changing room because she was tired. I was too excited to notice until the shop assistant suggested she have a glass of water.

When my sister and I went to the house, the new velvet jacket was hanging up in her wardrobe. I remember her saying that she was looking forward to meeting Chris' mother. We both had mothers then. Instead, we threw ourselves into planning the funeral. When I told Hannah that Granny had died, she cried immediately and later told me she cried every night after that, for weeks. They were very close. She was nine.

Two weeks is no time to grieve and focus on a wedding. But the wedding photographs show that I'm in a lot of pain. There were shopping trips to buy outfits with his daughters, arranging the cèilidh, wondering if it was too pretentious to have Guinness cocktails when we weren't even Irish, making sure Hannah was feeling included… none of which I did well.

At the time, I had a very affable literary agent who would occasionally take me to a 'chivvying up' lunch. Part of the chivvying was to wonder why I insisted on obsessing with TV scripts that kept getting rejected instead of writing a novel that might stand a chance. Luigi was always full of ideas. One day, shortly after he received his invitation, he called me up to suggest that *OK! Magazine* cover the wedding.

This was a very new area for me, I told him, conveniently passing over the fact I'd been in it already. But why would they want to cover my wedding? I didn't think Luigi quite understood my position. His confidence in me was flattering and the fact that he was baffled that I wasn't more successful was very nice, but really, *OK! Magazine* for a wedding? And Chris? He wasn't even a showbiz doctor. There'd be ordinary people there. I couldn't even guarantee Christopher Biggins… Of course, I remained hopeful.

'I'll call them,' he said.

Hours later he called back to say *OK!* were up for it.

'Really? Are you sure?'

'Totally,' soothed Luigi.

'Just tot up a list of celebrity guests to justify their… contract and we've got a deal.'

'How many do you need?' I asked doubtfully.

'How many do you know?'

'Two?'

He laughed and told me to make a proper list.

It felt very surreal. I tried to muster a list of all the famous people I knew, who would not only consider coming to the Irish Club in Eaton Square for a cèilidh, but would allow their photos to be taken. I only knew about the venue because Rik had his birthday there once and it was known as being rickety chic. If only more places could be roughed up like that; like a Soho House sanded down and covered in loose gravel with all the paintings removed.

I began with Ruby Wax, as she'd come to the last wedding. Tony Slattery could give me away again; he'd been perfect the first time. Chris Biggins was a yes, mercifully. John Hegley, he'd have to come even though he didn't do TV. And he'd be late because he was in *The Pajama Game*. Dawn French and Lenny Henry…

My list wasn't long enough. There was a polite request from Luigi to extend it. I tried to pad it out with some plus ones. Ivan Massow offered to bring Penny Junor. I said I'd look forward to meeting her and was a fan of her work.

This was getting better. Then Luigi called to say the *OK!* team had queried the name Felicity Montagu.

'You know Felicity,' I told Luigi. 'She was the PA in Alan Partridge. Don't they watch Steve Coogan?' I felt outraged on Steve's behalf.

Hannah and her best friend Emma giggled and snorted their way through the ceremony. I turned around to see my sister doing her best by glaring at them, but they were in their own little world of sabotage and hilarity and wouldn't be stopped. Hannah had just been to her first funeral, she had lost her grandmother, was in trouble at school (which I didn't know about), and now this, so we cracked on with the vows to a backdrop of very, very intrusive laughing.

After the legal bit, we all re-grouped at a Chinese restaurant because Hannah liked the food. My cousin Caroline presented me with Little Baba's silver serviette holder as a wedding present. I began to cry. Fortunately, Hannah's best friend Emma, who was enjoying someone's beer at the time, offered up a loud burp which lifted the mood. Then Hannah prodded the waitress' bottom with a fork. The waitress complained, and we hadn't even got to the reception.

At the Irish Club, I had a mild panic attack at the top of the ornate stairs while waiting to greet people. I didn't know a lot of them. I'd known Chris six months; I barely knew his children and my mother had just died. I suddenly thought, 'What have I done? Who is everyone? What do I say?' But once the band arrived, we were all forced into doing the polka with strangers and I was able to focus. Tony's surreal speech reassured me that I wasn't alone, and I accepted that alternating between happiness and crying would have to do. Hannah and her friends decided to perform an elaborate play about a terrible death in another room. Ruby Wax was fascinated and came to tell me about it. Then my new stepson's girlfriend was sick on the pavement outside. Hannah and Emma were overjoyed. It was the highlight of their day.

Chris and I spent the whole of the wedding night in a nearby hotel lobby talking to Tony. We laughed and we cried some more. Somehow, we had managed to assemble just enough famous people to cover the pages to fulfil our contract. *Just*.

The headline in *OK!* was at least more positive than the 'being ruined by an agent' one a few years before. Now I was dealing with grief and a second chance at a proper relationship.

'Star of TV's Ab Fab and Naked Video Helen Lederer – her joy at marrying Chris Browne and grief at the tragic loss of her mother.'

A few weeks later, I discovered there had been rumours in Warminster that we were going to cancel the wedding. When I heard this, I worried that perhaps it hadn't been normal to go ahead. But it had never occurred to me to do anything else. It was true, I was no longer as happy as I was before and wouldn't be again. Grief robs you of that freedom. Maybe we shouldn't have gone ahead. Maybe we should have postponed. But I knew my mother would have thought it wrong to cancel. She had met Chris and she approved. A 'good bedside manner' had been her verdict, which was her tongue in cheek way of saying something nice. I sensed her happiness that I was happy.

Christine suggested that she had waited to know that I was happy before she went. Her black velvet jacket hanging up in her wardrobe marked what could have been, but it also symbolised her pleasure, even if she wasn't there to wear it. The *OK! Magazine* piece would have made her laugh. She would have been both bewildered and amused. This time my showing off would have been allowed…

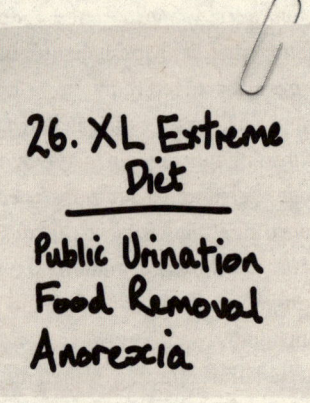

> **26. XL Extreme Diet**
>
> Public Urination
> Food Removal
> Anorexia

I'm in Islington at a wedding party. Simon Brint, half of Raw Sex, pretend uncle to Rowland Rivron and iconic musical genius, has just married Amanda. They are good people. I like Amanda's mother because I don't have one anymore and she is nice. Everyone is happy and excited for them. Me especially. In fact, I've been dreaming about this wedding for weeks. After three months of being off booze and normal food. I've forgotten what it feels like to hold a glass and eat a blini at the same time.

The restaurant is overrun with comedians, musicians and waiters with trays of fizz. I'm wearing a sleeveless grey silk bias cut dress with my mother's '50s bolero to cover the arms and I'm now drinking heavily.

The flutes of beautiful yellow fizz are whizzing around on trays and I've probably had about seven when the room becomes so spinny and lovely with all the guests greeting each other on a high, possibly none higher than me. This is very much a cool occasion and there is much love in the room.

And although this first taste of alcohol was heightened by the previous three months of booze abstinence as part of my new powdered food diet, I was still aware I was in very special company, and I mustn't let myself down.

There were quite a few guests present who I'd seen repeatedly at events over the years without knowing them personally. I know these types of guests must be given a certain respect. I don't want to make them think I want to be their friend just because someone I know knows them. And because they are famous.

So, to find oneself urinating in front of such a person is not ideal. Especially when wanting to achieve this nuanced balance of good manners. Not pushy, not obsequious but pleasantly friendly.

I'm on the way downstairs to empty my bladder when I get caught up with a couple of people I know in this way. Betty Jackson, the very spectacular designer, is a guest along with her distinguished husband. Somehow, I find myself speaking to Mr Jackson. I haven't quite made it to the entrance of the stairs. Instead, I've managed to get myself backed up against the stair rail. I'll need to turn and squeeze past to get to where I have to be, but I can't move on, without engaging first. I don't know what I say to him, but I feel I'm being appropriately nuanced in an animated and friendly way, and very, very, very pissed.

Suddenly I feel a sensation I've not felt since my waters broke. And, oh yes. There we go... I seem to be expelling a bit more liquid, all without me having to do anything. I'm wearing black tights. They feel... sticky.

This is now an official emergency. I'm talking to Betty Jackson's distinguished and altogether interesting French husband and, oh my god, I'm peeing all the way down my legs. It's positively gushing. Who knew that ten glasses of fizz could flow out and down, with such determination and for so long?? That's a lot of liquid to be teaming down my 50 denier opaques.

I think I manage to look as if this isn't happening and extract myself to tiptoe as quickly as is decent down the stairs to the loo. The lovely Frenchman may or may not have been aware he was talking to someone who was gently relieving herself. My dress is pale grey. I'm trusting the black tights have absorbed the urine, but I simply must go back upstairs, damply, to what is very possibly the most treasured wedding event of the alternative comedian's calendar.

Simon is about to play on stage. Rowland Rivron and Adrian Edmondson are ready. Simon has been working on the music for weeks. He is already up at the microphone.

I station myself at the back of the room and look around to see if anyone is pointing at my tights. Unbeknownst to me, the muscle wall in my stomach shrunk while I was busy losing the three stones, allowing the gates to open with the outpouring of fizz… I'm mortified.

Luckily, all eyes are on the couple. We toast again to our beloved friends. They are so happy. Happiness is golden. So is my urine.

* * *

Shortly after my own wedding, a theatre producer got in touch to suggest he produce and tour my one woman show. I was, as usual, reluctant but I didn't want Chris or anyone else to think I was work shy. I told him I only had half an hour of material that I was currently happy with. This wasn't a problem, he said, because he had another idea up his sleeve.

'Oh, yes?' I said, wondering, not for the first time, why managers and agents actually wanted to work with people like me. Surely they'd be happier with people who were actively promoting their live work with joy and enthusiasm.

The promoter suggested one of his clients, Tim McArthur, could sing his way through the first half, to save me worrying. This seemed like a solution. Apart from Bury, where we could hardly hear ourselves think above the glasses being smashed outside, and where the Mayor felt he had to write to us to express his and his wife's personal disappointment – we did OK. Chris would meet us in the bar afterwards and drive me to as many venues as he could. I'd never had this kind of support at the same time as working before. We had fun, we had drinks, we ate food. After a few months, I found myself returning to my lifelong belief system: that everything would really be so much better if only I could lose some weight.

I'd managed to lose a bit for our wedding, but it wasn't much. My body wasn't giving off the right image of power I wanted.

If I was a normal size, surely no one would be mean to me ever again.

It was 2003 and I'd been off the speed pills for at least 10 years. Perhaps I could learn new tricks? This was when I read about a powdered food diet in a magazine. It looked like the perfect solution. I phoned the number and was offered a local counsellor. I found David, a wonderful and rather large man who ran his own powdered miracle group from a rented flat in Norwood.

He operated from the ground floor of a 'safe house'. We clients would arrive with our plastic miracle powder carrier bags, nip briskly into the loo to test our own urine, and prove our loyalty to the cause before being weighed.

The cause required borderline starvation, gallons of water, and powdered food that became chunkier when mixed with water. Then we'd sit and try not to judge each other while we waited for David to finish weighing everyone in a smaller room. This took ages. Eventually someone would break the silence with a confession about eating a bread roll or an egg. We'd all nod in understanding about how awful that must have been, but tomorrow was another day.

Finally, David would emerge from all his weighing work to pull out his flip chart and advise us on how to stop being baffled as to why we were all so 'fat'. Being told what to do when faced with a groaning buffet table was particularly helpful. One suggestion was to leave the room, which I wouldn't have thought of.

Immersing myself in a world of chocolate and berry food packs was an effective way of removing myself from ordinary life. If I drank a gallon of water on the hour and stuck to the food packs, I would literally see the weight drop off.

It worked. I lost three stone in three months and I'm ashamed to admit that I didn't stop to think about how Hannah might react to her mother losing weight so fast. I would pack up my food bar and plastic shaker and go off to work while she went off to school.

Eventually I was told by another mother that my daughter had started making herself sick.

'I thought you'd like to know,' the mother said in a kind way as she came to collect her non-sick-inducing child after a tea.

While I was on my diet, and Hannah was having her fun teas with her pals, she was also being told she was fat by a group of boys in her class. She had just started senior school and I had got to know some of the boys and their parents. At first, I tried to blame anyone else I could think of. I was slow to see the connection. And finally, I blamed me.

I made an appointment for her to see a specialist. This doctor concluded that there was no evidence of anorexia at that time, but that Hannah had exhibited some anxiety that could put her at risk of further issues. Did this mean she had the propensity to be anorexic but that she wasn't…? Or that she might be? There was some relief and some concern. Hannah was such an energised person to be around. Even as a teenager, she was funny and kind. And now there was this new hidden thing.

Hannah and I talked about food, I bought lots of books and we both owned it. Up to a point. I had been unaware of the connection of my life long self-talk about my own body and the impact this may be having on a growing child.

Hannah tells me now; it was her own friends and pressures at school that influenced her body image and even though I knew this wasn't the whole story, there was a lot of it about.

Anorexia seemed to be the preferred ailment of choice in Hannah's mixed school, while more pupils were known to be self-harming at the posher all-girls one down the road. And even though talks were beginning to be offered, and the word anorexia was used a lot more frequently by both parents and pupils, I blame myself for not seeing a connection.

In my day, when I was head of babysitting at Blackheath, I was phoned up by a baffled mother who complained that one of the babysitters I'd sent her had consumed a whole leg of lamb from her fridge, which we both found hard to believe. It was later revealed that this girl had something called bulimia. It was very rarely talked about in the '70s.

By the time Hannah went away to university, I knew that what had been dismissed as a tendency, had become a serious problem. I would drive down to Bristol every two weeks just to see her, be close to her, and to know she was alive. I loved hearing all her news about being a student, and about the course that she loved and her new friends. But we knew there was something else that had to be addressed. I worried, I kept in touch, I sought advice, I read books, I spoke to experts. How bad was it? What could be done and by whom, especially as she refused to acknowledge it? I was told I had to let it get worse before it could get better. She was away from home for the first time, and I was powerless and frantic.

I was in *Cinderella* at Bromley when Hannah came back from university and came to a show. I hadn't seen her for a few weeks at this point and she looked so ill. Yet so cheerful. It was heartbreaking.

I'm ashamed to say I hurried her out of my dressing room because I didn't want the cast to see her. I would be judged, as indeed, I was judging myself. Here was a once beautiful girl who anyone could see was really ill.

At that time, we paid for treatment from the Capio Nightingale Hospital in London. This involved counselling and day patient physiotherapy during the first university holidays.

On Christmas Day, we had been told to spend a few hours at the table eating slowly. We had to do this together, without judgement and with acceptance. Hannah can look back at those photos now in disbelief about how she looked. But her thighs were narrow and her backside was tiny. I saw doctors. I read books. I talked to other people. I talked to Hannah. But being able to reason with anyone who has this disease is very hard. It is a mental disease. It was lonely for her and lonely for me. I would fear for her future and I would fear what damage was being done to her body. I thought she would die.

I would dream of seeing her fill out and have the same kind of figure as some of her friends, but I was in denial for a long time about how my own dieting may have affected her. So many of my generation had been on and off diets our entire lives. We were obsessed with food and body image. Some of us were slim, some of us weren't. Some of our daughters were slim, some of our daughters weren't. Some children were teased and didn't get ill. Some daughters never became anorexic. Some did. Hannah was one who did.

After several doctors, my sister told me about a wonderful one at the Priory in Bristol who made a real impact. The anorexia was an issue of control, but after that Christmas, Hannah never let it get that bad again. We just had to wait for 'nature' to do the rest. It was torture. Eventually the love and warmth of a boyfriend restored her confidence and she moved through it.

We managed to keep talking, no matter how painful. Our support was unwavering, along with the professionals, but ultimately this illness was defeated by the power of human interaction, time, and self-awareness. I had the joy of seeing her new body develop. A body that was not ill and a body that was beautiful in its health and strength. Those were the darkest days and to never know if it would go away was terrifying. But it did go away and now we are both wiser. Her empathy for others, open heart, and readiness to laugh at herself are proof that some challenges can be overcome, in spite of the parenting.

27. My Play
Miranda Hart
Crowd Pleasing
Not Really

I am officially nil by mouth. I go to a powdered food diet weight loss club once a week. Apart from three powdered food packs I can have 'unlimited' coffee, so I do. I can comfortably aim to consume up to four cafetières a day. After that I get palpitations, manic episodes, and visions – all calorie free.

I'm on my ninth cup (three per cafetiere) when I have the epiphany.

I must, I simply must, do a stage show with food.

It's been nine years since I've performed in Edinburgh and I'm feeling the itch to go back. I don't want to do a one woman show on my own as I'm scared of the exposure, and of failing. Instead, I embark on a plan to involve other people, so we can be exposed and fail as a team. We could be a gang.

It's 2004 and I've just seen the Spanish film Women on the Verge of a Nervous Breakdown. *My plan is to put that kind of hysteria on stage in a trio of heightened and aspirational women unravelling. But with food.*

This is it. This is the idea. I will write a comedy with food in it. And with actors.

Why hasn't anyone done this in Edinburgh before, I ask myself? I immediately call the Assembly Rooms and get put through to the press person which, I tell myself, is meant to be.

'Hi Helen, what are you up to?'

'Now, you mean? I've just had nine coffees.'

'That's a lot.'

'Yes, and I'm wondering, is the Wildman Room free this year?'

'Let me check.'

I crack open a sachet of Canderel. I hear a rustle of papers on the other end.

'Yes, the Wildman Room is still free. Did you want to do the whole run?'

'Whatever suits. Fantastico! Let's do it.'

From coffee and no food to booking Edinburgh for a show all about food – all on my own, with no producer, no agent, and no team. It took ten minutes.

* * *

My first action as a new playwright was to contact a kitchen company, offering the opportunity to support my show with a saucepan. Surprisingly, I got sent several, even though I had no use for a tower of five saucepans that could only work without a flame. But their arrival encouraged me to ask Cath Kidston for some floral PVC.

A few weeks later, a roll of her very kitcheny looking PVC fabric was duly delivered to my door, no questions asked. Empowered, I began to write a play around these props.

My challenge was to invent a setting where characters interacted with food and had a breakdown. Thankfully, my nine cups a day helped me solve this challenge with a few key ideas. *Flair4LivingTV* would be the pretend production company in charge of a chat show/foodie pilot called *Finger Food*.

Bella Le Pard (me) would be a divorced TV researcher with dreams of being a TV presenter while Brenda, the real TV presenter (proper actress), would fail to turn up in time, allowing Bella to step in and present the pilot instead. Aspiration, ambition, and disappointment all in one hour.

Unfortunately, if I'd bothered to check, all anyone wanted from me in Edinburgh in 2005 was another stand-up comedy show. Instead, I pushed on with the play.

A third character would be needed to play the *Finger Food* floor manager (a comedian), who would guide the audience into their seats and improvise with them before the play started. Suddenly, I was excited.

I just needed to find the right kind of actress to do this, but casting was already proving tricky. Felicity Montagu agreed to donate her voice to be used in a recording where she played the *Flair4LivingTV* boss. This was possibly a very kind way to avoid being in it. But I was thrilled at landing such a quality name for my audio section and took her to Simon and Amanda's house to record her lines. No one commented about the script because they felt it too soon to judge. That bit came later.

Brenda was easier to cast. She turned out to be a friend of a friend, played by Nicola Sanderson who was perfect in every way. The original Brenda had gamely grappled with the unfinished script for as long as she could, but when she was offered a proper job, she sensibly took it.

Nicola turned out to be friendly, fun and seemingly pleased to be doing my play. But I still needed Fiona the floor manager. Someone who could do comedy and improvise. I asked Jenny Éclair, who asked Richard Herring, who suggested Miranda Hart.

I had no idea who Miranda Hart was, but I phoned her and

explained I was the writer as well as producer which sounded better, and would offer a small wage for her talent plus free accommodation. Miranda suggested I come to the Battersea Arts Centre to meet her after a show she was in. Rudely, I didn't bother buying a ticket or check to see what the show was, as by now I was busy researching fire regulations for live cooked sausages, but I was keen to meet her.

We sat at a table on a landing in the middle of the Arts Centre. Audiences bustled past us on their way to a play or coming out of one. The more we sat together on the landing, the more I knew that Miranda was perfect. I asked her to do it immediately.

I had a slight worry when Miranda first emailed me saying she was 90% sure she was doing it because I didn't know what the 10% chances of her not doing it were. Perhaps she had read the script?

But I could see her with a clipboard. In fact, Miranda was so perfect for this role she played another person with a clipboard in the 'White Cube' episode of *Ab Fab* later that same year.

As I got pushed to find more material, I had to steal lines from my stand-up show and divvy them out. Fiona was given, 'So far, Bella's only done a non-transmissible pre-pilot called *When Vicars Attack* and a sewing show for the regions called *Stitch That, Jimmy.*' Lines that Ian Pattison had written for me for *Naked Video*.

And I recycled more: 'I opened my address book, then I closed it again because I'd had everyone in it and the rest were relatives.'

We are only a few weeks away from opening, and apart from a few last minute 'on the opposite side of slim' type jokes written by a paid helper, the play still didn't have a proper end. It did, however, have cooked food in the middle. And a song that had to be sung by Nicola, who had to double as an international top-selling cookery writer and campaigner for safe sex to make use of her versatility as an actress. And keep costs down.

Simon Brint offered to write the music for Nicola's food song and composed a *Finger Food* parody signature tune with the words: 'Finger Food, Finger Food, pop it in your tongue.'

The music and songs ended up being the most popular parts of the play. And taken as a whole, apart from the talents of Miranda and Nicola, everything else in the play was to form the base ingredients of a disappointing show – according to the reviews.

Extract from *Finger Food*:

Bella: Hello and welcome to Finger Food. I'm Bella Le Pard and I'm going to introduce you to some easy but stylish dishes for women who juggle their lives. And men and also youngsters, and old people including those in sheltered housing who can operate saucepans unsupervised as well as some children if they've washed their hands...this is one my favourites – it's called 'canapé heaven sue la mere.

[Bella starts cutting up a melon.]

Bella: Let's face it, everyone's got a melon, haven't they? Everyone's got a ham, and everyone's got a chicory – and if they haven't, they can go out and buy one. Now the theme is nautical and very summery, although not quite as summery as the 'Nigella Summer Cookbook' where she appears to be driving a toy car over a cliff for some reason, but who am I to question her profit margins – they certainly stick right out don't they?

[Bella places a coconut on a table and use strips of leg wax to remove the pubes.]

> **Bella:** I know some people are squeamish, so once you've defuzzed, you can go mad with your acrylic car paint...

And while my crafting may not have connected with every audience, the visualisation section I wrote for Miranda turned out to be universally alienating in a non-Brechtian sort of way .

Miranda's monologue had to be performed on a chair whilst acting out an orgasm. What was I thinking? Credit to Miranda – she went for it. Commitment is all. Miranda's mother was reported to ask 'Why?' or words to that effect, only more repelled, utterly shocked, and disgusted.

Each night, we would meet in the shared Assembly Rooms dressing room facilities. Miranda had been given a space next to comedian Natalie Haynes, so while Nicola and I would get into character (me with dread, Nicola with professionalism), Miranda and Natalie would share their passion for theories of comedy. Nicola wasn't a stand-up and, unlike me, didn't appear to have slept with any.

The pre-show nerves took up most of the day but at least waking up late meant I wasn't conscious for most of it. I'd have my powdered food diet sachet and then do the play. After that, I'd be in the bar. If it wasn't for the show, I'd have been in the bar earlier, along with all the other performers not doing a show and pining for the pain. One year, I was in the bar with Brenda Gilhooly (we were both visiting) when James Corden (also visiting) struck up a conversation. I may have said I was old enough to be his nan as a joke. Annoyingly, Brenda wasn't close enough to verify the content, but it was fruity.

In spite of it all, we still sold out. Nicola was amazing. So was Miranda. They would joke that my 'coachload from Fife' was in. And we did get laughs. From them. But this was before the killer masturbation scene and liquidised trifle finale.

I learned a lot. Namely that sorting props, posters, actors, accommodation, fire regulations and PR was best avoided on my own. And the fact that I'd persuaded a rep from Cointreau to turn up each night and hand out 150 plastic thimbles of bittersweet liquid to the Finger Food audience, would have been better if it was just money.

Essentially, I had no idea how to produce, be in charge of other people's professional needs, or write three acts of a play. Although I soon noticed that giving people money cheered them up a lot. The director always sat up straighter after he'd been paid.

But even with a propped-up director, I ran out of time to come up with an ending. Somewhere in my frenzy of caffeine and food powders, I'd hoped that an ending could be signalled by the turning on of a Magimix, with people shouting at each other. Surely this would be diverting enough to get us all off stage without too much disappointment. The beat of silence before people realised the play had ended helped us know the ending hadn't quite landed.

The one positive was that my extreme exile from normal food came to an end. I was planning which flavour crisps I'd be having as soon as we walked through the Assembly Rooms bar.

Just before Edinburgh, Miranda had been cast in a pilot set in outer space. Comedies at this time were thought to have more of a chance if they could be set in alternative 'precincts', which was a real word championed by the head of Sky Comedy at the time and had nothing to do with traffic.

When we came back from Edinburgh, Miranda's pilot went to series and she sadly disappeared from my life, next seen at Jennifer's 50th birthday and almost every other TV series with the word comedy in it from then on.

My gratitude knows no bounds. Miranda was funny. She was charismatic. She was particularly generous with props. Both carrying them onto the stage and taking them off. This was a

Viscomptress of Moldavia in *Bottom* with Rik Mayall and Adrian Edmondson on BBC 2

Fringe again Edinburgh. *Still Crazy After All These Years* show. Babar, Hannah, Vanessa, Tony and John in 1994

Single Minding Book on single parenting. Placed in both mental health and humour shelving, published 1995

Me and Jenny Releasing at the Brownswood Tavern, Finsbury Park with Jenny Eclair in 1988

Party like it's 1999 Gig poster with Barry Cryer and Sheila Steafel *(above)*. Slight turn due to Sheila's herbal supplements

Holding on My daughter Hannah and her friend Billie on the beach in 1995

Ab Fab Catriona keeping up with Edina in 1996 *(bottom right)*. The Last Shout

Another year in Edinburgh Myself and Tony Slattery at Edinburgh Festival

Wedding number two Kind contributors for the *OK!* wedding deal. I tried to muster a list of all the famous people I knew, who would consider coming to the Irish Club in Eaton square for a cèilidh. Here's me and Ruby Wax. I may be missing a tooth

A-list ceremony Absolutely no teeth. *OK! Magazine* wedding deal with Simon Brint in 1999

Joy and grief Two pages from the *OK! Magazine* coverage of our wedding. More people helping with the wedding deal. *(Left)* John Hegley and Tony Slattery

Acting daft *Calendar Girls* at the Noel Coward Theatre in 2009. Myself, Kelly Brook, Janie Dee, Arabella Weir, and Debbie Chazen. No one ate this cake. Probably

Photo credit: Alex Lloyd

Royal exchange Inviting closure from the Princess Royal re the speech that went wrong a decade earlier. If I'd ever been in any doubt that I was going down badly, it was confirmed when I resumed my place next to the Lady-In-Waiting to start my pudding. No one spoke

Catriona and Fleur *Ab Fab*. Catriona in rollers. Fleur with add on. Catriona and Fleur generally tried to join in, being pointless, but keen to be helpful to Edina and Patsy and generally getting in the way as time wasters on the magazine

Celebrations *(Above left)* with Miranda Hart and Nicola Sanderson. Party to celebrate end of rehearsals for *Finger Food*, Edinburgh. Smiling at this stage; *(Above right)* Me and Hannah. Eyeliner as at wedding of nice nephew

Muff dive In my swimming frock on *Splash*, ITV in 2013. The red light goes out. I tip myself forward and make myself fall into nothingness

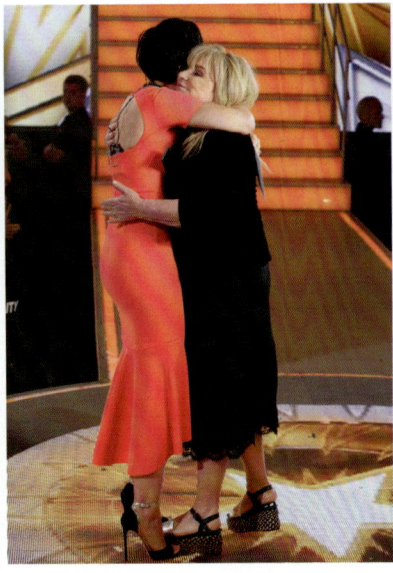

Big night out On our way to free drinks. *Ab Fab* wrap party. Julia Sawalha, me and Jane Horrocks in 2012

Big Brother Seriously hanging onto Emma Willis before entering the *Celebrity Big Brother* house in 2017

A different dive Interviewing Tom Daley for my Mr and Mrs section in 2022

Photo credit: Brett D. Cove

Saying yes to all manner of areas *(Clockwise starting top left)* in Auschwitz for documentary *War Hero In My Family*; Big Baba's papers from Czechoslovakia that got him the job as a 'Secret Listener'; *Ab Fab: The Movie*. Our scenes were in North London; Arts Theatre. *The Killing of Sister George* with lovely Meera Syal; quietly excited at Writers' Guild awards event with brainy, inimitable Caitlin Moran; With the late Bernard Cribbins waiting for the rain to stop while filming *Old Jacks Boat*

Photo credit: Donald Cooper

Women supporting women CWIP Winners' Event. *(Left to right)* me, Jo Brand, Sharon Horgan, Kathy Lette, and Meera Syal. If anyone asks about CWIP I say it's a 'passion project', which is shorthand for trying to make a platform happen that makes no money. But empowers. Always good to add the last bit

Pilgrimage: The Road Through the Alps *(Left to right)* comedian Daliso Chaponda, Harry Clark from *The Traitors*, sprinter Stef Reid, me with my Nordic walking poles, journalist Nelafur Hedayat, my new best friend Jay Slater, and Jeff Brazier

godsend as there was always a pool of blueberry juice on the floor, which didn't go down well with the next show.

Deservedly or not, we had queues for returns and extra shows added. But some reviews couldn't hide their misogyny, as they wondered what a middle-aged woman was doing 'bed blocking' a prime Assembly Rooms slot when she could at least have offered up a straightforward, stand-up show and save everyone a lot of bother. I agreed.

The kindest review says it was 'crowd-pleasing'. Which, as most people know, is always the kiss of death. The feedback from my own stand-up friends ranged from a cautious 'It's a romp' to 'I'm worried about you.' This was from Jeremy Hardy. The producer who had been anticipating a tour quietly stepped away, and I went on Prozac. An English woman on the verge of a nervous breakdown…

28. Reality TV
Being Filmed
Earning Money

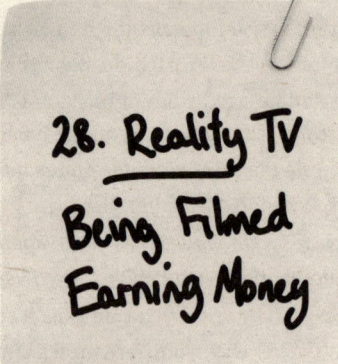

I'm being filmed in the back of a people carrier, talking to a researcher who wants to know how I feel. I don't have any feelings because I'm on Prozac.

'Excited?' I suggest.

'Have you any idea who you will be meeting tonight?'

'Celebrities?'

The researcher waits a beat so that bit can be edited.

'What would be your worst kind of dinner party food?'

'I might not be great with gristle.'

I'm being paid by Channel 4 to eat five meals every night for the next five nights, cooked by people I've never met before or heard of.

The first meal will be cooked by designer Ben de Lisi. He normally makes evening gowns but tonight he is doing us a broccoli pasta.

The cameraman leaps out of the cab to film me walking towards the door of Ben's smart, London mews house. I offer a slightly flam-

boyant ringing of the bell, but there's only so much a person who's mildly sedated can come up with on a porch.

Once inside, I'm filmed being poured a glass of fizz, and saying 'cheers then' to four celebrities in smart casual. We've all been given £1,000 in cash to eat each other's food on five consecutive nights, even though we are not real friends. There are cameras everywhere.

The person who gets the most votes for their supper wins money for charity. This is the pilot episode for Celebrity Come Dine with Me. *I'd been sent a VHS of the non-celebrity version to help me get the hang of the concept and at first viewing, it felt very slight. A host was filmed both cooking and serving a supper for five others to be eaten in a dining room that had to be brightly lit for the cameras. There wasn't a lot of conversation on the tape I saw, but I could hear the sound of people eating and noticed a few cutaways of contestants staring at their food in a worried way.*

Apart from a few interactive questions like 'Did you make this pastry?' Or, 'If you were an animal what would you be?', the dinner party chat was restrained. Without the £1,000 cash prize, there didn't appear to be an obvious reason why a table full of strangers would want to spend a week of their life scoring each other's casseroles out of a possible ten or poke about in the host's fitted wardrobe, trying to find a sex toy inbetween courses.

* * *

Reality TV hadn't quite hit its stride in 2005 and since Twitter and Instagram, etc hadn't been invented, the worst that could happen to any of us from this kind of exposure was running out of butter, or being a bit bored. And in my case, forgetting the serviettes.

The first thing I did with my £1,000 fee was invest in four white towels with a beige linen trim. The prospect of celebrities nosing about my bathroom had triggered a need for quality towels. Mixing linen as a frieze with terry towelling was ahead of its time in 2005 and those towels drew a few admiring comments both during the filming and for many years to come. Any cash leftover went towards the food, but the towels took up a lot of the budget.

David Quantick was a last-minute addition to the cast because Toby Young's child had measles and he had to cancel. I decided David would be my favourite. Ulrika Jonsson and Mica Paris seemed to have more in common early on, not least because they've both gone out with a football person, and I hadn't. They seemed nice and equally unafraid.

While Ulrika cooked her unusually massive fish, David and I decided to smoke in her garden and be cynical. I didn't smoke, but it was a quick way for us to demonstrate we were both innately humorous.

This was where I discovered David had used most of his cash to buy a nice new glass central ceiling light for his flat, which I agreed was also a sensible use of funds.

My mix of Prozac and alcohol meant the week flew by in a blur of other people's fizz. When Ulrika turned up on my hosting night, her greeting to me was, 'Great kitchen, bitch,' which I took as a nice compliment. By now, most of us had seen inside each other's downstairs toilets, which was helping with familiarity.

In the preparation for the cheesecake, I forgot to put the poppy seeds on the top of the cake before it went into the oven, so I had to take it out, half cooked, add the seeds, and blow them across the mixture. The voiceover remarked on my lack of hygiene as well as a few other snippy comments about my cooking. The recipe for the cheesecake seemed to be longer than when I last looked at it, the blender was missing its lid, and I just wanted it to be over.

The cooking was stressful. A new actor friend I'd met at a readthrough had taken the night off from *Jersey Boys* to help me cook. I knew this was a way for him to be on TV, and I was glad to offer him the slot. But on the night he got over-excited by the cameras and forgot to put wine in with the peas. When he forgot to turn the gas on altogether, I felt betrayed. I tried not to show it, but feelings were running high with three cameras documenting my every move.

The mushroom sorbet wasn't a success either. They didn't show that bit, but you had to be filmed going into a shop to buy interesting food. My local Londis didn't have a deli, so the researcher said, 'Try Harrods.' In the food hall, the Harrods press liaison person got very excited and insisted their sorbet person come up with 'something special' while the cameras were whirring. I thought sorbets were supposed to cleanse the palette, but since this one was mushroom, even I had my doubts. I was given a slab and served it between courses. I hadn't had mushroom sorbet before. Who has? Ulrika may have said it tasted like thrush, which I thought was funny, but led me to consider how anyone would actually know what thrush would taste like.

Between courses, Ben de Lisi kept himself entertained by sketching a series of dress designs for me. I would never have fitted into them, but I felt obliged to give one away to Ulrika because she looked like she would suit his style more than me. And I felt guilty about keeping them all. Then he got into bed with Hannah upstairs, who was 16 and possibly more interesting than the rest of us, while the producer had to deal with a TV researcher who had been traumatised by one of Little Baba's paintings in the front sitting room. The researcher had screamed when she saw a ghost looking out at her from inside the painting and was beside herself. The painting had to be removed by the producer and placed under a bed for safety. My meal came second from last, after David's. Also, my house was now officially known to be haunted.

Come Dine With Me was the first of many opportunities to 'be myself' without having to learn lines. The following year I was contacted by Reef Television and asked to choose my favourite garden for a series they were doing which was titled *My Favourite Garden*.

I didn't have a favourite garden. The only one I knew was the one I'd grown up with in Ryefield Road which had a modest, sunken rose garden and potato section. But since both had been completely flattened by the next owners, I didn't suggest a visit. This was lucky because the idea was to choose a public one that people could actually go and walk around. I went online and came up with RHS Wisley, as this was quite close and would be bound to have lots of plants in it.

Germaine Greer had already chosen her favourite one, so I felt I would be in the right kind of company for the series. I turned up for the hottest day of the year to walk around my favourite garden that I'd never been to before. I didn't mention this to the nice producers, in case they went off the idea.

I started off wandering up and down the paths, then a lake, stopping to point at a lily, sweating profusely, and getting shinier by the minute.

Then I was told to 'hit my mark' and stop in front of a large oak tree to conjure a horticulturally influenced memory. Having admired the trunk for a few thoughtful seconds, I began an anecdote about a snog with my first boyfriend which could have actually happened.

The reality TV offers kept coming. One minute I'm sketching a baby rhino in a Safari Park with Anneka Rice in a buggy, the next I'm watching Craig from *Big Brother* fit free decking on my patio. I'm also required to cook again.

I'm not proud of my *Celebrity MasterChef* debut in 2006. I was up against Rowland Rivron and weatherman Ian McCaskill. We were all pleased to be working together, although Ian had apparently just walked into a door and was looking rather bruised at the time of filming. I was happy to meet up with Rowland and enjoy his outrageous storytelling in-between cooking our signature dishes.

Our first test was to deal with a mystery fish. There were no obvious winners for this because we were all equally bad. But I wasn't put off, because I still felt extremely confident about my Moroccan couscous, seasoned with freshly squeezed orange juice, my honeyed chicken snippets as well as Little Baba's berry tart and kosher pastry (no lard).

I realised it best to leave the banter to Rowland and the boy chefs, since my jocular approach hadn't quite taken off. Ian wasn't asked too many things, as no one wanted to worry him.

Apart from the actual moment of walking up to present the two chefs my various courses when they don't smile, I felt safely confident that I would win. Ian's cooking didn't stand a chance and Rowland's pudding had a shop bought flake in it. Surely, I would walk it. We waited, exhausted in our aprons, for the winner to be announced. But it wasn't me. It was Rowland.

I was shocked. I felt there had been a massive miscarriage of justice. I became so convinced of wrongdoing I had to act. I urged my sister and cousin in Wales to write a letter of complaint to the programme. The complaint being that Ian's car crash, Rowland's flake inclusion and my tasty, delicate, well-presented meal had not been fairly compared or judged.

The letters were sent, and I should have left it there, but three years later when I was asked to do a series of *Celebrity MasterChef* involving all those who had lost in a previous series, I said yes.

I met my new fellow chefs in the Green Room while a producer talked us through how to walk and talk at the same time for filming purposes. We were required to take off our aprons, hang them up and then walk through a door. This proved quite a challenge for those of us who hadn't been to drama school but they needed to be used as fillers for the show.

Thankfully, Tony Hadley, Marie Helvin and I managed to walk

down the cobbled street at the same time as talking to each other and entering the studio building without any glitches. Then we met the boy chefs. If they'd known it was me who had instigated the complaint letters three years earlier, I would have died. I was so over it now, but this one extra fee for *MasterChef* was very welcome.

The contract stated that if any of us got through to the next round, we would have to be available for the next episode. But given my failure to get through the first time, I just closed my eyes and signed it. I was already rehearsing for a pantomime in Bromley, but at this stage I could take the time off. Any further time off into December would not be possible.

On the first day of filming, Marie may have told me she'd booked to go to Hawaii the following week. This was straight after I may have told her I needed to be at the tech rehearsal in Bromley. If this was true, it wouldn't suit either of us to win.

The next morning, I got up early to be driven to the kitchen of a famous restaurant in King's Cross for a famous chef to train us to cook lunch for his diners. Our score would go towards the final result. A concerned producer told us that Marie Helvin was feeling a little off and wouldn't make it. The competition would have to be between me and Tony. It was too late to get anyone else because they had already filmed the day before. Without Marie in the competition, there was a risk of winning the round. Marie was a good cook. Tony would be the first to agree he wasn't in the same league as the marvelous Marie. I would have to lose.

I would be needed at the Churchill Theatre in Bromley in a few days, especially as things weren't going well. Miming 'there will be miracles if you believe' was still rather new for me, so I couldn't afford to bunk off. I took the famous chef aside and asked him to score me low points. He didn't say anything, being mindful of breaking the law. Unlike myself.

On the third day of filming, the very charming but focussed Tony and I took our places at our kitchen islands. It was the only time in my life I wanted to lose anything. I had no choice but to smother the couscous with the salt and Tabasco provided. And burn the chicken. But under the pressure of the cameras, to purposely ruin a dish was surprisingly difficult. Would I get noticed?

Had I done enough? When judge Gregg Wallace came round to my island to taste the couscous, he gave nothing away, but surely his tongue was on fire. Maybe I'd been too cautious with the extra Tabasco? Making oneself over-season, turned out to be surprisingly difficult. As I watched him chew the food, he just looked thoughtful and didn't appear to even wince at the salt.

Had he been warned that there were members of my family who would break his legs if he didn't praise my food? I went to the loo in a filming break and, for the first time in my life, prayed that I would lose. On this occasion God answered. Tony Hadley was the declared winner.

In 2011, I found myself invited to take part in *Celebrity Coach Trip*. I was a late casting addition which persuaded me to say yes although I still wasn't keen. In an ideal world, I'd get chucked off the coach quite quickly, and no one would ever remember I'd taken part. Every participant had to travel with a friend. I'd never met my best friend, the very charming Sandra Dickinson, before but she turned out to be a great strategist. I hadn't bargained for the emotional catch of the show where each pair had to stand in a circle, look their fellow celebrities in the eye and crisply vote them off. This was quite sick making.

But trust in the workplace is usually well intentioned. I was booked to do the Exeter Festival called, rather optimistically, 'The Laughter Makers' with Barry Cryer and Sheila Steafel. I decided to reveal my nervousness because I was talking gibberish in the Green Room, and an explanation could help my reputation. I'd just met my new husband and he hadn't seen me do a gig before, which, I explained to them, was my kind of hell. They were very kind. Just before we went on, Sheila insisted I help myself to her herbal calm-you-downs, from inside a small snuff box. One minute I'm feeling grateful and supported, the next I'm keeling over the theatre stairwell with palpitations and about to faint. Somehow, I found the stage and did something on it, for 20 minutes. Barry called me a few times after Exeter to check I was still upright.

So, while trusting others is desirable, it's also tricky in a reality show when you have to be loyal to a partner you've only just met, especially if they have pink luggage.

The strategy for survival on *Celebrity Coach Trip* was simple but harsh. You had to make other couples think you were going to vote for them to get their loyalty, and then vote them off to increase your chances of staying in. I kept forgetting what I was supposed to say to people to achieve the outcome Sandra had devised.

Lembit Opik had been chucked off by the time we arrived, but Michael Barrymore, Lizzie Cundy and Brian Belo were very much present along with *Britain's Got Talent* duo Stavros Flatley, who turned out to be a rather thoughtful father and son.

When I was sheltering from the rain in a café in Pisa, the charming Brian came up to my table and asked me which way I would vote. I'd already been briefed by Sandra, so I told him that I was very sorry, I admired him as a good friend (this was the first day), but as we had discussed this as a pair, Sandra and I had decided to vote him off if that was OK. Sandra later said, 'You did what?' but I couldn't lie. I couldn't look at Brian ever again without sorrow and shame. And whenever I bump into Lizzie Cundy, I feel equally terrible that I voted her off as well. That's at least two potential friendships ruined.

And then somewhere in the midst of it all, and in a break from reality TV, I was asked to be on a CBeebies series called *Old Jack's Boat* with Bernard Cribbins. And since this didn't involve Tabasco poisoning or voting people off a coach, I was reminded that doing a job where it was all scripted was much less stressful. I was to play a rather bossy, robust lady called Miss Bowline Hitch, whose catchphrase was 'busy busy' and tended to only appear when she was on her way to do busy things.

I was shown my tricycle on the first day of filming in Staithes, North Yorkshire. It was set on a gradient, and it was raining. The camera crew were already halfway down the hill in waterproofs, when the director, Iwan Watson, called out 'action', which I assumed was my cue to climb on the trike and descend. 'One sec,' I replied before checking with the prop person if the brakes worked and, also, to ask where they were. The prop person showed me some wires and said, 'They should be alright, but yell if you can't stop', before giving a helpful shove.

I couldn't remember the last time I'd been on a tricycle, but at least this wasn't a two-wheeler. When I was given a second-hand two-wheeler for my tenth birthday my parents had placed blocks on the pedals for me to 'grow into'. Someone must have forgotten about the steroids stunting my growth because I never grew tall enough to reach the pedals with any confidence. Although this kind of weakness is not the kind of thing you mention on your Spotlight CV. The same with piano playing and riding a horse. According to Spotlight, I can do all of these with merit.

I set off down the steep hill and got quite far before I yelled. Iwan not only got a Bafta for the series, but also pieced together various shots that had me looking both pedal savvy and very busy.

The other worry was the corduroy trousers. I had specifically asked Robert, the costume person, 'Can Miss Bowline Hitch not wear trousers, please? I just don't see her in trousers. I think a kilt would work?' But apparently a pair of brown cords were unavoidable. Along with a rather fitting riding jacket that strained after meals and a flimsy floral cravat that kept moving. Robert had to tweak it for continuity before every take. Robert, me and the cravat became very close.

Bernard Cribbins played the Sea Captain who told wonderful sea stories and the series was a hit with the under-fives. Occasionally, I'd meet a father and child team where the parent liked me in *Bottom* and the child liked me on the tricycle.

The 'celebrity' game shows kept coming. There was an unfortunate moment on *The Chase* when my eyes seemed to trigger hysteria in Bradley Walsh for some reason and filming had to be paused while he composed himself. There was the episode of *The Weakest Link* where I may have been ganged up on by two women comediennes and voted off first, and an appearance on *Celebrity Eggheads*, where I let the team down for forgetting the word 'velouté'.

The only thing I did on TV with other celebrities that didn't lead to shame or regret was *Celebrity Pointless*. The first occasion was in 2012 with Harriet Thorpe where we both felt quite pleased that we didn't have to leave first. Far better than being teamed with poor Nicholas Parsons in 2016, when my wrong answer saw us leave immediately. This was heartbreaking. For him. But in 2018 and 2019, I won the Pyrex Pointless Pyramid of success. Without the pairing of my extremely brainy teammates Shaun Williamson and Cariad Lloyd, this would have been unthinkable. Another episode followed where I was teamed with a singer. This did not go as well, but I redeemed myself by saying 'Reykjavik', which is always a good answer, whatever the question.

Not that it's about winning. It's about taking people apart…

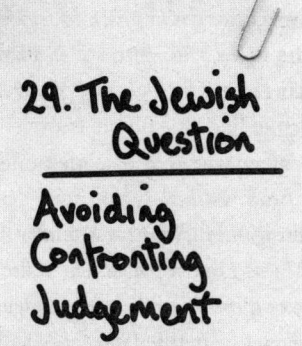

29. The Jewish Question
Avoiding Confronting Judgement

I'm waiting in a community centre attached to a synagogue in Prague, feeling conspicuous. I'm taking up space with a small film crew in a tiny vestibule while Czech Jews have to squeeze past me to get to a tea urn. Who do I think I am?

I was filming the poor man's version of Who Do You Think You Are *for Channel Five. This version was called* War Hero in My Family.

I'm about to be filmed entering a separate room and greeting a Czech cousin called Frantisek for the first time. I never knew I had a cousin called Frantisek. The two I knew about were called Vaclav and Verner and they were dead. Vaclav used to send Christmas cards, but Verner didn't because he lived in East Berlin and Little Baba didn't like him as much. Also, Verner had ended up on the other side of the wall after the war and was a Communist, which may or may not have clouded opinions.

This new person is alive. His surname is Lederer....

NOT THAT I'M BITTER

For the previous four days, I've been travelling with the crew through the Czech Republic and into Poland. We are making a documentary. When a producer got in touch to see if I'd like to take part in a historical series called War Hero in My Family, *I said, 'I'd love to.' Although, I wasn't sure if there were any war heroes in my family at the time of asking.*

'Was having one's own war hero absolutely essential, or could I do it anyway and get paid?' I asked.

Instead of answering, they told me it would be a journey. Last time I'd been to Prague I was 17 on a school trip to Russia. The tour guide fell backwards out of a coach while it was moving. She got straight back in as if nothing had happened and nobody dared laugh in case they got reported.

This time, the trip is much more emotional. Wherever I go, I meet another expert telling me more bad news about the Lederers. It's awkward. I'm a comedian being told about my people being gassed on TV. What is the correct expression? Neutral is cold. Knowing is disrespectful. Shocked and distraught could be seen as disingenuous and I needed to respect the content without milking it. Now it's the fourth day of my second-generation revelations, and I've been invited into an office to be shown yet more archives. The atmosphere shifts. The crew go a bit secretive and I'm sensing something is up.

Once the shot is set up, I'm told to open a giant-sized leather-bound book. As I turn the pages, I soon find what I am supposed to find. I see the names of people who actually survived the camps and the ghettos. Suddenly I find a Lederer. Frantisek Lederer. He is my cousin. Apparently, Frantisek gives talks to schools.

I hear myself saying, 'I want to meet him,' partly because I knew there had to be an end point for the edit but also because I wanted to.

On the way to the Community Centre, I'm made to watch a German propaganda film on a laptop so they can film my reactions.

The footage shows a selection of healthy-looking Jews, all smiling at the camera while taking part in sports or craft work inside what looked like a holiday camp. I'm told the film was made to deceive the Red Cross who later deemed the camps safe to live in. By the time I meet Frantisek, I'm feeling immersed in Nazi war crimes.

Now we are here to mastermind the denouement of the film, to make sure no drama is lost. I brace myself to film the reunion, although I don't speak Czech and I'm told Frantisek doesn't speak English and we're not in a cosy, country hotel with Davina McCall.

As soon as I see him, I decide that he does look a bit like my father might look. Probably. A bit. Pavel, the kind and empathetic translator, guides us both through this highly charged meeting. I tell Frantisek I feel guilty that my family came out and can't understand why the rest of the family didn't. He tells me, without bitterness, that it was a good decision that they did. I agree and hold his hand until the director says 'cut'. I don't take my hand away.

* * *

I'd managed to get this far into adulthood without watching too much footage about the camps. I'd made a point of avoiding it. If my grandmother and father didn't want to talk openly about it, then I wouldn't either. And it was easier to be in denial.

The itinerary was relentless. Everywhere we went, I'd meet another historian, all as keen as each other to share evidence of exactly who and how many of my family perished in the war.

The tour guide at Auschwitz was a particular enthusiast. She stood with me outside a hut and talked me through the likely conditions inside with unsparing detail. Then we went inside. I found myself saying 'Gosh' or 'God' as the information kept coming. The crew were quiet, and the ghosts could be felt. I'd only just recovered from this when another historian was arranged to walk me round Terezin, a ghetto for Czech Jews. It was foggy and rainy, and it almost felt as if he was waiting until the light was especially stark and sad to tell me that Carolina, my grandfather's mother, must have died three weeks after arriving here. She must have done, he insisted, waving a ledger book with her name in it as proof. I nodded and blew my nose.

By now I've been shown newspapers that describe Kristallnacht and the early ousting of Jews from their homes. I've seen a spread of photographs showing Lederers both as children and adults all neatly labelled and documented as to where they ended up and in what camp. I've walked through the barracks where people had to live without water or blankets and shown museum artefacts of hair, teeth, shoes and gas chambers. The guide asks me if I can feel the ghosts. I tell her I can and she nods.

The crew are quiet. We don't speak for a while. But hearing the name of my great-grandmother spoken out loud made me connect with conversations between my grandmother, my aunt and my father. Their lives became vivid. I could feel how they must have felt. And what Big Baba had to face in order to leave.

The family and friends they left behind all perished apart from the nanny who went to Canada and a cousin who came to England, where she was imprisoned in Holloway for having a camera. This meant she was an enemy. I'm glad to know my father went to visit her there. I had now seen first-hand all the stages before their deaths. I felt it. Denying their history was impossible.

No wonder the Lederers revelled in building a new life in England. Little Baba would visit art galleries and make careful notes about the artists in a special notebook. She wanted to know everything that was going on around her. She wanted to be part of a bright world. Life was for living and her standards were high. Family gatherings were frequent and full of food. They had to make up for what had gone. And they did. We had to have good manners and be told to say the right things at the right times. But she was always cautious. Little Baba wanted to know if we had told any of our boyfriends that we had Jewish blood in case it changed their view of us. The mix of pain, shame, pride and survival was hers to give, but for us to sort out.

When it came to the final edit, I was told the controllers of Channel Five were worried their audience might not have the attention span to follow just one celebrity's war journey on its own in one sitting. To work with their demographic, their solution was to blend two celebrities together per episode to keep people from switching off. This explains why one minute I'm seen wandering through Auschwitz on a dark afternoon, and the next Paddy Ashdown is to be found in a sunny French field reminiscing about his dad's horse jumping activities while he waited for the Germans to invade. At one point Paddy is found sitting astride a big iron cannonball in Flanders Field while I'm being shown someone's death certificate. The background music had to adapt discreetly to help the viewer segue through these very different scenarios.

I'd barely had time to go to the hairdressers before being picked up and driven to a location to do more filming.

The crew had arranged for a hired car to be placed in position, and the plan was to seamlessly drive it through the grounds of Trent Park and up towards the house itself, all while speaking to a camera set up on the dashboard about my cousin's discovery in Prague.

I'd managed to hold it together, more or less, during the camps, the ghetto, the reunion with my sad, survivor cousin who only survived because a guard came from the same town as him, but suddenly being faced with an automatic gear system I lost it. I couldn't make the car move.

'How can you expect me to drive an automatic?' I screamed. 'I mean, didn't you check? I drive a Ford Escort, for God's sake!'

Having let myself down badly, I managed to complete the driving sequence, by lurching up the drive to meet yet another historian. But instead of more news about my dead relatives, the next historian, Paul Reed – a military historian with a track record in TV programmes – had something else he was keen to share. I was still raw from the teary pieces to camera as well as the gear change mishap, but I sensed this new historian meant business.

The camera followed me, following him, down some stairs of Trent Park House and into a dark cellar.

'Hit me with it then,' I said off camera. And he did.

Instead of being safely recruited into the Home Guard to watch over Hampstead Heath from war torn Europe in 1939, as we all thought, Paul told me on camera, with a few dramatic pauses, that... Big Baba... had been... secretly recruited into... MI9.

This was quite a leap. Didn't you have to be Oxbridge to do spy work? As far as I knew Big Baba had been in charge of a large factory, making furniture, marquees and circus tents in Prague, and while they were rich enough to have maids, so did a lot of European businesspeople at the time. Did this give him the daredevil instinct of a spy? What was his memory like for coded clues? His sense of guile?

Paul was excited. He had found a letter written to Big Baba by a Major General Sinclair who was head of MI9 and showed it to me.

"I wish to convey my real gratitude for and appreciation of the assistance you have given to my interrogation organisation in respect of POWs captured during recent operations on the Continent. Your keenness and self-sacrifice in volunteering to assist in this work, and the efficiency shown in its execution, have materially contributed to these satisfactory results. Thank you again for what you have done."

In 1940 the War Office commandeered Trent Park – a stately home previously owned by Philip Sassoon – and turned it into a luxury prisoner of war camp for captured Nazi prisoners. They bugged the flowerpots, the grounds and the bedrooms. Everywhere the Germans went, their conversations were recorded. German-speaking refugees were to form a new army of 'Secret Listeners'. Their job was to obtain and translate information as it unfolded. Apart from the strategically placed microphones, there would be 'stool pigeons' posing as Germans while busily enticing loose talk from the captured, and mostly dedicated, Nazi generals.

The captured Germans had no idea their conversations were secretly manipulated and monitored. Big Baba's job was one of these. Apparently, he would listen and befriend them as a fellow sympathiser and direct the conversation to obtain any intelligence about future campaigns. Information that was found in this way apparently shortened the war.

There was a relief in knowing he did something. There was even speculation that he had been in the Czech Resistance and had had connections with the Czech government in exile. This was deduced from a letter in 1943 from the Ministry of Information. Big Baba's 'exposure of German wickedness' and 'expert knowledge to indicate the horrors of the occupation' of Czechoslovakia had revealed what was really going on. Particularly impressive coming from a man who was also pretending to his wife that he was in the Home Guard at the same time.

Big Baba went back to Prague after the war, possibly to do more secret work, I'd like to think, and to give Frantisek some chocolates from England. I wish he could have given him more. Like a house maybe. But Frantisek didn't seem too bitter. But I wasn't sure and I still felt guilty.

Of course, this new discovery was also fodder for the next therapist – to see if trauma can be passed on in the genes from one generation to the next, which might be handy to explain my attraction to fear and danger. But, when I see how my sister enjoys golf and how I still like to party, this second-generation avenue of blame seems unlikely. Although not impossible. The fact remains, they were migrants and England welcomed them. Does this connect with me never feeling quite worthy? Even from five years old, I can remember worrying about getting attention, even when people were being nice.

Five years later came another reality TV programme uncovering another family secret.

'Here we go,' I say to the agent.

A BBC crew asked if I'd take part in a series called *Home Front Heroes*. I assumed there'd be less travelling by virtue of the title and said yes again. Another reveal, another fee. The knowledgeable historian Dr Helen Fry was recruited this time to take possession of all the family documents and came up with more material and theories. I'm then whisked away up the M1 to be filmed in Hut 6, Bletchley Park, home to code breakers during the Second World War.

'So,' the in-house historian begins excitedly. 'The intercepted messages were gathered up from our radio operators, in five-letter patterns, and biked over here to be decoded.'

Before I can ask him to repeat himself, but slower, he's showing me an Enigma machine, where people like my mother had to find clues, before pressing lots of buttons, to tell us what the Germans were up to.

'What were the chances of her discovering anything?' I ask

'About one in one hundred and three thousand million, million,' he says.

'Yes, but seriously,' I say, thinking this might have been where my mother's passion for crossword puzzles began...

'I am being serious,' he says, and then he tells me that if any of the code breakers spoke of their work to anyone, it was treason.

'Treason,' I repeat, alarmed.

Fortunately, we end on a note of optimism. Even though the odds were against uncovering a pattern of clues to decipher a code which was changed every day by the Germans to trick us, apparently enough discoveries were made, by enough dedicated people, to shorten the war.

As they filmed my reaction, I felt very close to a young version of my mother and her life in this community. She was 20 when she was evacuated from King's College in London to Bristol during the war. But shortly after moving there, she was recruited to work at Bletchley Park. She became friends with Anne McDougall, who later married Labour cabinet minister Richard Crossman, who befriended my father.

He makes an appearance in *The Crossman Diaries*, written in 1977 as 'Peter Lederer, a Jew' which had a certain brevity about it. My mother, Anne, and another Bletchley friend shared a flat after the war and did racy things, as far as I could deduce from a few remembered conversations loosened by a Dubonnet and Bitter Lemon. I wished I'd asked her about the time before her marriage. Before she became a wife and mother who had to give up her job. Two war heroes, dealing with secret information in different ways. Secrets supposed to be taken to the grave... and outed by reality TV.

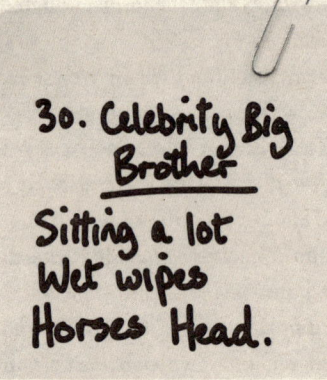

> 30. Celebrity Big Brother
> Sitting a lot
> Wet wipes
> Horses Head.

There's a horse's head in my bed. I feel violated. The cameras buzz into action. My violated reaction will now be part of tonight's episode.

It's August 2017 and I'm one of 15 housemates competing to win the 20th series of Celebrity Big Brother. Except I'm not competing. I'm just sitting. And when I'm not sitting, I'm keeping my privates clean with wet wipes to avoid the municipal shower. These are my main activities. Apart from stockpiling a daily collection of memories which will lead to my PTSD. Otherwise known as behaving very badly at the TV Choice Awards two weeks after my release.

The day of the horse's head incident started innocuously enough. I was in the storeroom, sneaking a slice of cheese, when a voice announced that two murderers were at large.

I ate the cheese and went into the dormitory. Shaun was lying on his bed looking at the ceiling. Brandi – Real Housewife of Beverly Hills – was filing her bikinis into genres. Small. Tiny. Very tiny.

'What's going on?' I asked.

'It's a new game,' said Sean.

'Someone gets murdered?' I asked.

Fifteen days in captivity had made this kind of exchange feel normal...

'Yes. And then they get put up for eviction,' Sean's voice sounded grave.

'How?'

Brandi looked up from her bikini work to explain that a horse's head in someone's bed would identify the murdered victim, who would then be put up for eviction.

'Oh,' I said. 'And who chooses the victims?'

I notice the large lump under my duvet.

'It wasn't me,' Shaun says too quickly. Shaun is my ally, apart from the snoring.

I pull back my duvet.

'Who put it there?' A horse's head stares back at me with sad, dead eyes. I look for somewhere to put it. There isn't anywhere obvious, so I end up holding it.

'Sam?'

Shaun looks uncomfortable.

I am gutted.

'He didn't want to do it.' He can't meet my eyes.

I was surprised how lonely I felt.

'He said Sarah told him to. He had to.'

Brandi goes outside to sit on a bean bag. Shaun needs to collect his laundry. I am on my own. No one likes a loser.

I know I'm supposed to know this is only a game but the incident with the horse's head has hit me hard. I'd had a few nice chats with both Sam and the late Sarah Harding. The fact I'd been chosen to be murdered was crushing. The clip of me finding the head is later shown in my 'best bits'. They don't have a section for the worst.

As it turns out, I don't get evicted on this occasion, so I must keep playing. I thought I had made a few friends. I am an idiot to think this. I am alone.

* * *

My first meeting with the charismatic and clever TV agent Melanie Blake – a well-known purveyor of highly prized reality TV contracts and talent agent – took place at the Langham Hotel in London. The white chandeliers, white chairs and white tablecloths felt slightly ethereal. I was either in heaven or a Philadelphia Cheese advert. Every so often a burst of 'Happy Birthday' would be played by a pianist followed by discreet clapping. This was very different from the agent's offices I'm used to, usually found five flights above a newsagent with no waiting area.

I may have sat on a low pouffe. Melanie may have sat on a chair. We were meeting to assess our chances together.

'People like you, but they don't *know* you,' began Melanie.

I said I hadn't been aware of this.

'You need to do a reality show, write a memoir and do a tour. It's going to be hard, but you have to trust me,' she told me.

I kept nodding. I didn't want to waste this very important person's time. I wanted to be the person she thought I could be. Melanie had said it would be hard, which meant that she understood me and that I must be worth it. I had to trust her.

After a nice exchange about her talented client in *Emmerdale*, Melanie said she would put a call in to *Celebrity Big Brother* and I went home, knowing that life would change. I could now be like other clients who had jobs on Emmerdale and did reality TV.

'Do you want the good news or the bad news?' said Melanie when she called a few days later.

'Bad news, please,' I suggested, as this would be more familiar.

They had said yes to me being in the show.

'Was this the bad news?' I asked.

'No' she said.

The bad news, according to Melanie, was the fee wasn't high enough. Melanie had driven an incredible deal. It was the most money I'd ever earned. Like the cost of a large caravan with a year's supply of *creme de la mer*. This would be even more money than doing the Finish dishwasher advert when I was given a rather garish £70,000 for one-and-a-half days' activity. One day to say, 'The best things come in small packages,' and half a day for the hand shot.

I knew if I was to go with Melanie, I had to do time in the house.

There was no audition, just a session with Gareth, the show's psychiatrist, to check I was stable. We both seemed to think I was, but I told him about the asthma just in case wheezing was considered a mental health risk. He assured me my Ventolin could come into the house with me once it was vetted.

After a brief discussion about humans being like cats and dogs, which I assumed meant not everybody would get on, we wondered how I could cope with inevitable quarrelling. The unflappable Vanessa Feltz had a meltdown in 2001. Trailblazer Germaine Greer walked out in 2005, even the resilient Sue Perkins needed a lot of Kleenex. In the end, we decided I would be fine.

By 2017 *Big Brother* had been on air for 17 years and the humiliation of contestants was a tried and tested formula. Manipulation of people's weaknesses was part of the game. Absurdist games offered entertainment, with a lot of compulsory dressing up to underpin our captivity and removal of power.

The final cast list would be a mix of people most likely to clash, compete or hate each other. Keeping it a secret was a big factor in the deal. Even the contract was in a fake name. The production company referred to itself as Haagen-Dazs. I was now working for a pretend ice-cream brand.

NOT THAT I'M BITTER

And since I couldn't tell anyone close to me about what I was about to do, I decided to tell a few people I didn't know very well in the Groucho Club instead. I couldn't resist the attention. Once they knew, waitresses were extra nice to me. Acquaintances seemed reassured that I was worthy of being cast. Melanie was right. I had to do what she said. Going into the house suddenly gave me a recognised role. It was just a pity I had to go through with it.

Haagen-Dazs had a lot of instructions. One of their strictures was that each housemate should bring three glamorous evening outfits. I had one black dress and one black jacket, and another black dress with a lace trim on the hem. This might pass as having three black outfits. My main worry was sleepwear. Pyjamas might show my front and back bottom, so I bought a nightie with sleeves for cover up. Then I had to buy white leggings to be worn underneath for modesty. And a flesh-coloured sports bra to avoid breast reveal. Bedtime would be extra warm.

Another requirement was to pre-record a short film to be shown just before entry into the house on the live show. The producer told me he did this sort of thing all the time. His job was to showcase the 'characteristics' of each contestant.

Once I was finished with extreme 'hair and make-up', I was asked to stand in front of a wind machine with my bare feet in a puddle of water and wink at the camera. The stage direction was: 'Think, "Hello, I'm interesting."'

'How would you describe yourself?' Yelled the producer over the wind machine.

'I would describe myself as someone who is obviously short and who likes a drink,' I said.

The producer wondered if I could inject more humour into my sound bite.

'I like to go out at least three times a week with vodka.'

'And how about saying something truthful?'

'I have a lot of fears about being incarcerated with strangers. I live in my head quite a lot of the time and I've been told I don't have a filter, so I might end up losing it.'

'And maybe say that with a different slant and in a funnier way?'

'This opportunity is like sex. If it comes up, never say no because it might never come again.'

'Great!' said the producer, and I was done.

The night before the first show, all the housemates were booked into the same hotel near the *Big Brother* set at Elstree Studios. We were allocated a chaperone to stop us from bumping into each other in the corridor and spoiling the surprise when we met.

My chaperone wasn't a smiler. It crossed my mind that she might have Googled me and found out about my shoplifting, because she was watchful and uneasy. Her main concern, she told me, was that I might wander off to buy a coffee unsupervised. I assured her this was unlikely, but she remained on her guard just in case.

I wasn't allowed to watch TV in the hotel room, so I sat on the bed in awkward silence, and she sat on the small chair looking responsible. Eventually, a man and an assistant arrived to make an inventory of all my clothes. He rifled through my suitcase, held up an item of clothing and gravely announced what he thought it might be to his assistant, 'One lace brief. Black.' The assistant duly marked this down on her clipboard. Eventually, all my items had been individually identified and noted onto the clipboard, and we could all breathe a sigh of relief.

DAY ONE

I had gone into work mode. I've done this before, I told myself. I've lived out of suitcases, I've changed in toilets and stayed in places where you can't lock your door, this will be the same. Once I'd been driven blindfolded to the set, interviewed live, and then walked through a baying audience and into the house, I felt like I'd just stepped on to a set of *Big Brother*. Which I had.

Was it my imagination or was there more than mild curiosity from Emma Willis in her quick interview as to why I was doing this show? I knew I'd let her down. Whatever personality I had when I said goodbye to Chris was already disappearing. The deep-seated fear that had driven me to seek therapy for the first time reared up again. The fear that I didn't have a personality. Entering the *Big Brother* house was a particularly bad moment to be reminded of this. Personalities would be at a premium. I knew if I went quiet, I would be a disappointment. Panic, regret and stage fright forced me into looking like a confident charity fundraiser person at a gala with a smile.

Once I'd walked down the staircase into the house, I felt I'd gatecrashed a drinks do without a host, in some venue off the M25. I didn't know who most of the people were. The most famous housemate was probably the late Sarah Harding, one of the singers from Girls Aloud. And I knew Sandi Bogle, who started on *Gogglebox*. We'd met a few weeks earlier doing a strand on *Good Morning Britain* somewhere near Malta, where we chatted to Dr Hilary on a cruise ship about wanting to be slimmer.

I also knew Shaun Williamson, the actor who had played Barry in *EastEnders*.

I couldn't understand why he was behaving so weirdly. This was disappointing. He later told me he was doing a secret task where he had to act increasingly nervous as each housemate entered the house. Once that was over, we connected.

I waved at Paul Danan thinking he was someone who'd been in the band Blue who I'd met on *Celebrity Pointless*, which turned out to be entirely wrong.

There was a medium called Derek Acorah, who has since died. I only discovered he was a medium after Paul told me he wasn't the footballer with white hair who did *Strictly*.

Every time a new person came down the stairs, we all looked up in hope, expecting someone more amazing to endorse the sparkle. But it was just us. We had to be the amazing people.

The other nine housemates were completely unknown to me. But I wanted to be nice and get to know them. The one thing we had in common was being locked up in the same house.

I connected with *Ex on the Beach* star Jemma Lucy early on because her Bulgarian buttock implants had only been inserted a few weeks ago and risked seeping if she sat for too long. Managing her leaky buttocks was an understandable health priority. I enjoyed her company, she was clever and playful, and we had a good alliance for a while. The tattoos over her body and face were blue and green. She reminded me of a muscly version of Cleopatra.

And the American internet sensation, Trisha Paytas, proved interesting. She'd had half her body fat removed, including some bones, to allow for an impressive re-shape. This enabled her to eat pizza and wear shorts at the same time. I liked her friendship. She let me play with her dressing up clothes, which would have been odd if we had not been in the *Big Brother* house.

One-on-ones worked best for Trisha. The rest of the time she felt attacked and misunderstood. I tried to persuade her to stay, which was later shown in a small section with me patting her while she cried, but she walked out of the house on day 11. I felt there was a meeting of minds even though, unlike me, her father was a country western singer, and she had a great command of general knowledge.

My first error was to allow a disagreement with Sandi on the first night. There were two dormitories, and we had to compete over who got a single and who got a double bed. I'd been worrying about how to nab a single bed without looking like I was doing it, so when I managed to bagsy one, I was thrilled. I wandered off around the fake grass with a drink to celebrate my ownership when Sandi approached me. Would I give up my single bed and share with her so that Derek, being the oldest person in the house, could have a bed to himself, she wanted to know.

Quick as a flash, I said no. *Why would I give up my bed?* I'm only a few years younger than Derek. I didn't want to touch pyjama bottoms with Sandi or anyone else. I hadn't even unpacked my nightie and bedtime sports bra at that point.

I should have said, 'Of course I'll give up my bed for a marginally older person – it'd be a privilege,' but I was too slow. And also, too reluctant. It would have been the decent thing to do and made both Sandi and I look kind. Instead, I looked mean, and I lost an ally very early on. We never quite recovered from my selfishness.

DAY TWO

The next morning everyone was talking about my 'row' with Sandi. Even Shaun, although he was trying to be helpful. I had to put it right and fast. I sat myself down next to Sandi on her bed and asked if we could talk about it. I could see I'd been a disappointment. Maybe she'd thought I was nice. I'm not nice. I'm selfish. I tried to tell her this but reaching out made me feeble and wheedling, so I didn't present well. This wasn't a great start. And if it weren't for the late Sarah Harding being given understandable airtime with her combination of talent, beauty and fragility, that first night row might have been shown on TV and, who knows, maybe I could have won for being the closet bitch.

On the second day the producers set up a talent show as a challenge. I was picked as a judge, alongside Sandi and Chad Johnson, an American estate agent who'd also starred in the US show *The Bachelorette*, as a bachelor. He seemed disorientated. I sensed Borehamwood wasn't an area he knew well. Or our pool was too small for him.

Sam Thompson from *Made in Chelsea* and Jordan Davies from *Ex on the Beach* decided to perform as *Magic Mike* strippers for the show. It all felt quite agreeable, until they invited Sandi and I to join them on stage for their strip. We felt slightly awkward, given the bed debacle, but we did it.

I tried to appear intrigued, as Sam did his best grind and twerk in front of me. But when he went for the oil, my heart sank. I knew what was coming.

He gestured for me to lie on the floor, so I, rather gingerly, lay myself down, while Sam placed his legs either side of me. I told myself the thrusting would have to end, eventually. I even managed a stiff little smile. But the kitchen oil he was pouring over his torso could not be ignored. The clip that was used of the grind/twerk routine has me shouting over the music, 'Do NOT get oil on my clothes Sam!'

Sam and Jordan ended up winning the talent show. They were now brothers for life. They were all our sons. Sandi's mostly.

DAY FOUR

This day probably marked my high point in the house regarding my place in the pecking order. Derek, Paul and I won the day's task, and our prize was to be members of *Big Brother*'s Private Members' Club. I was still new enough to take an easy win for granted. We won a life of luxury and immunity from the first evictions.

But popularity is always followed by a backlash, and I knew it would come.

Sarah and Chad started a flirtation early on and it was clear that they would be the house romance. No one else looked as good. Sarah was beautiful. Chad had a great body. They always looked perfect from where I was sitting on the sofa. I can't remember a time when they weren't a couple. Or when I wasn't on a sofa. They must have fallen in love within hours of arrival.

Sam and Jordan were also quick to bond as the cheeky boys who would provide the banter and flirt with the young women. And Paul Danan was wired. He had to be noticed. He had several explosive arguments with Sarah that helped with some of the more dramatic storylines.

I, on the other hand, was dull. Every time I crossed paths with Amelia Lily, a lovely 22-year-old musical performer/singer, our conversation almost uncannily reminded her of something her mother had said or done.

Sandi got the real mother role sewn up pretty quickly because she earned the position of 'cook'. Her spaghetti bolognese set the precedent for the meal of choice. There was one marvellous epicurean breakthrough when Brandi made us all a guacamole. I was beside myself with excitement. It was green.

The other occasion was when Sarah and Chad announced they would be cooking the supper. This initiative caused so much pain it wasn't repeated. I secretly cheered them on, but my cowardice wouldn't allow me to own it. Instead, I followed Sandi around the kitchen to ask her approval as to which dairy products should have foil on and which meat leftovers should be chucked. I have a lot of sympathy with obsessional behaviour and perhaps I hoped this would help us bond.

Sandi is very tactile. I am not. I could only look on in awe as she initiated, cuddled and soothed. She called the young people 'bubba'. I did not. I found myself envying the ease at which Sandi commanded attention. I can get on with young people, I told myself. But not if someone else is doing it better than me.

In the first few days, before we all stopped behaving as equals, I had my moment of power. It was Paul's idea; he encouraged me to do some improvised storytelling. Refusing Paul was unthinkable, so I suggested we all form a circle and begin telling a crazy, improvised story before handing it over to the person sitting next to me, and so it would continue until someone decided to end it.

I could see that the more Paul made out how brilliant I was, the more other people began to feel left out, and became critical and resentful. Especially the Americans, who hadn't seen me in anything on TV (apart from Brandi, who loved *Ab Fab*, which took us a long way). I didn't want to have the mantle of being good at storytelling foisted upon me by Paul if it wasn't going to end well.

The more people joined in to see what the fuss was about, the worse I became at the game. Either Paul had been clever to set me up to fail, or I was being triggered by the responsibility of popularity from my childhood. I remembered hating the burden when friends would bagsy the best places in the playground at break time. How could I choose who to play with? I'd have to let the other people down. This led to break away groups who would want to topple me. Popularity isn't easy. Hard when you have it. Hard when you lose it.

Brandi Glanville took on the cougar role. She was in her 40s, skinny, with stylish clothes. One of the first things she said to me was, 'You do you and I'll do me.'

'Doing her' meant drama with wine. 'Doing me' meant staying out of her way until elevenses the next day, when we talked about her books and any films we'd both seen.

So, there I was, for days and days, just getting on with it. I did the wet wipes in the loo because I couldn't face having a shower with other people judging my bad shower door and towel management. The bathroom was where the women would do their hair and offer up monologues to the camera, often these involved letting off steam about their parents. Brandi and I would find opportunities to join in without appearing old.

I found myself spending most of the time just sitting around on a sofa. I would land near someone and just hope they'd speak. If they didn't, I watched the pantomime going on around me.

At the start I thought, 'I can handle this, I can be funny.' But as other people's status rose higher, I tried not to resent being replaced. I had to disengage. A lot of the time I just walked around the garden in circles with Derek or Shaun while we asked each other questions. We were onto a winner when I asked Shaun, 'What's the capital of Norway?' And I saw the gleam in his eye.

DAY TWELVE

A low point. Our task was to form two teams and take part in a cheerleading competition, with the winning team earning immunity from eviction.

Sandi and Sarah were voted to be captains by the public and had to pick their teams. I was the last person to be picked. Derek was second to last. I smiled gamely for the cameras, but they were off me by then.

Our cheerleading team lost the task, meaning the winning team could choose which of us would face eviction. I was one of the chosen four.

Amazingly I survived the evictions. A tiny move up the pecking order.

DAY TWENTY

Surprisingly, I'm still here. Tensions are high, so, the producers created 'The Vault' to exploit any tensions that could be mined for a new storyline. 'The Vault' is a room of deposit boxes containing the chance of contact with a loved one for each housemate. Some people were permitted to meet their loved one for a few minutes. People without any loved ones had to make do with a visit from their agent or a flat mate.

Each housemate had to decide whether to accept their treat, or whether to sacrifice it in favour of somebody else getting theirs. Sam sacrificed his opportunity for contact so I could have mine. This meant I got to meet Chris for just a minute or two inside 'The Vault'.

When the time came and the door opened, I hugged Chris and felt tears come into my eyes. 'Don't say anything,' I said.

When I saw this on the 'best bits' I noticed *Big Brother* had added some string music to compliment the scene. The reason I asked Chris not to say anything was I was afraid of what he might say. A bit like when I begged my father not to sing in the school carol concert, or talk to any of my friends, in case it showed me up.

DAY TWENTY-ONE

By this point I'd given up. There's a clip of me on YouTube chatting on the sofa with Jemma Lucy. I was massaging her feet, something I would never normally do with anyone unless I was drunk, or if they were a blood relative.

Me: 'My daughter – she's 27 – she knows hundreds and hundreds of people in different worlds, because of all this internet business and Facebook. Whereas in our world you had your best friend, and you had your second-best friend. And that was it. Really good friends you could just phone up.'

Jemma: 'Yeah, but the thing about the world now, you have so many friends – Twitter friends, Instagram friends. But they're not your friends.'

Me: 'No because you never meet them. They just give you hearts. But that's easy. You just press a heart.'

Jemma: 'Yeah, and then it's like they love me, they're my friend. No.'

Me: 'Does that give you a rush? It obviously makes sense, but

I just don't get it. What would make someone give you a heart? What would you do on Instagram for someone to press heart?'

Jemma: 'Picture of my tits.'

So that's something I learnt from Jemma.

DAY TWENTY-TWO

I was feeling lonely and mad. Today's task involved dressing up as tacos and fast-food servers. At least there'd been no trousers in the dreaded dressing-up box that day. My fear of enforced trouser wearing was becoming an issue.

Without any normal recourse to conversation, love, sex, approval, shared outrage or friendship, I was defenceless against the group dynamic. We were all in the same boat. I could see how Vanessa, Germain and Susan had no choice but to let their own humanity show when stripped of familiarity and a sense of worth.

The tacos had to be filled with fish guts and cheese. I didn't question the nasty smell because this was my life now...

I was up for eviction from the house that night, along with five other people. It was to be a double eviction.

Sandi's name was announced first for having the least votes. I sat on the sofa and tried to look serene while I waited for the next name. Mine. We had to leave the house together. I grabbed her hand to show the audience that we were professionals and had never had a cross word in the kitchen area.

Immediately we were guided onto a separate stage to do a joint interview with Emma. Being free suddenly hit me. I felt drunk with it.

I wanted to be witty and funny, but I was also angry. The audience could see I had minded about other people, and I instantly lost my power. When I got home, I got into the bath. I would do that every evening and simply marvel at the experience of being in water with soap.

I wasn't really interested in what happened next on the show, but I watched on Day 25 as Sarah was announced the winner. It made sense. She was beautiful, she had the house romance, she played the game well. Her energy, her engagement and her declared vulnerability shone through. She wanted to do more. Everything mattered to her. That passion and hunger made her early death even more tragic.

I don't regret it, but I'm not proud of it either. And when I got offered *Celebrities Go Barging* the following summer, where five celebrities are inexplicably made to travel down a river together, on a barge, I told Channel Five that sadly the dates clashed with another job.

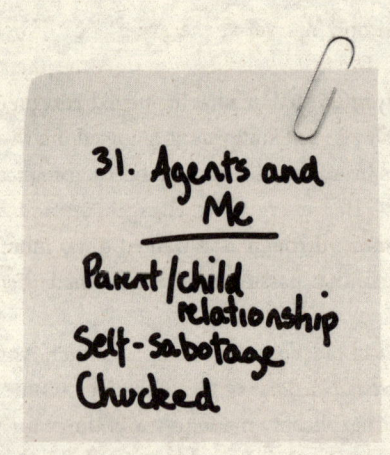

> 31. Agents and Me
>
> Parent/child relationship
> Self-sabotage
> Chucked

I'm back in my powdered food group in Upper Norwood, and keen to make full use of the free CBT (cognitive behavioural therapy) tips on offer. We are given 'workbooks' for making notes in, and to re-read if we ever get caught short near a doughnut unsupervised.

Today we are doing 'adult' and 'child'. There's a flip chart with two columns. One says 'adult' and one says 'child'. To the side is a column titled 'example of challenging scenario'.

In my 'challenging scenario,' I've already written 'trying to speak to an agent about wanting to be more of an actress.'

'What is your challenging scenario, Helen?' asks David.

'Trying to speak to an agent about wanting to be more of an actress.'

David changes his magic marker to fill in my challenging scenario in red. This takes a few seconds.

Then he swaps to green and taps the words 'adult' and 'child'.

'Which one are you Helen?' David asks.

'Child?' I say.

'Correct,' he says.

According to David (who'd lost five stone on the diet in three months before putting it back on again), I confuse agents with authority figures who tell me off. He suggests this is why I do things that cause them to tell me off, so I can feel aggrieved and act out 'my child'.

'It would be really nice to be an adult,' I say wistfully.

'Exactly,' he replies. 'And I'm thinking this connects with your biscuit issue.'

I feel we may be losing some of the group. I'm going to have to bring people up to speed about the Penguins.

'My mother had a tin of Penguins which she kept in the larder.'

'What's a larder?' asks a young person.

'A cupboard where you keep food.'

'Like a fridge?' she asks. The group talks about food a lot, so this question is quite typical.

'Almost, anyway she'd always buy a pack of Penguins and decant them into a big tin and then I'd have to creep inside the larder and open the tin very quietly and take out an individual Penguin to eat in secret. And then when I'd eaten that one, I'd have to do it again.'

'Why?' someone asks.

'Because I'd get told off if I went in on my own accord and helped myself,' I say.

David seemed pleased how this was going.

'And because you knew you would get told off if you ate an extra Penguin without your mother's permission, you wanted them even more – which is why you resented your mother and became more of a needy, angry child. So, you'd get found out and told off, because you wanted the freedom to eat when you wanted to – and resented her for having the power to control you and make you dependent on her to get her permission to feed your needs,' said David.

'I wouldn't go that far,' I say.

'Did your mother like Penguins?' asks someone.

'Let's focus on how the "Adult Helen" could have asked for a Penguin in order to serve her needs in a reasonable way,' said David, ever mindful of the CBT service.

* * *

Two weeks after celebrity *Big Brother* finished, I had to choose if I would go to the TV Choice Awards. So far, all I wanted to do with my free evenings was have baths. But my agent had invited me, and I had also been asked to present an award. It would be rude not to go. Each table was apparently prestigious and cost money. Not to buy, but to sit at. As it turned out, it was ruder to go.

I turned up in my usual black dress and pasted the eager charity fundraiser smile, but something felt different. Things started to unravel quite quickly. I spotted one of my agent's clients in the scrum area before we got seated. I asked her, in a smiley way, what it was like being a client. I felt curious, and it seemed a reasonable topic, since we were both clients. Less reasonable was asking more clients the same question when my agent was sitting at the same table at the same time, within earshot. In my head, I felt genuinely curious. In practice I'd forgotten how to behave.

Sensing a slight atmosphere, I focused on the person I was sitting next to who may have been a producer or a TV talent scout of some kind. I think I gave the person my business card. Clients don't give out their business cards. Not while the agent is two seats away... but I wasn't thinking.

A couple of regulars from *Loose Women* wafted over and quickly drifted away again. Perhaps they sensed the carnage.

At the back of my mind, I started to recall a conversation I'd had with Melanie on the phone a few days before. Maybe I had been bad?

Apart from being offered, rather unusually, to promote the GMTV competition slot which Andi Peters appeared to be doing perfectly well, there wasn't anything immediately comedic on the table. Like a handy cameo in a mainstream sitcom or a travel programme where I go round talking to people on my own.

Certainly, there was a discussion about writing a comedy show, but I was more hopeful about being offered a ready-made job. Which is why I may have raised my voice. All those hours locked up in a house trying to survive and not be funny had diminished me. Couldn't I have a reward like a proper job where I didn't have to write and push for it all by myself again?

But I wasn't fully engaged with the memory of this conversation. Instead, I was drinking and smiling and passing out business cards. My death wish kicked in. Words were coming out of my mouth, and I thought I was handling everyone very nicely and warmly but really, I'd lost a limb. My brain was not communicating with my heart.

I noticed that some of the producers I knew from *Big Brother* were sitting at the next table, so I turned around to talk to them. They appeared to be having a good time and instinctively, I moved my chair over. They made a space for me, and I began enjoying myself. Some of them wondered if I'd minded not being in much footage. Since I hadn't watched any, I merrily waved any concerns away and accepted their invitation of another glass from their bottle. I was free. I was connecting. I was drunk.

Presenting the award went relatively well, in so far as I didn't drop it, but back on my table, things didn't improve. I kept talking and trying. Eventually a colleague of the agent took me aside to kindly suggest that I was being embarrassing.

'It's normal for people to need to adjust after *Big Brother*, but it's been over two weeks now,' she told me sadly.

'Two weeks,' I repeated and managed to weave out of the hotel and get myself home. When I woke up, I knew it was over.

The adrenalin had been pumping for weeks. The same kind of adrenalin I felt when I nearly killed myself and Hannah in a hired car on a precipice in Italy, or when I watched my father have a heart attack on the bathroom floor. When events are out of my control, I freeze. In the army this is called PTSD. At the TV Choice awards it's called 'shoot me now'.

I had been bad. I had not allowed the agents to guide me, or appreciated the investment offered. Worse, I must have shouted a tiny bit on the phone. And asking other clients what they think of their agent when their agent is present (no matter how curious or innocent the inquiry) could only end badly.

I received an email from the agency and, by page four (or it could have been page five), I felt it was reasonable to deduce that it was very probably over. In response, I thanked them for their work and apologised. This apology took up less than half a page. I then received an even shorter reply, signing off with 'love and light'. I would have sent a one word reply, saying 'namaste', but less is more.

Agents continued to scare me. I saw them as a super class which in turn made me act like the needy, resentful child. All agents become my parents. I have huge expectations. They will all love me, nurture me, and fill in all the forms I need to have filled in, and then be thrilled for me when I do well and buy me lunch. And be kind to me when I don't.

The same teachings for 'buffet anxiety' came in handy for 'agent anxiety':

1. I start out thinking the new agent is going to change my life and do everything for me. <u>I am the eager pleasing child.</u>

2. I'm scared. I fear they aren't going to do enough for me, and I'll be stuck with them, and they'll be strict with me because I said I'll be with them, which means I can't work with any other agent who might get me another job because that would be a betrayal. I'm trapped. I start challenging the agent in my mind and assume they resent me back. I know I am their least favoured client. <u>I am the resentful child.</u>

3. *I have nightmares about the agent wielding power and control over me and I tell myself it is they who are holding me back from my true potential because all authority figures don't 'get me' including my headmistress which still hurts.* <u>*I am the rebellious child.*</u>

In 2000, one of my higher up agents was a nice woman at William Morris. And if she hadn't wielded such authority, or had such a big desk, I remember feeling I could easily have been friends with her.

Her office was very plush, and she had two cheerful assistants. I'd only been there a few weeks, when the assistants assured me they were writing up my CV, but due to other more pressing work, they hadn't completed it. I now became obsessed about having a completed William Morris CV. Quite why, I have no idea. It wasn't as if there was a requirement to be able to produce a completed CV, but the unfinished paperwork became an obsession, and I couldn't let it go.

It was during this period that a meeting was set up to introduce me to an American casting agent. We were to have a cup of tea with each other in a seating area, which happened to be next door to Susan, my pleasant high-achieving agent. Inexplicably, especially given the proximity of rooms, I began the interview by telling the American casting lady that the assistants hadn't yet finished doing my CV, in case she might find this of interest or perhaps share some of my disappointment.

I thought no more about it and went home hoping for stardom in America.

Needless to say, I didn't go to the States with this person, and I was asked to leave the agency.

My agent blind spot continued. As soon as I met an agent, I treated them differently. In 2009 I bumped into a very nice literary agent at the Soho Theatre. We were both going to the same show, so I decided to seize this moment of unexpected proximity to share my feelings about a recent rejection of a TV script.

I had been over-excited about my script, just as the nice agent had been, so when she had to be the bearer of 'bad news', the mix of anti-depressants and wine made the rejection seem quite personal, and I felt she might like to know that.

'You know what? You make me feel like a piece of shit on your shoe,' I explained conversationally, in case she felt she could make things better for me.

I was asked to leave her as well.

Interestingly, Dom Joly very kindly suggested years later that this nice agent might want to take me back and even went as far to inquire. She didn't. But on the plus side, she said, 'There are people worth hating and Helen isn't one of them.' So I'm now on an official list of people not worth hating, which isn't a million miles off being on a list of people who can't do games or who smell of oranges, which could be worse, while not being ideal.

There was also another nice agent, who happened to like the same boyfriend that I was going out with at the time. And the nice kind theatre one who nearly cried at my chucking letter ('because it was nice,' he later explained. I can't remember why I left him. Maybe it was going too well).

There were so many nice agents in my life, but for some reason, I'd mistaken them all for my mother. I saw them as the keeper of the Penguin biscuit tin who wanted to curtail my creative freedom for my own good.

I have since learned that the word 'agent' means 'representative', not 'God'. From the first agent who told me, 'You are only one part away from stardom,' to the one who sent the bike with the chucking letter, I wish I had understood that agents aren't priests.

Most of my working life I have feared agents for being my grandmother, my mother, my headmistress and any other strong woman who I respected and who told me off. And all men who did that as well. Now I just fear myself, which means I've finally cracked it.

> 32. Deathwish
> Royalty
> Puck fuck up
> Joan Armatrading

Have I Got News for You *was growing in popularity (I was also a single parent and didn't get out that often) so when I found myself standing next to the show's producer, Harry Thompson, at some event, I had to act. I wondered if he might need to put a face to my name.*

'Just wondering, Harry, why you haven't booked me for HIGNFY? Have you seen my stand-up?' I asked, adding, 'I've done The News Quiz *on Radio 4, so I think I'd fit in.'*

'All the agents have been given all the information about casting,' he replied smoothly. Which didn't answer my question but seemed all I was going to get.

This stayed with me, until many years later when a very nice agent, Debbie Allen, decided to get to the bottom of it, especially as I had been asked quite often why I hadn't ever appeared on HIGNFY.

'The thing is your old agent said you were a nightmare apparently...'

This may have been how I managed to stay on the 'who not to book ever' guest casting list for the next 30 years. On top of a range of other reasons, as the possibilities are endless.

* * *

My death wish isn't just confined to agents, dieting and sex, because my self-destruction doesn't seem to mind where it goes. It can appear in a venue as small as the Earth Exchange or indeed in front of royalty. Self-destruction doesn't discriminate.

I was invited to do a speech and present awards at a hotel in London in the presence of Princess Anne. The event was to honour the best in the fashion export industry, many of whom came from countries as far as Bali, The Dominican Republic and China. There was a clue in the brief which said something like, 'do make sure you are happy with any pronunciations'. I'd be fine, surely? Sandi Toksvig had done it the year before and what Sandi could do, I could do (only with fewer people knowing about it). Unfortunately for me, the event was to be held at lunch time which meant the audience would be more sober and less forgiving.

At what seemed like morning coffee time, I took my seat at the top table presided over by HRH. I was placed next to the Lady-In-Waiting who had been trained in the art of speaking to people like me. Before we had a chance to start passing the pats of butter, she had asked me a question about *EastEnders*. I knew I had to declare I wasn't a regular viewer before it got complicated, but undaunted Lady-In-Waiting switched to alternative TV shows that might chime. Anne, meanwhile, had raised a comradely twinkly eyebrow at me and I'd like to think we exchanged a few amusing comments. Then it was time to spoil it.

I'd cut and pasted some of my stand-up that had gone down reasonably well at comparable events, only not at lunch time, and not with HRH, and not with so many people from overseas not drinking wine.

I launched into my adapted Fashion Export Industry welcome, to be followed by material about meeting a Cuban at my salsa class, who I'd smuggled into an awards event under my sticky out skirt, and some other rude bits. This was the ice breaker. Which failed. I quickly self-edited and we came to the award section in record time. About three minutes in.

The main rule about the award section is not to lose your place, to keep smiling and to get people's names right. In the bright, lunchtime light of sobriety, I couldn't avoid seeing the event organiser wringing her hands as she handed each award to the person who had to hand the award to me, to hand to the person whose name I was mispronouncing.

If I'd ever been in any doubt that I was going down extremely badly, it was confirmed when I resumed my place next to the Lady-In-Waiting to start my pudding. No one spoke. Coffee had been poured, chocolate mints were left on their saucer and the royal party quietly removed themselves.

A normal award-giver would have left. But I was so aware that I'd failed, I went into survival mode and rounded up a few likely looking drinkers on another table and arranged to reconvene in the bar upstairs. Once we'd all got some drinks down us, I told everyone how awful I'd been. They agreed and the afternoon at least ended on a more convivial vibe. The company offered to pay some of my fee but not all. I accepted this generosity without question.

A slightly improved royal interaction was at Windsor Castle when I hosted a Prince's Trust event to celebrate how it changes young lives. The BBC were doing a documentary called *The Prince's Trust 30th Birthday* and my job was to interview a young beneficiary on stage and return to the top table and finish my supper. Jools Holland was sitting between me and Camilla, and as I sat down in a slight tizz, he told me my speech and interview had been 'authentic'. I didn't know what this meant. Camilla was friendly and welcoming in spite of my authenticity and I felt a definite vibe of the future Queen's warmth. Unfortunately, Charles had to make do with sitting next to Chris, who may or may not have been useful regarding the use of antibiotics if homeopathy were ever to let us down.

Another gig where me and the death wish worked well together was one that Sandi had turned down at the last minute. I can't say I was drawn to doing a speech for a firm of chartered accountants for their Christmas do on HMS Portsmouth or similar, but their trick was to give me a few hours to decide. So, I said yes.

The ship was very long: I was at one end, with lots of pillars in front, so no one could see me. And while this was good in terms of being quite near the exit, the organiser had other ideas. He'd installed a big screen to beam me out to the rest of the mostly male accountants, sat around trestle tables getting drunk on huge carafes of wine. I decided to do a meet and greet on each table to give myself a fighting chance before the speech. One accountant told me, 'Comedians have never gone down at the event. Ever. The last one was dire.' And another decided to take a selfie with me while miming (I assume) a wanking action at the same time. I mentioned the wanking action to the booker afterwards in case anyone in the accountancy firm might like to know. The booker reminded me it was Christmas. I said I knew this.

After my 'authentic' speech at The Prince's Trust event in Windsor, I was invited to take part in a fundraiser Mark Rylance had organised at the Globe. I arrived all set to do Puck's final speech from *A Midsummer Night's Dream* which was nice and short, and doable, I thought. When I saw Gwyneth Paltrow being loved up on the sofa next to Chris Martin in the Green Room, I started to worry if my Puck would measure up? In the make-up booth, Diana Rigg kindly pointed out it was only a few lines. As the day wore on, I counted them up. There were 15.

I started off okay, and anyway, some of the audience dressed in black tie and long frocks may not have done it for 'O' level, so I was safe.

> If we shadows have offended
> Think but this, and all is mended
> That you have but slumbered here
> While these visions did appear
> And this weak and idle theme…
> *…It was going well, so this was where the death wish came in*
> … No more yielding but a dream.
> *I was convinced there was hostility from the black ties…they were judging me.*
> People do not try to… bend?
> And, as I'm just a jolly Puck
> And if we get the worst of luck,
> Now to something of the tongue
> We will make amends for long.
> Else the Puck, another thing,
> Give me your hands if we be friends
> And Robin shall restore amends.

I felt there was some triumph in getting myself back to the last two lines, but when I saw Mark afterwards as I came off stage, he had his head in his hands. He may have just been tired.

Thankfully, not all royal encounters required me to do Shakespeare. When I met the Queen at Buckingham Palace, no performance was asked for. I'd been placed next to Ben Elton, who bowed nicely and said 'Ma'am', followed by a few witty words. By the time Her Majesty moved on to me she was still smiling so I felt there was nothing to add. I didn't ask her if she enjoyed *Naked Video*.

Although at the opening of Stella McCartney's shop in the early

'90s, Paul McCartney told me he'd been a real fan of the Girl at the Bar. He quoted a whole joke about me faking my orgasm and how I had to Tippex the sheets afterwards. His girlfriend Nancy kindly explained they didn't get *Naked Video* in the States and took his arm.

But more preparation was needed for a fundraiser gig in Scotland to celebrate Charles' favourite poet William McGonagall, who I'd never heard of but got to know quite well. When I was later introduced to Charles in a line-up at the PT headquarters in Regent's Park, I was keen to show my knowledge of our shared interest in ironic verse. I could see Camilla glancing over to check the reason for the hold up, understandably so, as I continued to wax lyrical about William and only let myself down when I strayed into the subject of baked beans. But he was kind, and the fact that he pronounced my name 'Laiderer' made me feel he had a real sense for authentic German pronunciation.

Some people learn from their mistakes. I tend to repeat them. In the autumn of my career, is it even possible to temper my behaviour in a non-self-sabotaging way and be more like the talented Emma Thompson, who continues to do good things.

My actions remain as mystifying as they are cringe making. I must have been at my peak of making errors in the 90s, when I cheerfully asked the fabulous Joan Armatrading why I had been left off the Women of the Year lunch guest list after 15 years of attending consistently. I wondered if she might know anything about that. She cheerfully informed me that as new chairperson she had made some changes to the guest list this year. That was my answer. I thanked her and put the phone down.

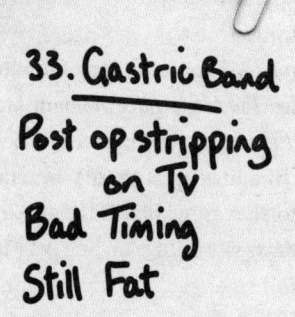

> 33. **Gastric Band**
> Post op stripping
> on TV
> Bad Timing
> Still Fat

It's June 2017, I'm sitting opposite Mr X and feeling hopeful. Even more encouraging was discovering that Mr X liked to draw. I wonder if, like me, he ever did a batik and figure drawing for A level art.

'This is the bypass,' he finishes his drawing with a little flourish of his pencil.

I stare at a drawing of a teapot with string.

'I see.'

'Or ...' he turns to a new page on his pad, 'There's the sleeve.'

Now he draws two ears separated by arrows.

'This is the removed stomach, and this is the new one.'

'Which do you think is best? Out of the two?'

He considers both drawings as if he can't decide between them.

'Both of these generate the most weight loss.'

'How much would you lose for each?' I ask, to push him.

'Three or four stone for both.'

I panic. There'd be nothing of me left to buy clothes for. And anyway, *wouldn't I miss my original stomach for opening doors when I was carrying a tray?*

Mr X begins another drawing.

'Or…there's this option?'

Now he draws an odd shaped sausage with a bulldog clip attached at the side. I could see indentations of previous sausages on his sketch pad. This must be the winner.

'The clip is the band. The sausage is your intestine.' He taps the sausage with his finger.

'That's a lot of sausage.'

'This offers the least risk.'

'I think maybe that one then?'

I was investing in some rather serious furniture for my gut. The Peter Jones of the abdomen. All I had to do was pay a deposit to one of the smart secretaries who had popped in to show me her card machine.

I thanked Mr X for all the nice drawings, and his time, and said I'd think about it.

He pats my shoulder. I wonder if he can tell how fat it is through my coat. Probably.

The secretary walks me to the lift and whispers she'll be sending me the invoice for the artwork under separate cover.

* * *

A year after *Celebrity Big Brother*, I sat down and thought what shall I do with all the money I'd been given? Buy a car, fix the roof – what is my dream? Then I thought, I know: my dream is to walk along the street in a pair of jeans and buy some nice wine without my thighs rubbing together. That's all. I've had enough of chafing. I've had enough of leggings on a hot day. I want freedom for my thighs. Six months later, I booked myself back into the clinic and this time I did it for real.

I was given my band date for early January, which meant I could really go to town at the *Mail on Sunday* Christmas party. I put on half a stone in three weeks, knowing what lay ahead.

I'd already been sent a nice brochure showing me what kind of room I'd have, so by the time I'd checked in and unpacked my sponge bag, I almost forgot I was in hospital and could pretend I was on a break in a capital city somewhere quite nice.

I watched a bit of television, until a friendly male nurse from the Philippines knocked on my door with some white socks. Either they were very tight, or I'd put on leg muscle over Christmas. He called me 'mamy', which only took some of the sting out of having to hang on to his shoulders while he tugged and hauled the hosiery up over my calves. Then came the gown without a back. My nice nurse helped with ties, so we could both pretend I was wearing clothes. No pants. The only words I had for him were 'thank you' and 'sorry'.

Once I was in the lift, I panicked, but I was on a trolley by then, with no pants and no obvious exit route. The indignity of sliding myself off and having to stand up while two porters and I travelled down to the basement together would be worse than staying put and pretending it wasn't happening.

When I woke up all I'd have to do is wait to be thin.

But contrary to expectation, it soon became apparent I was going to be one of those rare patients who actually put *on* weight after having a gastric band inserted. Luckily, I didn't know that when I heaved myself off the bed the next day to go home along with my new best friend, the rubber band.

But I sensed something might be up at my first appointment a few weeks after the operation. Mr X wrote in my notes: 'Overall, this lady is doing well. She has decreased levels of hunger though her weight in the clinic is practically unchanged.'

When I went back six weeks later to get the band adjusted, I had lost a few pounds. My world was now full of protein shakes, including a Kit Kat version, chewed 27 times in the third week when I was particularly fed up.

And there was also the morality issue. If I didn't tell people I'd done it, was I being deceitful? I felt I was carrying around a dirty secret. Not unlike the first time I had a Brazilian, but with more shame.

I decided to tell one or two people in case I fainted early on, and paramedics might need to be told about my rubber insert. And it was a relief that a small inner circle knew while I got used to it, because there were a few teething issues.

The first was in the car on the way to see Sam Bailey at the Orchard Theatre, Dartford in *Fat Friends*. I was sitting in the front, Chris was driving, and my two Scottish friends were sitting in the back. Luckily, these two well-brought-up brothers from the Highlands turned out to be the perfect kind of travel companions if ever one was to find oneself with guests sitting in the back of one's car shortly after a gastric band operation.

We were about halfway from East Dulwich to Dartford when the barfing started. I may have eaten something challenging (maybe a crisp), as it was easy to forget I should be on soft foods. A sudden lapse could render me barfing for 20 minutes. The sound is half human and half animal – a bit like a horse having hiccups.

I sneaked a look in the vanity mirror to see if David or Andrew had registered anything, but both boys were politely looking out of the window as if I wasn't choking on some kind of fish bone and about to expire on the front seat... This was kind. I had already told them about the operation since they were house guests and it seemed fair. They nodded and didn't say too much more about it, which was for the best. It was just a bit intrusive that the barfing continued all the way through the Rotherhithe Tunnel, Dartford town centre and the Poundland Car Park.

The barfing was still going strong as we got out of the car, showed our tickets, and found the bar. We all gathered in a slightly shocked group wondering if we could risk a water. What would we do? I couldn't barf during the show. These tickets were freebies. It would be so rude. But then suddenly, the barfing stopped, and I was able to visit the dressing room at the end of the show, to heap praise on the cast without fear. My friends have never referred to this again – and I thank them for that.

Far riskier was being seated at a birthday lunch in a restaurant with my sister and her husband. This time I wasn't with friends. I was with family. And I hadn't told them. I thought I'd chosen well from the large menu, but something got stuck. I briskly got myself downstairs to sit on a polished toilet seat and wait for the problem to resolve itself. Which is why I had to miss the moment when the waiter came over with the ice-cream cake piped with 'Happy Birthday Brian' in chocolate spread. Annoying, as I had arranged it. No one said anything about my absence. This reminded me how we'd lost touch as I'd never missed pudding in their company before. Or maybe they knew?

One of those in the know was my relatively new agent. She had rung me up before the operation with another 'factual entertainment' reality TV job offer. Instead of diving, this one required nudity. The timing couldn't have been worse. I had to tell her. Because, what if the hole gave me trouble when I was filming?

The job on offer was reasonable enough. It was to take part in *The Real Full Monty*, an ITV entertainment show where women with a TV profile are required to dance and take their top off in front of a live audience of 2,000 people.

'Are you sure they want me?' I asked.

'Yes.'

'But dance and take my top off? Why?'

'To help make people check their breasts.'

'Is there any other way I might help make people check their breasts but not have to dance?'

'No.'

It was this or nothing.

We discussed my operation in January. The agent decided I would be fine by March when the show started. I wasn't sure how she knew it would be fine. Maybe it was quite common for clients to have a band fitted and then strip off for a shimmy on live TV a few weeks later.

But gastric bands were still a guilty secret in 2017. Fern Britton and Anne Diamond were seen as having defrauded the public in some way. The only person who had made it work for her was Vanessa Feltz, who had provided her fans with so much detail that there was little appetite for any follow up.

Are comedians allowed to be vain? The only way I felt able to explain it was to pretend it was all a bit of a joke or to be in denial. Luckily, both options required hating myself – which was well within my comfort zone.

When I met up with my agent a few weeks after the operation I could see her trying not to look too disappointed at my unchanged appearance.

'Bang go the before and after pics in *The Daily Mail*,' I said.

'They could always photoshop you?'

'*The Mail* has very high standards of deception. I don't think I'd make the cut.'

The other condition of my involvement was that I was to turn up late and join the other women as part of the 'story'. This would mean I would miss the bonding and never be part of the group, but at least it would give an extra week for the hole to heal up. The line between factual entertainment and scripted documentary was interesting. We were expected to play 'ourselves' but make sure we were 'heightened' whenever we sensed the camera.

The Full Monty cast was headed up by Coleen Nolan and Victoria Derbyshire. They and the cast had already been filmed bonding while grouped around a kitchen island in a luxury townhouse the week before. By the time I joined them at King's Cross to board a train to Paris, everyone had chosen their besties. I was the new girl, with a gaping hole in my trunk that might weep at any minute and a restricted food channel that could cause barfing noises. Not only would I have to catch up socially, but I'd also have to learn a dance routine.

And even though the brilliant Ashley Banjo and his younger brother Perri were friendly and, in my case, patient, the steps didn't come easily. I'd stay at the back, sway about, and jump at the wrong time.

Ruth Madoc was the most senior *Monty* member, and excellent at dancing. I was the second oldest and worst.

Then came the meeting about our costumes. Coleen suggested we all wear black jackets, which suited me enormously. But the producers assured us they had come up with a very exciting concept and the black tux idea quietly disappeared. Instead, we were presented with the concept of 'rose-gold' evening dresses.

Being dressed as part of an ensemble of opera singers felt a little out there, but more worrying was the thought of the costume fittings. They would have to get close to my hole for my measurements. There would be no way to hide my new hole.

We had to travel to Sheffield for the performance, and after a quick run through of the steps and my continued confusion about how to hold my fan, we all had to take it in turns to be ushered into a tanning booth.

We had to be sprayed orange because it was ITV. I was directed into a tanning booth opposite Coleen, who'd sensibly, and professionally, removed her dressing gown for the scene to be filmed. I wondered how I could keep my dressing gown on during the spraying without it looking at all odd, as the dressing gown didn't need spraying. I knew I'd have to take it off. At least I was prepared. I had big pants on that pulled up over the torso.

The more my nice, smiley tanning person kept asking me to lift my arms, the more I smiled back and kept my arms down. We both kept smiling because we were being filmed and had to look committed. Eventually the tanning person had to give up and looked around for other body parts that were available for spraying. I nudged her attention towards my ankles. They ended up a chestnut brown.

When the spraying was complete, she said, 'I think you're all being very brave.'

I wanted to say, 'No, I'm not brave. They're being brave. I'm being greedy. I just can't seem to kick my occasional Kit Kat habit and I had some spare money for a luxury item, so I chose to violently sabotage an inner organ, that's all.'

I didn't say this. I did the dance. Badly. My fan may or may not have been held in the right way, but no one could tell me off by then because it was time to whip it away and bare the bosoms. The crowd roared. Then I got drunk. And met Joe Lycett's roadie in the bar downstairs who got me tickets for his Hammersmith show.

A few years after my TV Choice disaster where lessons were not learned, I was invited to a pre-BAFTA party. The production company who had made *The Real Full Monty* had been nominated for 'Best Factual Entertainment Programme'. The idea was to turn up to a pre-drinks event so all the nominees could be photographed, and the word BAFTA could be mentioned again in the press.

All I had to do was be engaging. And supportive. And congratulate people. And remember their names. And meet ITV's Factual Entertainment person. And be nice.

I arrived a bit late, started drinking, and instead of making sure

I got an introduction to the correct TV executive, I got talking to a documentary maker about Peru and the taking of Kambo, a hallucinogenic healing substance. By the time people started to leave I was still talking to him. Someone dragged me over to the crew, where I forgot the name of an assistant producer which was bad because we had been quite close. I had to ask Michelle Heaton to remind me what the producer was called in order to use the right name a bit later, but the damage was done. It was frosty thereafter.

Then someone else, whose name I did remember, guided me over to the important head of the important factually light department. She seemed nice, so I suggested we go out for a drink at the Groucho Club together and talk about 'ideas'.

This initiative was as bad as giving out my business card. If you are the 'turn' you must never ask a head of a department to go to the Groucho Club. They need to be protected from such enthusiasm and, also, they might not be a member. But I carried on chatting to her about daytime TV, wildly drawing on ideas that might be of interest to her. One of these topics was the recent suspension of a presenter, that in retrospect, was either a personal friend or her decision.

When I met this same group of people at the actual BAFTA event a month later, I knew I had done wrong at the pre-party. We met in a separate room to gather so we could all appear as a group when we walked into the main BAFTA event. I felt alone in a school playground.

I tried to find the loo for some respite and bumped into Steve Coogan, who was friendly. Thankfully, he didn't ask why I was there.

Phoebe Waller-Bridge gave a wonderful speech, and everyone knew they were in the presence of a new comedy class.

And then it was our category. I kept wondering what I would do if the programme won. I'd have to walk on to the stage and take a group bow for successfully taking my top off and making people more aware of breast cancer. Which was at least laudable.

We didn't win. I managed to stay until the second course of the dinner before sneaking out. A producer who'd been sitting next to me, texted me with a slightly baffled, 'Helen, you left your beef.'

When I went back to see Mr X a few years later to ask for the band to be taken out because of the trouble it was causing me, I'd put on another stone. There was no judgement. Just sadness and a quiet acceptance between the two of us that I had failed, although he was too nice to use that word.

It was my own fault. I'd gone for the least vigorous appliance for my fat fix-it device. Eating food has remained unchanged. I still do it. I blame myself.

> 34. 'Let go' from
>   Newsnight
> Uninvited
> Final Solution
> Legacy or Milestone

It's June 2017 and I'm sitting at my desk, feeling the humiliation of asking famous comedians to judge my Comedy Women's Literary Prize for no money, and wondering if the stress might be increasing my upper belly fat, or if it was the HRT, when I get the call from Newsnight.

Newsnight? Someone wants me to comment on something. I went through my specialist subjects. Old and New World wine? Dead People who were considered click bait who I'd slept with? But it was neither of these. Apparently, there'd been a story in the news that day, about there not being enough funny women on panel shows and would I come on the show and give my view?

'What time do you need me there?'

Obviously, I'd need time to write a dystopian feminist pamphlet about female omission in a post-war cultural landscape (Thank God for Wikipedia). Then I remember I've got a meeting in Groucho at seven with a producer I'd met at a Writer's Guild event who produces comedy scripts. Hopefully mine. He'd been tricky to pin down, which is another part of their job.

'About nine? Where do you need picking up from?'

This is embarrassing. I have to give the address of the Groucho Club which makes me sound like I sit about drinking in the daytime, looking at people.

I quickly add, 'I'm there for a meeting.'

A few hours later, I'm sitting with the producer, rather full of the fact that I'm having to leave early to APPEAR ON NEWSNIGHT, when the receptionist hurries over to say I have a message. I go to reception to use my phone.

'Hi there, I'm afraid tonight's been cancelled...' The researcher began, without sounding afraid at all.

My heart sinks with the dread of inevitability and rejection.

'What do you mean cancelled?' I ask.

'Well, we've got Maureen Lipman.'

'What do you mean you've got Maureen Lipman,' I say sharply. 'Has she been kidnapped?'

He laughs nervously.

'No, but we've got too many women on the panel.'

I'm still in the reception. People are coming in and out of the Groucho Club with no idea about the trauma I'm going through. I'm going to have to explain to the producer that I'm not going on Newsnight *after all. And everyone else I've told to watch me having my moment.*

Clearly the researcher has been busy since we spoke in the morning. I go on the attack to cover my sadness. I know this is pointless.

I say, 'Wait. You ask me onto Newsnight to talk about the lack of women on panel shows, and now you can't have me on, because you've got too many women talking about how you don't have enough?'

There's a pause before he says, 'Yes.'

'So,' I thought, 'Shall I leave it there?' And then I thought, 'No.'

I emailed Danny Cohen, then Head of BBC Comedy, to point out the absurdity of being asked to contribute to a debate on women's lack of visibility only to be dropped because there were too many women talking about how there were too few. I explained that by providing a 'turn' at the end, they had shown how much they didn't understand how to include original witty women's content, and had colluded with the very perception they were purporting to question.

Two days later, I received an email from Danny suggesting I come in to meet him. This was a result. I hadn't even mentioned the words Absolutely Fabulous.

I arrive. I wait. I go up in the lift talking to his PA about traffic. Five more minutes waiting for the tea and one minute in the meeting where he says, 'So, how can I help you?'

Where to start? I force an unnatural assertion out of myself about being a comedian in the '80s and how I was 'there'. He 'knows my work,' he tells me which could be a conversation stopper, if I let it.

I have to forget about the Newsnight *oversight. I'm sitting opposite a man in a suit who seems interested, almost human, and has the actual power to commission new programmes, with me in them, perhaps? This is my chance. Instead, I find myself talking about how the wonderful Miranda is everywhere nowadays. He agrees, and walks with me back to the lift.*

* * *

The idea for *Losing it* began as a radio play. But like most radio ideas, it didn't get commissioned. Fortunately, I'd already mapped out the beginning, middle and end which was enough to impress a publisher I'd bumped into at Jonathan Harvey's book launch. Years of writing to people and arranging meetings had failed. One book launch that I nearly didn't go to, and I was in.

I loved writing the novel. I loved the experience of being a first-time novelist. I loved fussing about the cover, fussing about the editor's notes, and fussing about the promotion of it. At the beginning I had no idea that fussing wasn't always popular with PR people and carried on excitedly with my fussing. I would query emails, details and promises made because I assumed this type of detail was expected from authors.

Everything about the publishing world was new and exciting and full of a genteel pleasantness. The biggest discovery was the joy of being a guest at the literary festivals. These were similar to doing stand-up comedy gigs, but with clapping.

My first time being interviewed about the novel was at the Hay Festival. I almost ran into the Green Room with excitement and met Alan Yentob by the plate of brownies. I introduced Alan to my literary agent. She smiled and said, 'Alan and I drove here together.' I may have said, 'How lovely.'

The event was restrained but jolly. I loved being in a marquee in front of a middle-aged, proudly grey audience, several in Pac a Macs, who had really come to see Andrew Marr. I loved being asked questions like '…And how much of Millie's character is really you?' Or, 'Which do you prefer – TV or writing?' as if my life had been a set of choices. There was an innocence from the audience, which made me feel protective of them. The saucepan handle story was left for another time.

When the book got nominated for the P.G. Wodehouse Comedy Literary Prize, I couldn't quite believe it. This was only my third time ever winning anything. The first was a position badge aged 10, for standing up straight at Blackheath High School. The second was winning a James Taylor LP from *The Daily Express* when I had to say why he was so great in 10 words. And now this. I mentioned it at every book festival and radio interview going.

The literary festival audience seemed reassured when I boasted about myself in an ironic way, which was a contrast to stand-up audiences, since boasting and stand-up comedy were not compatible.

It was worth waiting 50 years to get nominated for something that didn't hurt. From my David Frost sketch aged 10 to *Losing it*, 50 years later, I had come full circle.

In 2015, the genre of comedy female fiction was less publicised and less scrutinised. Language was less corrective, and I hadn't heard of 'trope' or 'agency' although I was aware of 'precinct' thanks to a SKY TV comedy commissioner who turned down my sitcom for being in the wrong one.

Being cancelled wasn't a thing then and I didn't consider that 'fat', 'man' or 'woman' could cause offence to people I liked and cared about. So, I just went for it. The baser the thought, the more hopeful I became about writing a hysterical scene.

Losing it was a simple story about Millie, a woman who's in debt, divorced and desperate. At one point, Millie has to visit her daughter in Papua New Guinea, which felt so real, I still believe I've been there. I visualised and sensed the jungle, the forest, the mud huts and even the road layout. I have even come close to recommending the hotel I invented. Papua New Guinea and I have such a connection that I won't have to go there now to see what it's like.

Armed with my copy of *Losing it*, I arrived at The Goring Hotel to celebrate the P.G. Wodehouse winners' event. This is the kind of hotel to offer free, made-on-the premises cheese straws, a chaperone to the powder room, and a place for the Middletons to use as a base when in London.

There were French people from Bollinger everywhere, pouring champagne and being glamorous with some of their team wearing white trousers, which was very bold. It felt very literary, plush and British.

This was the first time anything I created had ended up on a list of other writer nominees known to aim for humour. Alexander McCall Smith wins, while Caitlin Moran, Nina Stibbe and I don't. I don't mind. Nina and I hang around and amuse each other. Nina is reassuringly funny.

But seeds of doubt about female parity and a new interest in literary prizes has begun to feel important to me. I was sitting at my desk when I had one of my epiphanies. I vaguely started looking around to see if I could win a prize for women's comedy in fiction, but no such prize existed.

I'd been a judge for the Woman's Prize for Female Fiction, and ended up drinking a few glasses with the impressively accomplished prize boss Kate Mosse after a judging session. There was enthusiasm and passion galore, which sowed the seeds.

I would set one up myself. This time I hadn't been prompted by caffeine. There was a definite need for a prize and, more importantly, whenever I suggested this to people, no one said my idea was mad.

The only person who didn't go for it was a literary agent who said, 'I don't think there's enough women's comedy fiction to warrant a prize.'

To which I replied, 'Exactly! That's why we need one.' I used her quote as a way to amplify the cause and be passive aggressive about the agent at the same time.

Before anyone had time to say, 'Don't do it. You will be tied up with admin and managing volunteers who are often unhappy in themselves, cleverer than you and begging famous people for the rest of your life', it was too late. I decided to set up the Comedy Women in Print Prize. CWIP.

It was around this time that the P.G. Wodehouse received some attention. There was only one female witty author to win in 2005 after 15 years of its existence. And even though there were two women winners in 2016 and 2017, this made three female winners in 18 years.

My friend Karen, who worked for the Reading Agency and knew about books, tipped me off about an article written by the hugely successful Marian Keyes. Marian had called out the lack of winning women authors and seemed quite 'annoyed' – according to *The Times*.

This was the same year the P.G. Wodehouse Prize decided not to run because there were no books deemed funny enough to be judged, so the timing was right. It made me bold enough to ask Marian to be a judge for CWIP. When she said yes, I got goosebumps.

All my anger at being overlooked, mocked, and sidestepped at parties would now be channelled into making something happen that was actually real and would make a difference to women who were good at being witty but wanted to be visible as well. I now had a famous but well-respected name on board. I had to do it.

But I was also doing a new stand-up show in Edinburgh in 2018. I wanted to perform a mix of shocking and passive aggressive stories without being sued. I called it *I Might As Well Say It*, because, as I justified to myself, if not then, when? The show sold out and I ended up owing the producer £800 – normal for Edinburgh.

Since I was in Edinburgh, where I assumed there'd be at least some press amenable to a free croissant in the daytime, I decided to launch the prize before doing my evening show. The Pleasance Theatre gave me a free room and invitations for a soft launch went out to anyone who might be in Edinburgh, liked witty women, pastries and preferably be a bit famous.

'You only need one or two shots,' reassured the photographer as we stacked the chairs to make the room look less empty. He was right. He took one photo of Tony Slattery talking to the one woman witty author – the handily Scottish Gill Simms – and another of Janey Godley and Jenny Colgan doing their best in front of an ambitiously hired mic stand. The nice PR went home with the uneaten croissants (still warm) and I knew then that the first CWIP winners' event would have to avoid daytime and pastries.

At this point, I had no idea that setting something up from nothing could feel so humiliating at times, but it also became my thing. It became a way to address my anger from the '80s, while giving something back and producing something real. In 2018 the lack of parity for either winning or published witty women writers (compared to men), proved there was a case for a prize.

But the leap from my being overlooked as a comedy person to becoming versed in social media analytics, budgets, spreadsheets, step and repeat boards and, worse again, the emotional needs of other people, was as incongruous as it was lonely. A bit like swapping ballet for becoming an accountant overnight with no friends.

I enlisted two fierce and intelligent women, who I only later discovered didn't get on, to help set it up and then begged the two Scottish brothers to always check my emails before I sent them out, in case people became alarmed or thought they were spam. My lack of spelling and direct approach had already caused one quietly spoken, book-y person with a growing family to leave. She hadn't realised CWIP was 'such a start-up', she said – nor had I.

I was now a 'founder' of a prize although it took me a couple of years to work that out and write that at the bottom of an email. From doing the circuit, writing and acting, I was now a woman who had meetings and who waited in reception areas of big offices to talk to CEOs about my 'business plan'.

It was as if my death wish needed an extra push. What else could I do that would keep the anxiety in play or, at the very least, still be as fulfilling and nerve-racking as stand-up? Inventing and running a prize, with people I depended on but couldn't manage. Perfect!

Within a year, we secured a panel of famous judges, including the one and only doyenne of witty words, Marian. A well-known publisher offered a book deal for the winner of the unpublished prize, a university offered a place on an MA in creative writing for the runner-up, and there was actual cash and publicity for the published winner.

The winners' event was held in November 2019 in the fanciest of clubs in Conduit street London. A wonderful Welsh woman and event organiser, also called Helen, secured the venue along with a plinth for me to stand behind and loads of other things I never knew we needed – all for free.

Unlike the Edinburgh soft launch, we had so many guests saying they would come that we were over our legal capacity – so I gave a pretend guest list of a hundred names to the organiser and got a volunteer to hang around upstairs to rush anyone who looked even remotely famous down the stairs. The thought of Stanley Tucci being turned away unwittingly was a worry. Mercifully, he was let in.

When Marian Keyes arrived, there was a palpable buzz of excitement from the writers. Not only was Marian endorsing the prize, but she would also be making a speech. I was already worrying that I'd spoken too much in the judges meeting out of obsequiousness, even though I wasn't a judge and had promised to be silent. But it was too late now to change anything. Even so, by the time Jilly Cooper arrived, in readiness, to receive her honorary 'Witty Writer of the Year' award, I chose to lose it.

'Can someone get Jilly a chair for God's sake!' I screamed to the PR team of three (we had a team this time, but no croissants). I was suddenly gripped with a fear of Jilly becoming crushed or overcome with fumes from other witty writers, but mostly I didn't want her to die. Surely she'd need a chair. One of the PR women disagreed and told me that, actually, Jilly absolutely didn't need a chair at this juncture. The PR person was so firm about this, I felt as if I'd been slapped in the face and it was all I could do to keep my hands by my side.

NOT THAT I'M BITTER

It would have been awful if I'd made the Diary page, 'Lederer slaps PR for refusing Jilly Cooper a chair'.

Instead, I checked myself. CWIP had grown from an angry thought to a winners' event with invitations, celebrities (including one American male actor), free drinks and quality goodie bags. And no deaths, thankfully.

* * *

There's music, people in posh outerwear, a PR team, a drink company with their own PR, individuals with their own PRs. There are almost more PRs than writers. But famous people, publishers and genuine friends who've done so much work for free are also there, and this time, the room is full. Suddenly I'm on the stage, but before I jump in – I look out into the audience.

I've never seen women celebrating each other like this before. Georgia Crandon cracks out the CWIP song with her saxophonist and it's loud. This is a loud book prize, with real clapping, cocktails and cleverness.

Everyone is glad for each other. There's a sense of new beginnings in the room; the start of a community where we care about wit and writing and bigging each other up. Would this have happened in the '80s? There were never enough of us at once, and if there were, we competed, rather than championed.

Somewhere, all that stand-up, writing and performing and not being on the winning team had led to this. My old sparring pal Jenny Eclair was there to banter on stage with me. Everyone gets it. A new alternative establishment – witty women's writing is finally on the map and, for now at least, there's an absence of anxiety.

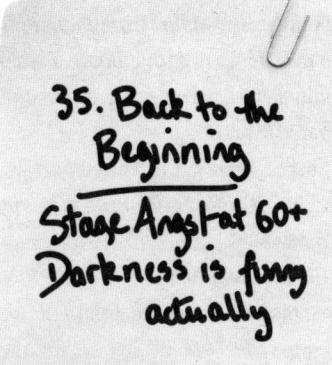

> 35. Back to the Beginning
> Stage Angst at 60+
> Darkness is funny actually

It's 2022 and I'm in a dressing room waiting to go on stage. The misery won't be over until I finish the show and insert the straw into my wine. I've brought my own bottle and plastic glass in case no one else brings me a drink for when I come off stage. I've also laid out a room spray, rescue remedy, CBD oil, loo paper and matches for the toilet – old actress' trick, one strike of the match and no one need know you've done a number deux.

I'm practising my four breaths, in and out, anchoring two fingers to simulate a feeling of past success and passing a small ball from left to right to bring about a calm, before tapping my collarbone for a reason I can't quite remember. I am very unhappy. And although I've been diving into the unknown for 35 years, I still get the same dull ache of fear, rendering me unable to communicate even slightly normally.

'Why don't you just enjoy it?' Asks the 27-year-old in the adjacent dressing room, who's been on a burlesque course. She stands back

to give her thong a happy tweak. The rest of her is naked unless you count nipple tassels as an item of clothing.

I avoid looking in the mirror apart from making sure my lace skirt won't catch on the over-strappy gothic boots. Falling in public is to be avoided, especially before my opening gag about Prince Andrew which is mercifully still current.

The audience is tanked, there are three hen parties, seriously drunk people, tourists and me. It's like performing in a wind tunnel.

And I want to do this.

In fact, I was thrilled to be asked.

And I want nipple tassel to think I'm great.

* * *

I've been invited to host a cabaret show in London. Thursday, Friday and Saturdays have to be spent as if I'm preparing for an operation. I can't allow myself any fun in case I jinx it. Suffering is essential. Sunday is spent in recovery due to the post-show wine intake, and because Saturday nights can be messy. As soon as I'm off stage, I seek out the performers who I've bonded with, sling my straw in my glass and suck out the wine.

'Did you see the woman stage left behind the twat with the drunk woman staring at Lydia's Tampax string…'

'Henry told me there was a man wanking in the toilets in the interval – his wife was outside…'

I'm the least fun pre-show companion to share a dressing room with and the most disloyal one afterwards but, somehow, I get home.

On Mondays and Tuesdays, I'm still worrying about what I might have said on Saturday night. But because I have to manage people who volunteer to help with CWIP, I swap to worrying about them instead. Volunteers are doing this for no money, and I am grateful. The rest of the time I have to fundraise to pay the ones who need to get paid.

I need to accommodate their needs without coming across as weak, controlling or an egomaniac. Which is impossible as any dictator knows.

There are also famous people's agents to be humble with – some of whom I've chucked and some who have chucked me. I need celebrity judges, so grovelling is part of this job.

I've unwittingly created a machine that employs people with administrative skills, professional expertise and a need for investment, which are all depressing words.

If anyone asks about CWIP I say it's a 'passion project', which is shorthand for trying to make a platform happen that makes no money, but needs money and, in year three took my money, which I gave with a mix of grace and gritted teeth.

In peak prize season, CWIP also takes up most of my working day. Luckily, I have a shoe box of business cards I've stuffed down my top from parties, in the days when we had them. These form my database.

My emails start:

Dear name,

It's been too long! It was such fun when we last met all that time ago, and I have some exciting news...

Four years after it began, CWIP has become my child, and financially I have to support it when the sums don't add up. But it's not a working model. I want people to support CWIP because there is a need to champion women's wit, and even though the world has changed since the '80s, we can't pack up just yet.

My other child lives in Ibiza, and I struggle with how to be in her life and how not to be in her life. I follow and comment on her relationships via WhatsApp and make phone calls and visits. But she is an adult and I have to let her go, which is hard for someone who likes to control. It was always Hannah and me from the day Roger left when she was one. We were a team. We had a similar sense of the absurd and wanted to hear each other's opinions. Especially during adolescence and her anorexia, we were there for each other. She was always in my thoughts. The strange misshapen clay ashtray she made me as an outpatient at the Capio Nightingale Hospital is a reminder. We both think it's funny. Sort of.

All those years of taking her to places, of looking behind me to make sure she hadn't wandered off, of thinking up ideas for things to do together, of providing protection, this doesn't stop. It changes. We learn as we go.

And for younger women today, their world is light years away from my twenties. We have evolved to a place where young people are sure about boundaries – which ones to challenge and which ones to implement. Back then, my top three achievements amounted to living with a Marxist to escape suburbia, being around different kinds of feminists at once and going on an assertive training course to practice a 'no' face.

It wasn't until I wrote this book, I started to wonder if something harmful had occurred without me being conscious of it at the time. I still use self-deprecating humour (the kind that was reviled as 'un-feminist' in the '80s) because making things sound absurd against myself distances me from my own shame and awkwardness and makes it safe in its ridicule. Making fun of the bad stuff, and caring about the bad stuff, can be done at the same time.

Over the years, the saucepan story became my party piece. I got to tell it so well, no one was outraged, including myself. If people didn't laugh, then I assumed they weren't on my wavelength.

I placed myself in situations that today's generation might question. The goal of the extra 'psychodrama sessions' was to become a better actor and any unpleasantness was lightened by mocking it.

Up until now, I have felt in control of my actions more or less, but looking back, I can see that people in power can wear their power well, or they can abuse it.

My mother had fewer expectations of herself than I did. She was told to leave her job when she got married. With her education, if she was born ten years later, I believe my mother would have done more with her work life. She had knowledge and intelligence that must have left her unfulfilled at home, but '50s housewives just didn't. Society didn't encourage her, and for a person who was naturally modest and quite shy, she didn't push for more.

But she didn't judge me – even when I told her I was on the pill she carried on cutting up her homemade fudge into chunks. The knife didn't waver. Telling me not to get over-excited and laugh turned me into the hysteric that I have become, because breaking rules became important to who I was. But my mother did this to protect me.

I grew up with my father's gratitude to Britain and need to contribute. Refugees may be displaced but they are not inferior. Yet somehow, the Lederers felt they were. We were brought up to be polite, to write thank you letters, to be grateful and at some level not to expect everyone to like us because of our background. Deep down we had a secret that could offend so we had to fit in. To pull our weight. And not to be lazy.

As a result, I will always be wary of elites; I hate privilege and I will never be normal around famous people, which is awkward, especially when I want things from people who are. When the cabaret job is over, I miss it. Being funny is the one certainty I have in my life. The loneliness in the lead-up to a gig is worth it. Darkness is needed.

My instinct to perform was about not being good enough. I loved the bliss of creating a laugh from an audience. When I did it for 'work', I hated the anxiety of fighting other women, and longed for a world where funny women were not seen as odd or 'trouble' because they had the power to draw a crowd.

Women are more present than ever. They are collaborative, they run companies and they are allowed to do this while having fun. I had to fight off the competition of other women most of my life, and rarely experienced the pleasure of female camaraderie.

I have done my best and my worst to still be here; making mistakes, getting upset, upsetting people, relishing the laughs, and hopefully coming to a stage near you soon with this story.

I won't read from it, as there'd be no surprise, and comedy is all about surprise. Or as I like to describe it, seeing someone fall over and then pretend they haven't.

> 36. Showing Off
> God
> ~~Laughter~~ More
>   Laughter

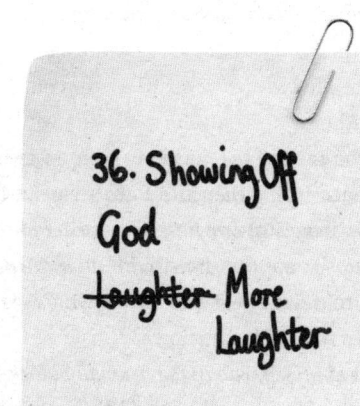

An agent calls.

This is the same agent who keeps asking me to do Celebrity Mastermind, *even though I told him the first time, 'Why would I want to do that to myself?'*

'I've had an inquiry for you to take part in a programme for the BBC.'

BBC? Where were they between 1981 and 2023? Maybe one of their team saw me at the Hay-on-Wye Festival, where I had to share the stage with Doon Mackichan because we were both comedy women with memoirs, and to save on space.

'What kind of programme?' I ask.

'A religious programme.' There was an upwards inflection on 'programme' to take away from the word 'religious'.

Religious? This was akin to doing a programme about storms.

'When for?'

'September.'

'I can't. I've got loads of book festivals lined up.'
'How many?'
'Two.'
'Can you cancel?'
Cancel? Was he mad? For the first time since 1982, women were coming up to me and saying they knew exactly what I was talking about. I was the messenger of our times! No longer ahead or behind – I was connecting, for the first time, with an audience who liked me, found me funny, clever AND who were buying my book. I didn't have to mind that I wasn't Dawn French.

This is how I found myself walking up a small hillock in Austria to meet six oven-ready celebrities, all hand-picked by a casting director for their ability to walk and talk at the same time, and looking like I had no regrets about my two cancelled gigs.

* * *

I'd been busy touring book shops and literary festivals with my memoir – which you are kindly reading as we speak – and was in the habit of calling ahead to see if wine was provided. The first event banned wine, which is how I learned to check. This was the same bookshop gig where the interviewer thought it might be interesting to do a 'body count' on how many people I might have shagged 'back in the day' and kept mentioning Harry Enfield when there was no need to.

Apart from the Scarborough Literary Festival, where the social worker (who I mentioned in an earlier chapter) turned up; Yate Library where two men in the audience had to help me put up my screen; oh, and the interview with the ex-BBC radio commissioner on stage, in a field of feminists, where I reminded her (smilingly) that she never gave me any jobs – the book touring had been positive. Even Robin Ince said he felt he knew me having read it and, as long as we skirt round the chapter about the saucepan handle, I took this as an affirmation from one of my peers...

So, it seemed that all the self-promotion and DIY PR had led to an offer for a TV show.

'Not quite *The Masked Singer*,' I told my other agent to play it down. 'It's more *Lorraine* with an element of *Sunday with Laura Kuenssberg*,' I said.

I was going on 'a pilgrimage' for the BBC and all I had to do was buy some walking boots and make sure I actually walked in them for the next three months – just so I could see what it felt like not to sit in a car.

Which is how I found myself filming my religious 'backstory' in my sitting room two weeks before flying to Austria. Every pilgrim has to have one of these.

'Do you believe in God?' Toni, the series producer, begins.

'I don't not believe in God.'

'Do you think there is something... other?'

'I don't think there's not something other.'

Silence while Toni and the camera director wait. I've signed the contract now, so I'm being paid to have an opinion.

'Yes, I do think there is something other,' I say, nodding assertively.

'And your family are Jewish?'

She's like a dog at a bone.

'My mother's from the Isle of Wight.'

'Was she religious?'

'Yes, they would have gone to church. For events...'

'But your father's family were Jewish?' I can see her point – this issue is going to crop up on The Alps so we might so well get it over with.

'They were cultural Jews. They weren't religious.'

'And when did they come over?' She added, 'to this country?'

I tell her the story, then I cry. It reminds me of when I did the Channel 5 documentary and met the historian who first 'outed' my grandfather's past – prompting a trip to Auschwitz. This time I find myself talking about inheriting my grandmother's silver serviette holder. Then I feel foolish because I don't want to be seen as the kind of person who boasts about having a serviette holder.

To prevent further spiralling, it's suggested we all use the label 'mixed-heritage' as a multi-purpose all-rounder. Satisfied we've solved the conundrum, they prepare to leave, and I settle back and wait to get cancelled.

Just before they go, I remember asking what the point of the programme was. I'd like to think writing this memoir has reminded me to be a bit more discerning when it comes to saying 'yes' to reality TV – especially after an alleged sighting of one's escaped camel toe on *Splash!* in 2013.

'Is this a reality show where the fastest pilgrim wins?' I ask. 'And also, do you have to show your upper arms?'

Turns out, *Pilgrimage* sees what happens when seven celebrities from different religious backgrounds – or even none which is also allowed – join up to walk several miles a day, sleep in modest accommodation – already a worry – without a phone and see if this pared-back existence gives them greater clarity about themselves.

'Do we have to sleep together?'

There's a slight pause.

I take that as a yes and start worrying about sleepwear because, frankly, no one gets to see my nightie...

The kit list is daunting. It's two pages long and includes the words 'sweat-wicking', which I have to look up. It was like boarding school. You had to have one long sleeve t-shirt, and two short sleeve ones, which is worrying. Why can't I have two of each? Leggings are discouraged in favour of walking trousers – which I discover are designed to emphasise the crutch area in a very big way – with an elasticated waistband that came in two very sad colour ways, very beige and lesser beige. And who knew you had to be fitted with a rucksack as if it were a bra?

Three months later, I'm standing with my appropriately-sized rucksack at Heathrow. I've cancelled the gigs where I'm shining like I've never shone before and I'm buying lipstick in the duty free.

I was halfway through the flight when it hit me. I'd left my kohl eyeliner on the make-up counter at home. I was distraught. My eye pencil is the one staple that can get me from 'forgettable' to 'dressed' in seconds so I knew any filming at this stage would be out of the question. I could barely look at anyone going through customs. My first words on Austrian soil were: 'Tom. We need a chemist, okay? Is there a chemist near here? We need to find a chemist now.'

Tom, my designated pilgrim handler, was now looking quite scared. What did I need? Could it be a sanitary pad (unlikely) or blood thinners? He didn't ask and I didn't specify.

I let Tom drive us frantically in and out of unlikely chemist shop areas until he scraped his front wheel. I pointed out to him that a bit of the bumper had fallen off. Or was it a hub cap? In any case, I felt I should tell him I'd seen a bit of his van on the road because he was being very kind to me.

Eventually we found a chemist and I went straight to the Austrian Maybelline section and bought my liner. Tom offered me some sweets. He was stuck with the nutter and must have been wondering what the other six pilgrims were like.

When we finally found a bit of hillock that was the designated 'holding area', I was told to hide in the van until we got the sign to start walking.

'And why am I hiding?' I asked, accepting Tom's kind offer of a packet of Mini Cheddars from the back seat.

Apparently, I was to be the last pilgrim to join the others for the first 'meet-and-greet scene' which required a bit of stage-managing. I could hear a pilgrim walk past me... Would Tom say 'action' I asked. I was getting nervous. Tom thought about this. 'I'll just say go,' he said.

And why was I going last again? I wondered. We'd nearly run out of sweets. Tom assured me being last was most definitely the best position to be in as a celebrity. Before I could ask why that might be, he said 'go!'

I eyeballed the other pilgrims. I didn't know any of them. Actually, I did. I knew the one with what might have been a side parting. It was Jeff Brazier. He smiled at me but didn't reference the GMTV health strand we did together on a cruise ship with the dashing Dr Hilary. Nor did I. Then I saw a young man who I thought was AJ from *Strictly*, but in fact was Harry from *The Traitors*. Same hair. Beside him was an athletic-looking woman who Jeff introduced as a sprinter, Stef Reid, and a smiley tall man who nodded at me as if he was a shepherd (prompted partly by a stick he was holding, which looked a bit like a crook). Next to the shepherd was a woman called Nelufar, who made documentaries, and then a shorter man who I was told is a comic, Daliso Chaponda. For some reason, because the shorter comic was not looking directly at me, I assumed he was blind. So, I stand in front of him to speak clearly in his eye-line so he can 'sense' me. When we got to the hotel, I quickly realise he was not blind but could see. Quite a lot actually.

So, by now I've met all the pilgrims. There's Jay (tall shepherd) who is a lapsed Catholic, Harry, an active Catholic, Stephanie (the athletic person), a very active Christian, Nelufar (film maker) of Muslim heritage, and the man comic Daliso, who leans towards something called Baha'i, which no-one has heard of. It's going to be the sharing of religious beliefs that will link us all. Except for Jeff who believes in nature.

The walking starts. It's immediate, and it's uphill. I forget to look at the scenery as I'm making sure I keep up and try to appear likeable.

Hundreds of miles later (seven) it's a relief to arrive at a convent to have a sit down and pray for guidance. Sister Nathanja – businesswoman turned nun – tells us her venue is a powerful place for pilgrims to recharge. Let's hope. I'm knackered. But there's a problem. There's only one single room. Who will have it? The group must decide. There's a bit of an exciting *Celebrity Big Brother* moment, when all three cameras start whirring as we are filmed showing our true characters. I get in quickly and say I absolutely don't mind where or who I sleep with. This is a lie obviously.

I end up sleeping with Stef, which turns out to be a blessing. We both check in about how we are 'coming across' and start a nice pilgrim friendship. Just before lights out Stephanie asks me, 'I don't know if anyone told you I have one leg?' I pause and say, 'It has been mentioned,' then to be extra helpful I add, 'How would you like to play this – do you have a torch?' Just in case the leg needed to be put on (or off) during the night for a loo visit. I never find out what system is preferred because I turn to my side of the wall and shut my eyes. Tightly, out of respect. I love her.

The following morning we're invited to sit in a circle with the main nun who is the businesswoman and two other nuns, one with a guitar and another who looks shy – but it's hard to tell their mood. Nuns may not have moods. We're handed some words on a piece of paper and invited to sing them out loud. I decided to commit to this – even if singing in front of celebrities, three nuns and a camera crew, wearing climbing trousers with rouched ankles, feels a bit out of character.

I'm singing next to Jay, who I've since discovered is from a boyband called 'The Wanted' and who sings in a way I've never heard before – it's sweet and pure. I'm singing between him and the not-blind-at-all comic Daliso, who's giving it a good go – like a hymn at a wedding. Jay's voice gets to me. I start to cry. People look concerned. Am I trying to get camera time? No, I'm trying to make sure my nose isn't dripping. I may be falling in love with Jay. He is 34. I am 69 and seven eighths.

We leave the nuns to do more walking. And because there's nothing else to distract us, I start worrying that I may be flat-footed, which won't be a good look from the drone shots. We finally reach a ski resort for posh people and meet a handsome ecologist called Martin who everyone decides should be my love interest. He can also yodel which, while being a skill, is also a surprise when it happens.

We do a long walk with a big drop if you look down. I don't. Jay chooses a different crook each day – I play safe and use the same Nordic poles. When we go up steep bits, I find myself having to grunt to help shift myself upwards. This can be quite loud, but there's no choice – it's a case of grunting or risk being last. Jay has his sticks. I grunt.

As we continue to walk (I try not to look ahead too much), I'm trying to work out what I'm feeling that's different. Being unable to shop for tights or see how well other people are doing on Instagram has left me with a gap and I'm filling it with new feelings. Was my family background a bigger part of me than I'd ever allowed? There is definitely a change taking place. When Daliso and I pause to sit on a rock we find ourselves talking about the Mauthausen concentration camp which is close by, I surprise myself with more crying, but before I can adjust my Austrian eyeliner, we have to gather around a shrine to film the next scene.

Daliso is telling us a complicated story about a shepherd who spots dead pilgrims in the snow along with a live baby, who then ends up building a hostel for pilgrims. It starts out well, but then – perhaps because of the altitude or a lack of sandwiches – the usually brainy Daliso loses his way in the storytelling. Either the baby appears to be dead; or the dead pilgrims are suddenly alive, or the hostel doesn't get a mention… By take ten, everyone is mouthing at him 'dead pilgrims', 'baby', 'alive', …and he gets a round of applause

That night I discovered a domestic fridge full of dead chickens near my sleeping section in the pilgrim hostel. The owner lets people stay in exchange for free labour. We don't do any work, but we do have a party – mine. It's my birthday. It amuses the crew and cast to give me a framed photo of myself and Martin, the friendly yodeller – we do look very good together, like a retired couple on an Alpine chalet break. And although I never expected to have my 70th birthday party in a pilgrim hostel with straw, dead chickens and a shared lavatory – there was more hysteria here than I would have got at home. All of which slightly beats the room above a pub with a buffet table of Ottolenghi side salads that I might have gone for.

At the Jewish cemetery the next day, I find myself having a filmed conversation with Stephanie (Head Girl Christian and Paralympian roommate), who is speculating about whether they drink coffee in heaven. At first, I think I've misheard but can't focus because something has disagreed with me (could have been one of the dead chickens not properly defrosted) and as the cameras continue to roll, I'm dangerously close to defecating in public, on TV, in a cemetery. I worry I might be looking inexplicably furtive in the group shot while I hold it in. I don't want to stall Stephanie's speculative heaven, coffee, resurrection theory, because understandably everyone is riveted, but it's touch and go.

We do the scene; God helps me out of the cemetery to find a hedge.

After more walking in the rain, which is quite wonderful – but only to look back on – Jay invites me to talk about the death of his close bandmate, Tom Parker. More crying from both of us. I find myself telling him there may be a God, to cheer him up, and because he asks. He says that's nice, but he doesn't think so.

The final 'mixed-heritage' riddle takes place with Esther – a very jolly woman with dogs – whose mother was Jewish and her father a Christian. We sit down for a chat about the contradictions and 'nuances' of being 'mixed-heritage'. I say I'm not a spokesperson for anyone. On the one hand, I'm confused about the shame of not owning my background more, but on the other, I worry I'm over-claiming it for the purposes of the programme – because no-one likes a pretender, do they? Esther brushes my worries aside and tells me I'm coming back to my roots. I am reassured, although the mention of roots is diverting. I know my highlights need doing…

By the time we reach our final and rather large destination, an abbey, we must decide whether we have changed. Jay links his arm in mine as we look at the Madonna and I try not to think about how we are getting to the airport and who will sit next to who on the plane home.

Have I changed? Maybe not so much. But I am on a high – not just because we're 880 meters above sea level – but because I've been laughing more than usual. It took a trip away from home with complete strangers to bring me back to my true self. It was there all along, I just forgot sometimes.

When I was asked at the beginning of my pilgrimage if I believed in something 'other', I wasn't sure. But now I am. And while I've gone for truth telling in this memoir (which has variously been received as #awkward #painful #hilaire), humour offers the one visceral, failsafe, belief that we can be happy and without judgment. And we can also unite with others. Maybe we should worship humour?

Laughter can be transformative – and it embodies all that I believe in and know to be true – especially if it's at my expense…

And in even more good news, the main takeaway from my experience is that I can go on location, make temporary friends and finally get to be in the cool van with the cool pilgrims where the driver snuck the beers in – especially for us. Touring this book gave me my voice, even if it's to just 20 people at the Chiswick Book Festival in an annex above the main theatre with Janet Ellis – I've done it. Thank you, reader.

Epilogue
Tony Slattery
RIP

I get a text. Tony Slattery, my friend, comedy champion and soulmate, has had a heart attack. I read the text twice. He'll be alright. Surely? People aren't suddenly fine and then die from a heart attack, do they? Ok, there was that one time with my father… but not Tony.

Given Tony's track record with agents – involving a few messy endings or polite disengagement from TV bookers – there is no showbiz management announcement, so a few shocked friends cautiously WhatsApp each other asking if they can do anything. Mark, Tony's life partner, begins to arrange the funeral.

I send Mark a bumper stash of casseroles from 'Cook' (frozen ready meals), including a sausage one, because I know he likes them. It makes me feel better. But not much.

There's shock, the beginning of grief, but mostly a dull ache of feeling alone. No one else could give me away (twice) at my weddings. No one else will ever be as kind or as dangerous or as loyal. And no one else had the grace, wit and intelligence to land a line with such precision and delicious cruelty. Everything Tony did – people noticed and wanted more of him.

A month later, we arrive early at the crematorium and spot a group of sad-looking adults waiting in the car park. I glance back to get a better look, but I don't recognise anyone. This is because it's not Tony's funeral. We wait further down the road until it's the right time to go. I become hysterical when I realise Chris is about to drive us into the 'exit' instead of the 'entrance' section of the car park. Luckily, my screams prevent this awkward faux pax, but it's a close call.

I'm still hysterical when I spot Josie Lawrence in a group of people I don't know very well. It triggers a need to connect. I do this by grabbing her wrist and looking into space.

Then I see Hugh Laurie. This time, I avoid the wrist area and try speaking.

'White shirt,' I say.

'And?' he replies.

'You're wearing one?' I am mad, but no one minds today.

We walk towards the building, and for one moment it feels as if we had just met in the queue for a BAFTA dinner at the Dorchester – but it wasn't – it was Golders Green crematorium. And this was our friend's funeral. I have no idea if crying might happen during my speech.

I am sitting next to Hugh in a pew. I kick my handbag out of the way in case Stephen Fry or Hugh has to suddenly squeeze past in an emergency of some kind. It's fashionably large and a nightmare to find anything in. I need a pen. Crying would be preferable to the kind of covert rummaging I was doing.

'Have you got a pen?' I whisper to Hugh

'No,' he says. He looks at Stephen who doesn't have one either.

I focus on listening to Al and Erica's speeches – two kind NHS workers with a keen interest in comedy who have resurrected Tony's career in the last few years. They created a podcast with Tony and booked gigs around the country which gave him purpose. Erica is talking about when she took Tony to see 'Steps'. Her idea, she adds. No one would dispute this.

I need to make a list of the famous names who are there, in case I miss anyone out, which I know would trouble me for a long time to come.

I give the giant suede hold-all another final rummage and find a pencil.

Hugh nods wisely at it.

I quickly scribble names of a few people I need to include. I feel Tony would understand my need to network, even in death.

Then I need a tissue, so it's back to the bag. No tissue.

I reach into my pocket and locate an old one that is yellowing and marked. Please God it won't be needed.

Before it's my bit, we hear 'A Different Corner' by George Michael. We all look stoically ahead, but inside is turmoil.

I step up to the plinth and pray I'll do justice to Tony. There are no press. I can say celebrity names and I can be bad. Always freeing.

'I made some notes,' I say, sounding cheerful.

I start in 1983 and start listing a few shared disasters before we get to my favourite anecdote.

'It's 2007 and we're guests on a programme called Hell's Kitchen,' I begin. 'For those who aren't familiar with this programme, it's where people who can't cook learn to cook a meal for celebrities and get shouted at by a chef who has to be quite angry. The meals take a very long time to arrive because of this.

'It took place somewhere in Wandsworth in the rain, in a marquee with a very small and sodden red carpet we had to walk across for guest celebrities like ourselves – after a free meal. We are drunk when we arrive and make short work of more free booze. We look around to see who else is doing the same thing and then say hilariously nasty things about them – as well as the director and the producer of the programme. Carol Decker is at the next table… only near the end does she tell us that the fake rose in a vase in the middle of our table conceals a microphone. We are asked to leave. But not before being interviewed by a model – very possibly on her first outing as a celebrity interviewer. We are wasted and the word 'vermin' is offered by way of a response. Tony finds this so funny; we have to be loaded into our free cars before there's a fight. As you know, Tonys' laugh is the most hysterical connecting laugh ever and will need to be remembered going forwards at times of darkness.'

The celebrant also mentioned Tony's laugh. I resolve to make the celebrant a new friend. He is clearly okay with dangerous people.

After a heartfelt and tender farewell from Mark, the door is opened by an undertaker, wearing slightly weather-beaten slip-on shoes and we can see bright sunlight and blue sky outside. I wonder if Tony would enjoy me noticing the slips-ons. I miss him.

Now we must drink. Lots of people appear to be getting into Chris' car – particularly in the back seat where I am and I start to worry about halitosis. We find the pub for remembering Tony and I chuck my coat down on a table lined up with ketchup and mustard and invite the celebrant, whose name is Gavin, to do the same. I feel dangerous and I feel Tony right there with me.

I discover that white wine – lots of it – on an empty stomach can be quite beautiful at a funeral. A wedding would inspire more caution, but Tony is dead now and I must drink him well.

Gavin is able to be naughty with me while emotionally present with everyone else. He will be the one I ask for when my time comes.

I shout across to Neil Mullarkey, 'Hand us over a bottle, will you,

Neil? White! Yes, white!'

It's handed across and I tuck it under my arm to look more lairy until Hugh removes it.

I find myself talking to Stephen and Gavin – my new best friend – about AI. I offer up some thoughts about Alan Turing (well, one thought actually, which was just the name check) and then I start to wonder why I, of all people, am trying to tell Stephen Fry everything I know about AI?

When we get to the question 'can machines think' I know I am reaching my limit, but I'm saved by Gavin who mentions Thomas Aquinas. This is received with interest by Stephen which was lucky because Thomas Aquinas is one philosopher I know absolutely nothing about. If only it could have been Descartes – I might have plundered a soundbite from my philosophy module, but the subject had moved on by then.

After another glass I decided to tell Stephen I'd quite like to slap some people for no good reason. He replied that this was entirely understandable with so much emotion going on. I love him for that. And it helped. I didn't slap anyone.

Tony was our gift, and a champion of all things good – and we all know that. Whichever incarnation he had, just think of his laughter… that should get us through the next bit.

ACKNOWLEDGEMENTS

In 2017, I invited friend and writer Terry Ronald to start recording memories, mainly because I wasn't quite sure if I'd even had a life. Was I alive even? Terry assured me I was and we ended up with many leaves of paper. And then stuff happened and we let them gather dust for a few years. But as soon as journalist Liz Hoggard introduced me to Marcus Field, who happened to be clever and empathetic with a track record of writing and journalism, it felt right to jump back in again.

Marcus would arrive with his tape recorder, ask questions, probe without judgement and go away to assemble my answers for review. He also had the idea of recreating a 'scene' at the top of each chapter. His skill in locating dates, titles and places (he even found the bar I'd been in with Lenny Henry on his birthday) was extraordinary. Without Marcus, I would never have jumped back in or been made to feel I had a story to tell at all. I owe so much to him – as a master conduit, champion and enthusiast… And thank you Liz for introducing us.

And then there was the much needed Faith. Not just in the book, but as in Faith Bleasdale, my friend. Unlike normal people, Faith can go shopping, do the gardening, write her own novels, but also be relied upon to cut to the chase with intelligence and knowing when it's required. Faith suggested I needed to get brutal with the leaves or I'd still be faffing about with this at 80. I didn't fancy sharing a book tour with a carer, so I surrendered to Faith's instinct. Her skills as a writer and content whisperer are second to none and even her notes of 'too much?' and 'do we need this here?' made me laugh. Mostly. Everyone needs a Faith, and I was so lucky with mine. I have changed names in some places and not others. I have remembered events from how I felt and I have not made things up (well, not knowingly). But where I have 'conjured', I have owned up to it.

Thank you so much to James Wills and Helena Maybery at Watson, Little for believing in the book from the outset and telling me in an email that they were actually laughing as they read the manuscript in the office. I never asked which bit, but I am eternally grateful to them.

Thank you to the commitment and enthusiasm of Mirror Books and especially to Paul Dove and Steve Hanrahan who championed this from the start, and later, to Chris Brereton. To my extremely clever and patient editor Christine Costello, along with the marvellous Claire Brown and the talents of Rick Cooke, Colin Harrison, PR Sarah Harwood and Tony Woolliscroft – all part of an amazing team at this fabulous publishing house.

And a big mushy, understated thank you to David and Andrew Colthart who I met in Glasgow and never looked back. Their continued voluntary work, as my friends and for this book, is a marvel. Assembling the photos, the graphics, the social media hoo-haa… They want me to succeed. I owe them. Thank you.

Thank you to John Saddler for imparting such valuable knowledge on all areas. Huge thanks to Kevin Tewis-Allen for troubleshooting as well as Tom Gribby. Thank you to the fine agents and adults who variously believed in me: Jessica Adams, Gina Anderton, Katherine Armstrong, Tom Collinson, Peter da Silva, Jenny Drewett, Emma Engers, Dawn French, Georgina Godwin, Anita Hanson, Katie Kendrick, Claire Kissane, Suzy Korel, Kathy Lette, Kate Lyall Grant, Heather McGlone, Caroline Newte Hardie,

Bjarne Nørum, David Oppedisano, Orlando Ortega, Mark Pollard, Nick Portelli, Sue Sian, Simon Spencer, Frog Stone, Julie Tamblin, Mahvash Tavassoli, Iwan Watson, Simon Wilson, Simon Withington, Mel Woodbridge, and Siobhan Wykes.

To Oliver Double who introduced me to the British Stand-Up Comedy Archive at the University of Kent and located leaflets, posters and all manners of proof of existence. To the great writers who cheered me – DJ Connell, Faith Bleasdale, Chris Manby, Jessica Adams, the late Mavis Cheek, John Hegley, Liz Hoggard, Marcus Field, and Katie Glass.

To my loyal sister and dear cousins who got asked the same questions over and over again. I love them. To my very loved Hannah, who generously let me share her story and to Chris who hasn't thrown in the towel and always believes the glass is full. And who is the best ever. To my friend Ian Pattison who wrote my best stuff. To the friends I've wronged... think there's about three so far... so at least you're not alone.

To my colleagues and famous contemporaries for their generosity to endorse: Jo Brand, Jenny Eclair, Ben Elton, Dawn French, Stephen Fry, Joanna Lumley, and David Quantick. These: Mark Arden, Owen Brenman, the late Simon Brint, Arnold Brown, Lee Cornes, John Dowie, Jenny Eclair, Steve Frost, Ronnie Golden, Abbie Grant, Jo Good the late Jeremy Hardy, John Hegley, Richard Herring, Jane Horrocks, Mark Hutchinson, Barb Jungr, the late Rik Mayall, Tim McArthur, Max and Phil Nice, Nick Revell, Rowland Rivron, Julia Sawalha, Jennifer Saunders, Tony Slattery, Arthur Smith, Sol, John Sparkes, Steve Steen, Jim Sweeney, Harriet Thorpe, Richard Vranch and the late June Whitfield. The people whose stories matter greatly: Alexanders, Helena Appio, Virginia Crossman, Christine Folker, Howards, Gerry Keehan, Katie Kendrick, Thralls, Lederers, Fiona Maddocks, and Robarts.

To the people and friends who made CWIP happen: Beatrice

NOT THAT I'M BITTER

Aidin, ALCS, Isabel Appio, Martha Ashby, Fran Bailey, Lisa Batty, Claire Berliner, Black Girl Writers, Fanny Blake, Susie Blake, Faith Bleasdale, Katy Brand, Amanda Brint, Sarah Carson, David and Andrew Colthart, Paul Cullen, Peter da Silva, Jamie DeAth, Pete Duncan, Kath Eastman, Ed PR, Janet Ellis, Daisy Francis, Llewella Gideon, Michael Green (very much, to whom CWIP is so grateful), David Hansom, Barbara Hayes, Abbie Headon, Liz Hoggard, Fiona Hughes, Jake Hussey, Farrago Books, HW Fisher, Andrew James, Sally James Gregory, Katie Kendrick, Zoë King, Tony and Clare Langham, Kathy Lette, Simon Mackay, Deborah McClaren, Pauline McLynn, Karen McPherson, Sally Miller, Shazia Mirza, Sam Missingham, Gemma Murray, Jo Overfield, People in Harmony, Laurie and Kat Peters-Fox, Annabelle Pounder, Anna Pitt, Teresa Randall, Andy Ryan, Joanna Scanlan, Alex Scott, The Sister Squad, Simons Muirhead Burton, Maureen Stapleton, Nina Stibbe, Meera Syal, Arabella Weir, Paula Wilcox, Andrew Wilson, Writers' Guild and Jennifer Young.

To Marian Keyes whose support for CWIP in the first year was a gamechanger. Her chairing of the prize – wonderful. To all the funny, passionate, and clever CWIP judges. To the authors. To the sponsors. The talented interns.

To the new friends and the old friends without whom there'd be no laughs and without laughter, it's all unthinkable.